THE ART OF COOKING

THE ART OF
COOKING

Crescent Books
New York

First English edition published by
Marshall Cavendish Books Limited 1979

© Marshall Cavendish Limited 1979

Library of Congress Catalog Card
Number: 78-21554

This edition is published by
Crescent Books, a division of
Crown Publishers, Inc.

abcdefgh

Printed in Great Britain

ISBN: 0-517-27465-5

CONTENTS

INTRODUCTION

Eating well every day is a pleasure, cooking well-balanced meals every day is an art. And given the pleasure that good food can give both to the chef and the diner, good cooking is an art well worth cultivating.

The Art of Cooking provides in one book a complete cooking course. Every major area of culinary expertise and technique is covered in comprehensive text and step-by-step colour photographs. There are whole chapters on the crafts of stock- and soup-making, sauces and pastry-making – and anyone who's ever been lucky enough to taste a good home-made soup or stock or had a perfect puff pastry melt in the mouth, will already have been converted to the idea that home-made is not only often cheaper but almost always tastes better. The everyday basics are not forgotten either: whole sections deal with fish, meat, poultry and game, desserts and many others; how best to cook different cuts of meat, or different types of fish, how to make chicken portions from a whole bird, the best way of cooking vegetables – all are covered in detail. And in addition to technique there is a whole host of recipes, easy-to-follow and delicious-to-eat dishes ranging from a homely apple pie to an elegant roast, from a classic stew or sauce to a hearty, warming soup. *The Art of Cooking* is an invaluable aid to better and easier cooking.

STOCKS AND SOUPS

Stocks and soups form the basis of every cuisine. Without stock there would be no base for soups or sauces, or gravy for meat, vegetable or fish casseroles. And although one can be instantly created from a cube, home-made in this case does taste infinitely better and is very little trouble to make. Stock freezes well too—so a large batch can be made at a time, with any leftovers being stored. To save space you can freeze concentrated stock into ice-cube trays and use as you would stock-cubes.

Soups are among the easiest and most satisfying dishes both to make and eat. They are also versatile in that they can be first course, 'appetizer' or an entire meal; and they are rich in vitamins and other nutrients being made usually from a mixture of fresh vegetables, meat and/or fish.

STOCK

A stock, or bouillon, is a liquid made by simmering bones and/or vegetables with herbs and water and straining. It is used as a basis for soups, gravies, casseroles and sauces and greatly improves the flavour of the finished dish.

Storage

The old-fashioned habit of keeping a 'stock-pot' into which odds and ends were popped periodically, is not to be recommended. Bacteria develop rapidly in such a warm, moist situation. It is better to buy bones or collect them in the refrigerator, and make stock in one batch. Refrigerate the stock and use within a few days, or freeze it. Stock freezes extremely well, so it is sensible to prepare a large quantity at one time and freeze it in measured quantities for future use. If you do not have a freezer it is just as worthwhile to make stock in small quantities. Do remember that flavour intensifies with freezing and also with reducing, so it is best not to salt stock until you use it.

Ingredients

The best meat and fish stocks are made from fresh bones (or fish trimmings). But leftover cooked bones can also be used. When you buy meat for other dishes and the butcher trims or bones it, be sure he gives you the trimmings or bones to use for stock. Ask him to cut the bones into short lengths.

Beef and veal bones and chicken carcasses make the best all-purpose stock. Ham, pork and lamb bones have distinctive flavours, so do not use too many in an all-purpose stock.

Some raw meat can be added when making stock to give it a stronger flavour. Cheap cuts such as shin and neck are suitable.

The vegetables most often used in meat and fish stocks are onions, leeks, carrots and celery. Use fresh vegetables—cooked vegetables make stock cloudy, as do starchy vegetables such as peas, beans and potatoes. Turnips, cauliflowers and cabbage can be used in vegetable stock but are too strong for meat and fish stocks.

The herbs normally used to flavour stock are parsley, marjoram, thyme and bayleaf. They can be added conveniently in the form of a bouquet garni. Peppercorns are sometimes added, and a little salt.

WHITE AND BROWN STOCK

If the ingredients are browned—in the oven, or by frying in a little fat, butter or oil—before the water is added, the stock is known as a brown stock. If not it is a 'white' stock (though the colour can be pale brown). Meat bones are browned either in the oven or by frying, vegetables only by frying. Fish stock is always white. Classic chicken stock is a white stock, but a brown chicken stock can be made; brown the bones by frying, never in the oven, where they tend to burn.

Basic white stock

This all-purpose recipe can be made with beef bones, veal bones, chicken carcasses or whole boiling fowl (stewing chicken), and sometimes pork, lamb or ham bones. A white beef stock is unbeatable for many sauces, soups and casseroles. A mixture of veal and chicken bones makes a more delicate white stock ideal for cream soups, white sauces and aspics. A good chicken stock is the basis of many sauces and soups, and is ideal for moistening white meat casseroles and pies.

When making chicken stock, use the giblets, excluding the liver. Lamb bones make a meaty stock usually used for Scotch broth and barley soup; pork or ham stock is good for soups and purées made with pulses (dried legumes), such as lentils and dried peas.

Basic Stock

	Metric/UK	US
Bones	2.25kg/5lb	5lb
Cold water	7L/12 pints	7½ quarts
Onions	225g/8oz	½lb
Carrots	225g/8oz	½lb
Celery stalk	1	1
Leek	1	1
Bouquet garni	1	1

Place the bones in a large clean stockpot and cover with the cold water. The water should cover the ingredients by 2.5cm/1 in. Bring to the boil slowly, to extract full flavour. Skim off the white scum, and add the whole, peeled vegetables and bouquet garni. Partially cover and simmer for 3–4 hours or until the liquid has reduced by one-third. Skim off any scum as necessary. Add more water if the level falls enough to uncover the ingredients. Do not boil rapidly or fat and scum will amalgamate with the stock and it will become cloudy.

Strain the stock through a fine strainer. Cool as quickly as possible. Refrigerate or freeze. To remove surface fat when hot, soak it up with pieces of bread, paper napkins or kitchen paper towels.

Pressure cooker method

Stock can also be made in a pressure cooker. Allow about 40 minutes at 8kg/15lb for the simmering time and then follow the instructions above.

Fish Stock

For a good fish stock use the bones and trimmings from a firm fleshed fish such as sole or plaice (flounder). Shells of prawns (shrimp) and lobster may be added.

	Metric/UK	US
Butter	50g/2oz	¼ cup
Onions, blanched and shredded	225g/8oz	½lb (2 cups)
Parsley stalks	50g/2oz	1 cup
Juice of 1 lemon		
Fish bones and trimmings	1.75kg/4lb	4lb
Cold water	4 L/7 pints	4½ quarts
White wine	300ml/½ pint	1¼ cups

In a large pan, melt the butter. Add the onions, parsley and lemon juice and lay the fish bones on top. Cover with buttered greaseproof or waxed paper (or foil) and a lid. Sweat slowly for 10–15 minutes, but do not allow to colour. Uncover, add the water and wine, bring to the boil and skim off any scum. Simmer for only 20 minutes, strain the liquid and then use immediately or freeze.

Another method of making fish stock is simply to put all the ingredients in the saucepan, bring to the boil and simmer for 30–40 minutes.

Veal Stock

Veal stock is used in many classic recipes. Make it the day before, chill it and remove the fat before reheating in a recipe.

	Metric/UK	US
Veal bones, cut into 5cm/ 2 in. pieces	1kg/2lb	2lb
Knuckle (shank) of veal, cut into 2.5cm/1 in. pieces	½kg/1lb	1lb
Onions, sliced	2	2
Small turnip, chopped	1	1
Carrots, chopped	4	4
Button mushrooms, sliced (*or* mushroom stalks, sliced)	100g/4oz	1 cup
Bouquet garni	1	1
Fresh marjoram sprigs	2	2
Peppercorns, crushed	8	8
Lemon rind	1 strip	1 strip
Water	3L/5 pints	3 quarts

In a large saucepan, blanch the veal for 5 minutes, drain and rinse. Return to the pan and add the rest of the ingredients. Proceed as for Basic White Stock.

Brown Stock

Brown stock is used as a base for brown sauces and gravies, and for moistening red meat casseroles and pies. It is usually made with beef shin and marrow bones and meat, but can include veal and/or chicken bones.

	Metric/UK	US
Beef bones, chopped	2.25kg/5lb	5lb
Bacon trimmings	225g/8oz	1 cup
Onions, diced	225g/8oz	½lb (2 cups)
Carrots, diced	225g/8oz	½lb (2 cups)
Celery stalk, diced	1	1
Leek, diced	1	1
Water	7L/12 pints	7½ quarts
Bouquet garni	1	1

Preheat the oven to moderate (180°C/350°F, Gas Mark 4). Place the bones in a roasting pan and brown evenly in the oven. Fry the bacon to extract the fat, add the vegetables and fry to light brown. Drain off the fat. Put the bones in a large stockpot, add the vegetables, cover with the water, bring to the boil and skim. Add the bouquet garni and proceed as for Basic White Stock.

Vegetable Stock

This is an excellent stock, but does not keep well. It should be used within one day of making, or it tends to lose its flavour and even turn sour. It makes a nourishing thin soup when served with grated cheese.

	Metric/UK	US
Butter	15g/½oz	1 Tbsp
Carrots, sliced	½kg/1lb	1lb
Onions, sliced	½kg/1lb	1lb
Celery, sliced	½ head	½ head
Turnip, sliced	small piece	small piece
Bouquet garni	1	1
Salt		
Hot water	3.5L/6 pints	7½ pints

Melt the butter in a large pan. Add the vegetables and cook over a low heat until brown. Add the bouquet garni, salt and hot water and bring to the boil. Simmer for 3 hours, then strain carefully.

Three marvellous examples of the art of stock-making: at the top of the picture, a nourishing chicken stock, on the bottom left-hand side, a quick-cooking fish stock and on the right, a rich, beefy brown stock.

Economical Vegetable Stock

A good way to use up scraps. Use any of several of the following: celery stalks and leaves, leek and carrot trimmings, watercress stalks, mushroom peelings, outer leaves of lettuce or cabbage, young pea or broad (lima) bean pods, and cooking liquids from any of these vegetables. Proceed as for Vegetable Stock. Use the stock for soups, braising vegetables, or cooking pulses (dried legumes) or rice.

Game Stock

This method is the same as for Brown Stock, but use carcasses and meat scraps of any game birds, as well as some beef bones and a vegetable such as celery, and herbs.

SOUPS

Hot or cold, heavy or light, soup can provide the perfect start to a meal, or with bread and cheese make a meal in itself. As an appetizer, soup should be light when the main course is rich, and substantial, thick or creamy if the main course is plain and light.

TYPES OF SOUP

Soup can be roughly divided into thick and thin soups. There are three kinds of thick soup: purée soups, cream soups and velouté soups. The last two are thickened with a thickening agent. The 'thin soups' are based on unthickened stock and there are three types: broths, minestrone-type soups and clear soups.

Enriching soup

This is an optional extra to most kinds of soup, done just before serving to add a creamy flavour and smooth texture. Stir in small pieces of butter or a little cream or sour cream. Warm the soup over a gentle heat but do not allow to boil.

An egg yolk will thicken as well as enrich soup. Allow 1 egg yolk per 600ml/1 pint (2½ cups) soup. Cool a small quantity of the liquid and blend it in a small bowl with the egg yolks; then stir in a spoonful of the hot soup and keep adding until the bowl is full. The mixture is then returned to the rest of the soup. An easier—

Melt the butter and add the prepared vegetables. Cover and sweat over low heat for 5–10 minutes.

Now season and add liquid to the pan. Cover and simmer gently for 15–25 minutes until tender.

To purée the mixture using a vegetable mill, hold the mill over a saucepan and turn the handle.

To purée the mixture using a strainer, pour the mixture into the strainer and press through.

To purée the mixture using a blender, pour the mixture into the goblet and blend.

Finally, reheat the soup over low heat. Adjust the seasoning and enrich if you wish.

and richer—method is to blend the egg yolk with 2–3 tablespoons of single (light) cream in a small bowl, stir in a spoonful of the hot soup and then proceed as above. Soups thickened with egg yolks should not be allowed to boil again, or the eggs will harden like scrambled egg.

If freezing soup, do not enrich until immediately before serving.

1. Purée soups

Purée soups are made with fruit or vegetables, puréed in the liquid in which they were cooked. This is the simplest method of making soup. Potatoes, Jerusalem artichokes, carrots, parsnips, peas and pulses (dried legumes) all make good purée soups. Vegetables such as mushrooms, lettuce and watercress are often used, with a starchy vegetable such as potato as a base. The purée does not usually require the addition of a thickening agent.

Proportions vary enormously according to the vegetable used. As a rough guide, allow 25g/1oz (2 Tbsp) butter and 600ml/1 pint (2½ cups) liquid to ½kg/1lb vegetables.

First clean and dice or slice the vegetables, then sweat them in the butter over a very low heat, shaking or stirring to coat them with butter. Cover and cook for 5–10 minutes very gently. They should absorb the butter but not become brown. Fast cooking will give them a hard outer skin and spoil the colour of the soup.

Next add the liquid. Chicken or other white stock, vegetable stock, vegetable cooking water, or milk diluted with stock or water can all be used. Season with salt and pepper. Bring to a boil and simmer until the vegetables are quite tender. Do not overcook. The ingredients are now strained or blended with their cooking liquid. Reheat the purée gently, check the seasoning, and add more liquid if the soup is too thick.

In plain soups made from one vegetable and chilled soups such as Vichyssoise, fat tends to coagulate on

Celery Soup with Almonds is an example of purée-type soups. For decorative effect, swirl cream into the soup and sprinkle over toasted almonds.

top, spoiling the appearance. The sweating stage can be omitted to avoid this; simply cook the vegetables in the liquid and purée.

Purée soups can be enriched before serving. They freeze very well, but should be underseasoned; check the seasoning when reheating the soup.

2. Cream soups

Cream soups are fine in texture and richer than purée soups. They can be made from fish, shellfish, poultry or vegetables but not fruit or red meat. The ingredients are simmered in the cooking liquid and the liquid is then strained and thickened with a starch to make the soup; the original ingredients are discarded, though a few pieces may be saved for garnishing. The cooking time is longer than for purée soups, to extract the full flavour. Vegetables for cream soups are sweated in butter as for purée soup, but fish or poultry are never sweated—they are added to the simmering liquid. The liquid used is a suitable stock, or mixture of milk and stock.

Thickening cream soups

Flour and butter, just flour, or cornflour (cornstarch) or arrowroot are used to thicken cream soups. Flour and butter can be added in two ways: by the roux method, as if making a Basic White Sauce, using the cooking liquid as the liquid in the sauce, or by adding beurre manié. Flour, cornflour (cornstarch) or arrowroot can be added by the flour blending method: mix the thickening agent [allow 25g/1oz ($\frac{1}{4}$ cup) per 600ml/ 1 pint ($2\frac{1}{2}$ cups) soup] to a smooth paste with 1–2 tablespoons of cold liquid in a small bowl. A cooled portion of the soup itself, or water, can be used. Now add a ladle of hot soup, gradually blending it in. Finally add the mixture to the soup bowl, stir it in and bring the soup back to the boil, stirring until thickened. Once the soup is thickened, check the seasoning. Cream soups can also be enriched before serving.

3. Velouté soups

These combine the methods used for purée soups and cream soups; they combine the solidarity of purée soups with the richness of cream soups so are quite substantial. Poultry or white fish can be used, but vegetables are usually the main ingredient. Distinctively flavoured vegetables such as asparagus, celeriac, Jerusalem artichokes, leeks or Florence fennel are particularly suitable. As the finished purée will be thickened, there can be more liquid to solids than in a purée soup.

Sweat the vegetables in butter, add the liquid (and poultry or fish if used) and simmer as for a purée soup. Blend or strain to a purée and thicken as for cream soups. The best thickening for velouté soup is to add cornflour (cornstarch) by the flour blending method; this gives a really smooth finish.

Another, simpler way of making velouté soups is to cook the solid ingredients gently in a little butter until tender. Stir them into a thin Béchamel Sauce and then purée.

Velouté soups are often thickened and enriched further with egg yolks and cream.

4. Broths

Broth is made very much in the same way as stock, by simmering meaty bones for a long time in water, with the addition of some vegetables, which can be fried in butter first to give the soup colour. The resulting liquid is not thickened, but the meat is picked off the bones, which are discarded. The meat is stirred back into the broth before serving.

Unlike stock, broth cannot be made with cooked bones. It would not have enough flavour. Suitable vegetables to add at the beginning of cooking are root vegetables, onions, leeks, barley or pre-soaked dried vegetables such as lentils or split peas. Fresh green vegetables which cook quickly, such as peas or cabbage, can be added shortly before the end of cooking time.

The fat can be skimmed from the top of freshly-made broth before serving. To remove all the fat, chill the soup overnight, remove the hardened fat, reheat and serve.

Broth can also be made with fish; Bouillabaisse is an example. Fish broths need a shorter cooking time, as fish bones give a bitter flavour if cooked too long.

5. Minestrone-type soups

These consist of a good, flavoursome stock, in which solid ingredients are cooked for a short time to give the soup body. The stock is not thickened in any way, except when the ingredients do this naturally, as when potato disintegrates into the soup. Chicken, meat, game, fish or shellfish stock can be used. The solid ingredients can be rice, pasta, grated cheese, strips of cooked ham or bacon, eggs, bread or vegetables. The ingredients are only cooked for a short time in the stock, so they do not impart as much flavour to it as with the long, slow cooking of a broth. This is why it is important that the stock has a good flavour to start with.

6. Clear soups

Clear soups, or consommés, made from clarified stock, are not too filling, but the flavour should be very savoury and strong, so not much is needed per person. They can be served hot or cold. When cold, clear soup is a soft jelly which is usually chopped before serving.

This consommé-type soup has vegetable strips floating in the strong broth.

Consommé

Cook the bones to extract the fat and fry for 15 minutes. Add liver, vegetables and sugar, pour on Marsala and 2.3 L/4 pints (5 pints) water.

Boil and skim off fat. Add herbs and seasoning and simmer for 4 hours, topping with water if necessary. Strain and cool. Degrease as above.

Chop the meat and vegetables for a second cooking. Add, with orange rind, egg white and shell to the stock and whisk until almost boiling.

A foamy white cloud will form on the surface. Stop whisking, reduce the heat to low and simmer, uncovered, for 1 hour.

Very slowly pour the contents of the pan through a strainer lined with cheesecloth, which has been placed over a large bowl.

Season, then strain again. Degrease and stir in Marsala. Cover and simmer for 30 minutes. Set aside until cold. Reheat to serve hot.

	Metric/UK	US
Beef and bones	1.2kg/2½lb	2½lb
Knuckle (shank) of veal	1	1
Ox (beef) liver	225g/8oz	½lb
Large onions, sliced	2	2
Large carrot, chopped	1	1
Celery stalks, chopped	2	2
Sugar	2 tsp	2 tsp
Marsala	125ml/4fl oz	½ cup
Bouquet garni	1	1
Black peppercorns	6	6
Bayleaf	1	1
SECOND COOKING		
Lean beef	175g/6oz	6oz
Celery stalk	1	1
Carrot	1	1
Small onion	1	1
Zest of 1 orange		
White and shell of one large egg		
Marsala	3 Tbsp	3 Tbsp

It should not be ice-cold. Hot clear soup is often garnished with croûtons or strips of meat, or very thin blanched strips (Julienne strips) of vegetables. With the last, it is known as Consommé Julienne.

To make a good rich stock for clear soup, you can use veal bones and 1kg/2lb rolled rib of beef with its bones. Other good bones to add for gelatinous stock are chicken bones, a pig's trotter (foot) or half a calf's foot. Brown the bones first as for Brown Stock, to give a good rich colour.

The stock for clear soup must be strained well, degreased (by chilling overnight) and clarified.

Clarification

Both stock and wire whisk must be absolutely grease-free. Turn the cold stock into a clean enamel saucepan and warm over low heat. When the stock is liquid but still cool, whisk in one large beaten egg white and crushed egg shell per 1.2L/2 pints (5 cups) of stock. Whisk vigorously; an anti-clockwise movement mixes

Croûtons

To make croûtons, first take slices of slightly stale bread. If you are using flavouring, spread it on four thick slices.

Now pile up the slices, one on top of the other. Remove the crusts with a sharp knife and cut the bread into small cubes.

Put a large frying pan (about 25cm/10in in diameter) over moderate heat with about 50g (2oz/¼ cup) of cooking fat.

When the fat has melted and is hot, add the small bread cubes and gently spread them out in one layer in the pan.

Fry the cubes for about 2–3 minutes, turning them frequently with a spatula or slice to brown them evenly on all sides.

Finally, lift the now crisply fried croûtons from the pan and drain thoroughly on paper towels before serving as a garnish.

in the white more thoroughly and avoids splashing.

As soon as the stock boils, stop whisking and allow it to rise slowly to the top of the pan. Remove it from the heat and allow it to settle for 10 minutes. The egg whites form a crust and attract all the cloudy particles, leaving a clear stock below. Put it back on the heat and allow it to rise again, taking care not to break the egg white crust. Put the pan aside, wait, and repeat a third time. Let it stand for 5 minutes.

Strain the stock through a scalded flannel cloth or a strainer lined with damp cheesecloth. Do not squeeze the bag or break the crust. Strain again if necessary.

Garnishes for soup

The final touch to a delicious homemade soup is the garnish. This should be neatly prepared and not overpowering in size or flavour. Garnishes can be made from:

Herbs—parsley, chopped chives, chopped dill.
Vegetables—brightly coloured cooked vegetables, such as carrots cut in thin (Julienne) strips, sprigs of watercress, thinly sliced cooked mushroom.
Fruit—thin slices of lemon on lentil soup, on a summer soup such as cucumber, or on cold soup.
Pasta—tiny shells, noodles or broken-up spaghetti: all can be cooked in the soup.
Dough—small light dumplings poached in the soup, which make it more filling.
Bread—croûtons, which are small cubes of stale white bread, grilled (broiled) or fried to a golden brown, and scattered on the hot soup as it is served.

Dumplings, pasta and Julienne vegetables are suitable for clear soups, herbs and croûtons for thick soups.

Melba toast

This crisp light toast is served wrapped in a napkin to accompany soup. Slices of white bread, 5mm/¼in thick, are toasted on each side to a golden brown, then split with a sharp knife to make two slices. The uncooked sides are then toasted until brown.

RECIPES

Scotch Broth

A filling, meaty soup, Scotch Broth is thickened with pearl barley and dried peas.

	Metric/UK	US
Neck of mutton or lamb, trimmed	1.35kg/3lb	3lb
Water	1.8L/3 pints	7½ cups
Salt	1 tsp	1 tsp
Black pepper	1 tsp	1 tsp
Pearl barley, blanched	50g/2oz	¼ cup
Green split peas, soaked overnight in cold water and drained	50g/2oz	¼ cup
Carrot, chopped	1	1
Onion, chopped	1	1
Leeks, chopped	2	2
Celery stalks, chopped	2	2
Turnip, chopped	1	1
Chopped parsley	2 Tbsp	2 Tbsp

Cut the meat into medium-sized pieces, place in a large saucepan and pour in the water. Bring to the boil over a high heat. Skim off and discard any scum which rises to the surface. Add the salt, pepper, pearl barley and peas. Reduce the heat to low, cover and simmer for 1½ hours.

After this time, add all the chopped vegetables. Re-cover the pan and continue cooking for a further 1 hour or until the vegetables are very soft. Remove the pan from the heat.

Using tongs, or a slotted spoon, transfer the meat to a chopping board. Slice the meat from the bones and discard them. Return the meat to the pan and cook for a further 5 minutes over a moderate heat. Taste and season further to taste. When ready to serve, ladle the soup into a warm tureen or individual soup bowls and sprinkle with parsley.

4-6 servings

Potage d'Hiver

This classic purée soup is made with dried beans and split peas which are puréed with fresh vegetables. The fact that dried vegetables are often used in winter is thought to have given the soup its name.

	Metric/UK	US
Water	1.35L/ 2¼ pints	1½ quarts
Dried kidney beans, soaked overnight in cold water and drained	175g/6oz	1 cup
Dried yellow split peas, soaked overnight in cold water and drained	225g/8oz	1 cup
Dried butter (lima) beans, soaked overnight in cold water and drained	175g/6oz	1 cup
Butter	50g/2oz	¼ cup
Onions, very finely chopped	3	3
Carrots, parboiled for 5 minutes, drained and finely chopped	3	3
Dried thyme	½ tsp	½ tsp
Salt	1 tsp	1 tsp
Black pepper	½ tsp	½ tsp
Chicken stock	900ml/ 1½ pints	3¾ cups
Bouquet garni	1	1
Spinach, cooked, drained and puréed	225g/8oz	1 cup

In a large saucepan, bring the water to the boil over a high heat. Add the kidney beans, split peas and butter (lima) beans to the water, a few at a time, so that the water does not stop boiling. Reduce the heat to low, cover the pan and simmer the beans and peas for 1½–2 hours, or until they are tender. Set the saucepan aside.

In a large frying-pan, melt the butter over a moderate heat. Add the onions to the pan and fry, stirring occasionally, until they are soft and translucent. Add the carrots to the pan and fry for 5 minutes or until they are tender. Remove the pan from the heat. Purée the onions, carrots, beans and peas in a food mill or electric blender.

Transfer the mixture to a large saucepan and stir in the thyme, salt, pepper and stock. Add the bouquet garni. Place over a high heat and bring the soup to the boil. Reduce the heat to low, cover the pan and simmer for 15 minutes. Discard the bouquet garni. Stir in the spinach and cook, stirring occasionally, for 5 minutes or until the soup is hot. Ladle the soup into a warmed large tureen or individual soup bowls and serve immediately.

4 servings

Filling and nutritious, Scotch Broth is thickened with dried pulses–in this case barley and dried split peas. It makes an excellent meal in itself served with crusty bread and butter.

Borscht

A beautifully coloured beetroot (beet) purée soup.

	Metric/UK	US
Large, raw beetroots (beets), peeled and coarsely grated	5	5
Cold water	1.8L/3 pints	7½ cups
Onion, chopped	1	1
Tomato purée (paste)	75ml/3 floz	⅓ cup
Lemon juice	1 Tbsp	1 Tbsp
Salt	1 tsp	1 tsp
Black pepper	½ tsp	½ tsp
Sugar	1 tsp	1 tsp
Sour cream	300ml/½ pint	1¼ cups

Put the beetroots (beets), water and onion in a large saucepan over a high heat. Bring to the boil, cover the pan, reduce the heat to low and simmer for 45 minutes. Add the tomato purée (paste), lemon juice, salt, pepper and sugar. Cover and cook the soup over a moderately low heat for another 45 minutes. Remove the pan from the heat. Strain the soup into a warm soup tureen. Discard the vegetables. Serve with sour cream.

6 servings

Cream of Shrimp Soup

	Metric/UK	US
Butter	50g/2oz	¼ cup
Leek, sliced	1	1
Potatoes, sliced	½kg/1lb	1lb
Fish stock	900ml/1½ pints	3¾ cups
Milk	300ml/½ pint	1¼ cups
Celery stalk, finely chopped	1	1
Salt	1 tsp	1 tsp
Egg yolks	2	2
Single (light) cream	150ml/5 floz	⅔ cup
Cooked, peeled shrimps, coarsely chopped	225g/8oz	1⅓ cups

In a large saucepan, melt the butter over a low heat. Add the leek and potatoes and cook for 10 minutes, stirring frequently. Do not allow them to brown.

Cover the potatoes and leek with the stock and milk. Add the celery and salt and bring to the boil over a high heat. Reduce the heat and simmer, covered, for 15–20 minutes. Purée the mixture. Return the soup to the saucepan and bring back to the boil, then remove from the heat.

In a small bowl, beat the egg yolks and cream together with a fork. Add a little of the warm soup and mix thoroughly. Add the mixture to the soup and mix it in

well with a wooden spoon. Put in the chopped shrimps. Return the soup to a low heat and warm gently until the soup and shrimps are hot, but not boiling. Serve at once.

6 servings

Minestrone

This nourishing Italian vegetable and pasta soup makes a hearty meal on its own, served with rolls and butter.

	Metric/UK	US
Water	900ml/1½ pints	3¾ cups
Dried kidney beans	100g/4oz	⅔ cup
Dried chick peas	50g/2oz	⅓ cup
Salt pork (fatback), cut into cubes	175g/6oz	6oz
Olive oil	4 Tbsp	4 Tbsp
Onions	2	2
Garlic clove, crushed	1	1
Potatoes, diced	2	2
Carrots, in 12mm/½in slices	4	4
Celery stalks, sliced	4	4
Small cabbage, finely shredded	½	½
Tomatoes, peeled, seeded and chopped	6	6
Chicken stock	2.4L/4 pints	2½ quarts
Bouquet garni	1	1
Salt	½ tsp	½ tsp
Black pepper	1 tsp	1 tsp
Green peas	225g/8oz	1⅓ cups
Macaroni	100g/4oz	1 cup
Parmesan cheese, grated	50g/2oz	½ cup

In a medium-sized saucepan, bring the water to the boil over a high heat. Add the beans and chick peas and boil for 2 minutes. Remove from the heat and leave to soak for 1½ hours.

After this time bring the water to the boil again. Reduce the heat to low and simmer the beans and chick peas for 1½ hours until almost tender. Remove from the heat, drain the beans and peas and set aside.

Fry the salt pork for 8–10 minutes in a large heavy-bottomed saucepan over a moderate heat, until it is golden brown and has rendered most of its fat. Remove from the pan with a slotted spoon and set aside. Pour the olive oil into the pork fat and add the onions and garlic. Fry until they are soft and translucent, stirring occasionally. Then add the potatoes, carrots and celery and cook for 5 minutes. Add the cabbage and tomatoes and cook for a further 5 minutes. Pour in the chicken stock and add the bouquet garni, the reserved chick peas, beans and salt pork, and season to taste with salt and pepper. Bring the soup to the boil, reduce the heat

to low, cover and simmer for 35 minutes.

Take out and discard the bouquet garni. Add the green peas and macaroni and cook for a further 10–15 minutes until the macaroni is just tender. Serve at once in individual bowls with a generous sprinkling of Parmesan cheese on each.

8 servings

Cream of Carrot Soup

This substantial and attractive velouté soup is thickened by the roux method and enriched with single (light) cream.

	Metric/UK	US
Carrots, sliced	700g/1½lb	1½lb
Chicken stock	900ml/ 1½ pints	3¾ cups
Salt	2 tsp	2 tsp
Butter	2 Tbsp	2 Tbsp
Flour	1 Tbsp	1 Tbsp
Tomato purée (paste)	2 tsp	2 tsp
Single (light) cream	175ml/6 floz	¾ cup
White pepper	½ tsp	½ tsp
Chopped parsley	1 Tbsp	1 Tbsp

Place the carrots in a medium-sized saucepan and add enough of the chicken stock to cover. Add 1 teaspoon of salt and put the pan over a high heat. Bring to the boil, then reduce the heat to low. Cook the carrots for 30 minutes, or until they are soft, then purée.

Minestrone, a thick tasty vegetable soup with pasta, is Italian in origin.

In a large saucepan, melt the butter over a moderate heat. Remove the pan from the heat and stir in the flour with a wooden spoon, mixing to a smooth paste. Return the pan to the heat and gradually stir in about one-third of the remaining stock, and then the carrot purée. Add the remainder of the stock, stirring to mix well, and bring the mixture to the boil.

Remove the pan from the heat and stir in the tomato purée (paste) and the cream, mixing briskly. Return the pan to a low heat and warm gently until hot, but not boiling. Season with the rest of the salt and pepper as necessary. Pour into a warmed tureen and sprinkle with the chopped parsley.

4–6 servings

Consommé Madrilène
(Tomato Consommé)

This chicken consommé with tomatoes is usually served cold and jellied, but it can be served hot or with crisp melba toast. The recipe includes clarification.

	Metric/UK	US
Egg whites	2	2
Tomatoes, chopped	½kg/1lb	2 cups
Canned pimento, drained and chopped	1	1
Strong, cold chicken stock	1.2L/2 pints	5 cups

Dry sherry	75ml/3 floz	$\frac{1}{3}$ cup
Lemon rind	1 slice	1 slice
Celery stalks, chopped	4	4
Salt	1 tsp	1 tsp

In a small bowl, beat the egg whites until they are frothy. Put the tomatoes, pimento and stock into a large saucepan. Whisk in the egg whites and sherry and add the lemon rind and celery. Place the pan over a moderate heat and bring to the boil, whisking constantly. When the mixture comes to the boil, stop whisking and let it rise in the pan. Remove the pan from the heat.

Reduce the heat to very low, return the pan to the heat and simmer gently for 45 minutes. Then let the consommé stand for 15 minutes. Lift off the egg white

This classic Onion Soup is garnished with garlic-flavoured French bread slices toasted under the grill (broiler).

crust and place it in a strainer lined with cheesecloth. Pour the consommé through the strainer into a large bowl. Taste it and if necessary add salt. Pour the consommé into individual soup bowls and chill until set.
6 servings

Onion Soup

This is a classic French recipe, fortified with toasted French bread and cheese.

	Metric/UK	US
Butter	75g/3oz	6 Tbsp
Onions, sliced in rings	4	4
Flour	2 Tbsp	2 Tbsp
Salt	$\frac{1}{2}$ tsp	$\frac{1}{2}$ tsp
Black pepper	$\frac{1}{4}$ tsp	$\frac{1}{4}$ tsp
Beef stock	900ml/ 1$\frac{1}{2}$ pints	3$\frac{3}{4}$ cups

	Metric/UK	US
French bread slices, toasted	6	6
Garlic cloves, halved	3	3
Parmesan cheese, grated	75g/3oz	$\frac{3}{4}$ cup

In a medium-sized flameproof casserole, melt the butter over a moderate heat. Reduce the heat to low and add the onions to the pan. Cook them, stirring occasionally, for 25–30 minutes, until they are golden brown.

Remove the pan from the heat and stir in the flour and salt and pepper with a wooden spoon, mixing to a smooth paste. Return the pan to the heat and gradually stir in the stock. Bring to the boil over a high heat, then reduce the heat to low, cover the casserole and simmer for 20 minutes.

Preheat the grill (broiler) to high. Rub each toast circle on each side with a garlic half. Float the toast slices on the surface of the soup and sprinkle Parmesan cheese generously over the top. Grill (broil) the soup for 5 minutes until the cheese is golden and bubbling. Serve at once.
6 servings

Gazpacho

Another classic soup, this time from Spain, Gazpacho is served cold with several garnishes, such as croutons, chopped olives, hard-boiled (hard-cooked) eggs, cucumber and onion.

	Metric/UK	US
Brown bread slices, cubed	3	3
Canned tomato juice	300ml/ $\frac{1}{2}$ pint	1$\frac{1}{4}$ cups
Garlic cloves, finely chopped	2	2
Cucumber, peeled and finely chopped	$\frac{1}{2}$	$\frac{1}{2}$
Green pepper, seeded and finely chopped	1	1
Red pepper, seeded and finely chopped	1	1
Onion, chopped	1	1
Tomatoes, peeled, seeded and chopped	700g/1$\frac{1}{2}$lb	1$\frac{1}{2}$lb
Olive oil	90ml/3floz	$\frac{1}{3}$ cup
Red wine vinegar	2 Tbsp	2 Tbsp
Lemon juice	1 Tbsp	1 Tbsp
Salt	$\frac{1}{2}$ tsp	$\frac{1}{2}$ tsp
Black pepper	$\frac{1}{4}$ tsp	$\frac{1}{4}$ tsp
Dried marjoram	$\frac{1}{4}$ tsp	$\frac{1}{4}$ tsp
Dried basil	$\frac{1}{4}$ tsp	$\frac{1}{4}$ tsp
Ice cubes (optional)	4	4

Place the bread cubes in a medium-sized mixing bowl and pour over the tomato juice. Leave the bread to soak for 5 minutes, then squeeze to extract the excess juice. Transfer the bread to a large bowl and reserve the tomato juice.

Add the garlic, cucumber, peppers, onion and tomatoes to the soaked bread and stir. Purée the ingredients by pounding with a pestle and mortar and rubbing through a strainer or by putting them through a food mill. Stir in the reserved tomato juice.

Add the oil, vinegar, lemon juice, salt, pepper and herbs to the purée, and stir well. The soup should be the consistency of thin cream, so add more tomato juice if necessary.

Turn the soup into a bowl and chill in the refrigerator for at least 1 hour. Just before serving stir well, then drop in the ice cubes. Serve with chopped garnishes of your choice, to be added at the table.
4 servings

New England Clam Chowder

	Metric/UK	US
Salt pork (fatback), diced	75g/3oz	3oz
Onions, finely chopped	2	2
Water	175ml/6floz	$\frac{3}{4}$ cup
Milk	250ml/8floz	1 cup
Potatoes, chopped	4	4
Clams (24 fresh, scrubbed and steamed for 8 minutes, broth reserved, or 450g/1lb canned clams, juice reserved)		
Salt and pepper		
Paprika	$\frac{1}{2}$ tsp	$\frac{1}{2}$ tsp
Double (heavy) cream	250ml/8floz	1 cup
Butter	15g/$\frac{1}{2}$oz	1 Tbsp

In a saucepan, fry the salt pork over a moderate heat for 5 minutes, or until it is golden brown and has rendered most of its fat. Add the onions and fry until they are soft and translucent, stirring occasionally.

Pour the water and milk into the pan and add the potatoes. Bring to a boil, reduce the heat to low and simmer for 10 minutes, or until the potatoes are tender. Stir in the clams with broth or juice, the seasoning and paprika and bring back to a boil. Stir in the cream and heat gently until it is hot but not boiling.

Stir in the butter until it melts, then serve at once.
6 servings

Cream of Chicken Soup

This tasty soup is an excellent way to use leftover chicken. It is thickened by the roux method and is made extra smooth by the addition of eggs or cream.

	Metric/UK	US
Butter	40g/1$\frac{1}{2}$oz	3 Tbsp
Flour	3 Tbsp	3 Tbsp
Chicken stock	600ml/ 1 pint	2$\frac{1}{2}$ cups
Milk	600ml/ 1 pint	2$\frac{1}{2}$ cups

Chicken, cooked and finely chopped	225g/8oz	1⅓ cups
Salt	1 tsp	1 tsp
White pepper	½ tsp	½ tsp
Dried basil	1 tsp	1 tsp
Egg yolks	2	2
Single (light) cream	125ml/4floz	½ cup
Chopped parsley	1 Tbsp	1 Tbsp

In a large saucepan, melt the butter over a moderate heat. Remove the pan from the heat and stir in the flour with a wooden spoon, mixing to a smooth paste. Return the pan to the heat and gradually stir in the chicken stock and milk. Bring to the boil and stir constantly. Add the chopped chicken, salt, pepper and basil, reduce the heat to low, cover and simmer the soup for 15 minutes. Remove the pan from the heat.

In a small bowl, mix the egg yolks and cream together with a fork. Mix in 3 tablespoons of the soup and stir this cream and egg mixture into the soup in the pan. Return to the heat and cook gently until it is hot but

Traditional Cock-a-Leekie is Scottish in origin, and as the name suggests, has chicken and leeks as its tasty and nourishing main ingredients.

not boiling. Serve at once, sprinkled with parsley. *4–6 servings*

Cock-a-Leekie

As the name suggests, this traditional Scottish broth is made with chicken and leeks.

	Metric/UK	US
Chicken	1.35kg/3lb	3lb
Water	2.5L/4 pints	2½ quarts
Leeks, sliced coarsely	7	7
Celery stalks, chopped	2	2
Pearl barley	50g/2oz	¼ cup
Bouquet garni	1	1
Salt	2 tsp	2 tsp
Chopped parsley	1 Tbsp	1 Tbsp

Place the chicken in a large saucepan with the water, making sure that it is completely immersed. Bring to the boil over a high heat, and skim off any scum that rises to the surface. Then add the leeks, celery, barley, bouquet garni and salt. Reduce the heat to low, partially cover the pan and simmer the chicken for 1½–2 hours, until the meat is almost falling off the bones.

Remove the pan from the heat and transfer the chicken to a chopping board. Leave it to cool slightly.

Meanwhile skim the fat off the surface of the cooking liquid with a metal spoon. Remove and discard the bouquet garni.

Detach all the meat from the carcass and discard the skin and bones. Slice the meat and return it to the liquid in the saucepan. Simmer the soup over a moderate heat for 5 minutes or until it is reheated through, then remove from the heat and transfer it to a warm tureen. Sprinkle over the parsley and serve at once.

6 servings

Vichyssoise

A well-known cold cream of leek and potato soup.

	Metric/UK	US
Butter	100g/4oz	$\frac{1}{2}$ cup
Leeks, chopped	1kg/2lb	2lb
Potatoes, peeled and chopped	$\frac{1}{2}$kg/1lb	1lb
Celery stalks, chopped	2	2
Chicken stock	600ml/ 1 pint	$2\frac{1}{2}$ cups
Milk	600ml/ 1 pint	$2\frac{1}{2}$ cups
Salt	1 tsp	1 tsp
Black pepper	$\frac{1}{2}$ tsp	$\frac{1}{2}$ tsp
Sugar	$\frac{1}{2}$ tsp	$\frac{1}{2}$ tsp
Grated nutmeg	$\frac{1}{4}$ tsp	$\frac{1}{4}$ tsp
Double (heavy) cream	300ml/ $\frac{1}{2}$ pint	$1\frac{1}{4}$ cups

In a large saucepan, melt the butter over a moderate heat. Add the leeks, potatoes and celery and fry, stirring continuously for 8 minutes. Pour in the stock and milk and bring the mixture to the boil. Season with salt, pepper, sugar and nutmeg.

Reduce the heat to low, cover the pan and simmer for 30–40 minutes, stirring occasionally until the vegetables are soft. Then remove the pan from the heat and either pour the mixture through a fine strainer, rubbing the vegetables through, or purée them in an electric blender. Stir half the cream into the purée and set aside to cool. Then place the soup in the refrigerator for at least 4 hours before serving. To serve, divide the soup among individual bowls, pour a little of the remaining cream into each and garnish as preferred, with chopped chives, parsley or even a little curry powder for added zest.

6 servings

Vichyssoise is the invention of the French chef Louis Diat–based on his mother's puréed potato and leek soup. It is served chilled.

SAUCES

A good sauce can enhance the flavour of food in many different ways. It can complement it or subtly contrast with it. It may form an integral part of the dish, where the juices of the dish are the basis of the sauce or it may be made separately. Some piquant sauces form a very sharp contrast to the food they accompany, such as mint sauce with lamb, or sauce tartare with fish; their intense and distinctive flavour means that only a small quantity is needed. The softness of a sauce can add a welcome change of texture to an all-crisp meal. Sauces look good, too. The appearance of a dish can be greatly improved by coating the food with a smooth, glossy sauce, as with a cheese sauce; or a sauce can add colour, as with the rich, red glow of tomato sauce, or the bright fresh green of parsley sauce.

The three basic types of sauce are white, brown and egg-based. In addition there are butter sauces, and sauces made from flavoured purées of a single ingredient, such as tomato, apple, mint, and bread sauce, and pan gravy or deglazing sauce. Sauces can be hot or cold, sweet or savoury, and the interesting thing is that however often you make a sauce by the same recipe, it will never taste exactly the same. Sauces are very individual, and once the basic sauces have been mastered, you can produce endless variations by the judicious addition of herbs, seasonings and spices.

White sauces

Both white and brown sauces are made from a combination of equal amounts of fat and flour, known as a roux, which is the basis of many classic sauces. In white sauce the fat is usually butter. Milk, or a mixture of milk and white stock, is blended into the roux over low heat and the sauce is stirred until cooked and smooth. White sauce can be almost infinitely varied. The milk can be flavoured first with herbs and other seasonings, when the sauce is called Béchamel. Béchamel is richer than a simple white sauce and is a delicious base for other sauces, using mushrooms, cheese, tomatoes, shrimps and many other additions. These can also be added to a plain white sauce.

Brown sauces

In a white sauce the roux is cooked for only a minute or two before adding the liquid; it is known as a *roux blond*. If the fat and flour are allowed to colour to a rich brown before the liquid is added, the roux is a *roux brun*, the basis of many brown sauces. Care must be taken not to burn the roux, or the sauce will have the bitter taste of burnt flour. The fat used in brown sauce can be cooking oil, dripping or vegetable fat (shortening), giving a more robust taste than butter, and liquids such as brown stock or red wine are used. A brown sauce needs longer cooking than a white sauce to develop the flavour.

Egg-based sauces

These rich sauces make use of the ability of whisked egg yolks to absorb a surprising amount of butter or oil. The butter or oil is gradually whisked into the yolks to make a shiny, creamy sauce. Made with butter in a bain-marie or double boiler, to protect it from direct heat, this is Hollandaise Sauce, traditionally served warm with asparagus or salmon; made cold with olive oil, it is Mayonnaise. These sauces are not hard to make if certain points are remembered: the egg yolks must be well beaten first, and the oil or butter must be added in tiny amounts to begin with, until the sauce begins to thicken.

Butter sauces

Sauces based on butter, without flour or eggs, are lighter than the rich egg-based sauces. Vinegar is flavoured with herbs and reduced to make it more potent, and the butter is whisked into it. Perhaps the best known of these sauces is *Beurre Noir*, or black butter sauce, often served with fish but just as good with eggs, chicken breasts or calves' brains.

Consistency of sauces

A pouring sauce, at boiling point, should just coat the back of a wooden spoon. A coating or binding sauce is one which coats the back of the spoon well and is too thick to pour easily. Sauce for coating must be used at once, and the food to be cooked should also be hot if the sauce is to stay smooth. A thick white sauce can be used to bind together small particles of food, as when making croquettes.

If you are making a roux-based sauce, a roux of about 25g/1oz (¼ cup) flour and 25g/1oz (2 Tbsp) fat will thicken 600ml/1 pint (2½ cups) of liquid to a pouring consistency. To make a coating sauce, use about 50g/2oz (½ cup) flour and 50g/2oz (¼ cup) fat to 600ml/1 pint (2½ cups) of liquid.

A pouring sauce or gravy goes further than a coating sauce; 300ml/½ pint (1¼ cups) will serve 4–6 people, while the same quantity of coating sauce will coat four helpings of meat, fish or vegetables.

Thickening sauces

There are three basic ways of thickening sauces, apart from making a roux; sometimes a sauce recipe combines more than one of these, but it is useful to know the principles. If a flour-based sauce is too thin any of these methods can be used to thicken it, but they are not suitable for egg-based sauces.

1. Reducing The sauce is simmered gently; some of the water in the sauce escapes as steam, making it thicker and more pronounced in flavour.

2. Adding flour or arrowroot Flour, cornflour (cornstarch), potato flour or arrowroot can be used. Arrowroot gives a rich, clear, shiny finish to a sauce. A small quantity of the liquid to be thickened is cooled and then thoroughly mixed with the measured quantity of the thickening agent. The mixture is added to the rest of the liquid and the sauce is stirred briskly over a low heat until it is smooth.

Flour can also be added to sauce or stew in the form of a *beurre manié*.

3. Adding egg yolks As in 2 above, a small quantity of the liquid is cooled and then blended with the egg yolks, and the mixture is then returned to the rest of the liquid. After adding the egg yolks be careful not to boil the sauce, or the eggs will harden and scramble.

Step-by-Step to Basic White Sauce

Melt the butter slowly in a small saucepan. Be careful not to let it sizzle or become brown, or it will change the colour of the sauce.

Remove the pan from the heat and stir in the flour to a smooth paste. Return to the heat and stir for 1–2 minutes until smooth.

Either heat the liquid in a separate pan until it is as hot as your finger can bear (do not let it boil), or add straight to the roux.

Now remove the roux pan from the heat and gradually add a little liquid, stirring continuously until all the liquid has been added.

When the mixture is blended, return the pan to the heat and bring the sauce to the boil, stirring continuously. Season to taste.

Reduce the heat to low and cook for 5–7 minutes to cook the flour—you can either cover the pan or not, as you prefer.

Basic White Sauce

This is the foundation for many of the popular sauces.

	Metric/UK	US
Butter	25g/1oz	2 Tbsp
Flour	25g/1oz	$\frac{1}{4}$ cup
Milk	600ml/ 1 pint	$2\frac{1}{2}$ cups
Salt	$\frac{1}{2}$ tsp	$\frac{1}{2}$ tsp
Pepper	to taste	to taste

To make the roux, melt the butter over a low heat. Remove the saucepan from the heat and stir in the flour with a wooden spoon, mixing to a smooth paste. Return to a low heat and stir the roux for 1–2 minutes, so that it bubbles gently. Remove from the heat, let it cool slightly, then gradually add the milk, mixing it in vigorously with the spoon. If the roux is too hot when the liquid is added it can make the sauce lumpy. Return the sauce once again to the low heat and keep stirring until it thickens and is smooth and shiny, and the flour is cooked. This takes about 5–7 minutes. If the flour is not cooked long enough the sauce will have the rough taste of raw flour. Adjust the consistency, if necessary by adding more liquid and add seasoning.
About 450ml/$\frac{3}{4}$ pint (2 cups)

Béchamel Sauce

This variation on a basic white sauce can be enriched with a little cream, egg yolk or both. (See method 3 under Thickening above for adding egg yolk.) If you add either cream or egg yolk, remember that you must not let the sauce come to the boil again.

	Metric/UK	US
Milk	450ml/ $\frac{3}{4}$ pint	2 cups
Bayleaf	1	1
Peppercorns	6	6
Grated nutmeg	$\frac{1}{8}$ tsp	$\frac{1}{8}$ tsp
Butter	40g/1$\frac{1}{2}$oz	3 Tbsp
Flour	25g/1oz	$\frac{1}{4}$ cup
Salt	$\frac{1}{2}$ tsp	$\frac{1}{2}$ tsp
White pepper	$\frac{1}{4}$ tsp	$\frac{1}{4}$ tsp

Put the milk, with the bayleaf, peppercorns and nutmeg, in a small saucepan over a low heat. Warm it for 10 minutes, but do not let it boil. Strain it into a bowl and set aside to cool. Now make the roux as described previously, then add the flavoured milk as for Basic White Sauce.
About 300ml/$\frac{1}{2}$ pint (1$\frac{1}{4}$ cups)

Milk, eggs, onions, cheese, mustard, shrimp, mushrooms—only a few of the many ingredients which flavour the sauces described here.

Variations on White or Béchamel Sauce

Name	Addition to 450ml/¾ pint (2 cups) White or Béchamel Sauce	Variations in Method	Name	Addition to 450ml/¾ pint (2 cups) White or Béchamel Sauce	Variations in Method
Anchovy Sauce	3 tsp anchovy essence (1½–2 Tbsp anchovy paste) 1 tsp lemon juice	Use fish stock as part of liquid. Add essence (paste) and lemon juice at the end.	Mushroom Sauce	75g/3oz (¾ cup) mushrooms 1 tsp lemon juice	Finely chop the mushrooms and cook in butter. Add the flour and use this as the roux. Add lemon juice at the end.
Cheese Sauce	3 heaped Tbsp of dry, grated cheese ½ tsp made mustard, shake of cayenne pepper	Use all milk in the sauce, Add the cheese, mustard and cayenne and stir until cheese is melted. Sprinkle the completed dish with extra cheese. Brown under grill (broiler).	Shrimp Sauce	75g/3oz (½ cup) chopped peeled shrimps, ½ tsp anchovy essence (1½ tsp anchovy paste), 1 tsp lemon juice	Add shrimps, essence (paste) and lemon juice to the completed sauce. Warm thoroughly.
Caper Sauce	3 Tbsp capers, roughly chopped 3 tsp vinegar	Use fish or meat liquor from the dish as part of liquid. Add capers and vinegar at the end.	Parsley Sauce	¾ Tbsp finely chopped parsley	Add parsley to the sauce and cook for 1 minute.
Herb Sauce	2–3 heaped Tbsp of finely chopped mixed fresh herbs, e.g. basil, chives, fennel, parsley etc.	Add herbs to the hot sauce and simmer for 1 or 2 minutes.			
Watercress Sauce	Small bunch of watercress 1 tsp lemon juice	Plunge watercress in boiling water. Chop finely, drain and simmer for 2 minutes in completed sauce. Add lemon juice at the end.			

Sauce Espagnole

This strong, rich-flavoured sauce, is based on a roux noir. It may accompany steak, vegetables, game or eggs, or it can be the basis for other sauces.

	Metric/UK	US
Fat (dripping, lard, butter or margarine)	100g/4oz	½ cup
Medium-sized onion, sliced	1	1
Medium-sized carrot, thinly sliced	1	1
Lean veal, finely chopped	50g/2oz	⅓ cup
Lean cooked ham, finely chopped	50g/2oz	⅓ cup
Parsley sprigs, chopped	4	4
Flour	75g/3oz	¾ cup
Beef stock or brown stock	2L/3½ pints	4½ pints
Mushroom peelings	2 Tbsp	2 Tbsp
Cloves	2	2
Bayleaves	2	2
White wine	450ml/¾ pint	2 cups
Salt	½ tsp	½ tsp
Black pepper	½ tsp	½ tsp

In a heavy saucepan heat the fat over a moderate heat. Add the onion, carrot, veal, ham and parsley. Cook, stirring occasionally, for 15 minutes, or until the vegetables are tender. Sprinkle on the flour and stir with a wooden spoon to make a roux. Reduce the heat to low and cook until it is brown, but not burned, stirring continuously. Remove from the heat and gradually add the stock, stirring continuously. Return to the heat and, still stirring, bring the liquid to the boil. Add the mushroom peelings.

Reduce the heat to very low and add the cloves, bayleaves, white wine, salt and pepper. Simmer the mixture gently for about 1 hour, regularly skimming off scum and fat.

Strain the sauce through cheesecloth over a bowl. Rub the solid ingredients in the cheesecloth with the back of a wooden spoon, to press out the juice. Discard the pulp left in the strainer. Rinse out the saucepan and return the strained sauce to it. Bring it to the boil over a moderate heat, then reduce the heat to low and simmer. As the fat rises to the surface, remove it with a metal spoon. Taste and add more salt and pepper if necessary.

Since this sauce freezes well and is so useful, it is well worth making a large quantity at one time and freezing it in family-size cartons.

About 1.8L/3 pints (7½ cups)

First, warm the goblet of your blender. (To do this, fill it with hot water, leave it for 5 minutes, then rinse out and dry.)

Meanwhile, put the vinegar, peppercorns and bayleaf in a pan and boil over moderate heat until the liquid is reduced to 1½ Tbsp.

Strain the vinegar into a cup and set aside. Melt the butter over low heat, then pour it carefully into a small jug. Set aside.

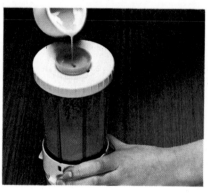

Put the egg yolks into the goblet of the blender, then carefully pour in the reduced vinegar mixture. Blend for about 4 seconds.

While blending, gradually add the melted butter in a very slow trickle through the top of the blender, until the sauce is thick.

Season to taste with salt, pepper and lemon juice. Blend for a further 10 seconds, then turn into a sauceboat to serve.

Sauce Diable

The piquant flavour of this sauce, based on Sauce Espagnole, complements steak or chicken.

	Metric/UK	US
Butter	1 Tbsp	1 Tbsp
Onion, finely chopped	1	1
Garlic cloves, crushed	2	2
Salt	½ tsp	½ tsp
Black pepper	½ tsp	½ tsp
Cayenne pepper	⅛ tsp	⅛ tsp
French mustard	1 Tbsp	1 Tbsp
Vinegar	1 Tbsp	1 Tbsp
Mango chutney	1 Tbsp	1 Tbsp
Worcestershire sauce	1 Tbsp	1 Tbsp
Tomato ketchup	2 Tbsp	2 Tbsp
Dried tarragon	½ tsp	½ tsp
Dried thyme	½ tsp	½ tsp

Sauce Espagnole	600ml/	2½ cups
	1 pint	

In a medium-sized frying-pan, melt the butter over a moderate heat. Add the onion and garlic and fry them, stirring occasionally until they are soft and translucent. Using a slotted spoon, transfer the onion and garlic to a medium-sized saucepan.

Stir all the other ingredients into the saucepan and cook the sauce for 25 minutes over a low heat, stirring occasionally.

Serve in a warmed sauceboat.

About 600ml/1 pint (2½ cups)

Deglazing Sauce

Deglazing sauce is a simple brown sauce made with the juices left in the pan after roasting.

	Metric/UK	US
Brown stock	300ml/	1¼ cups
	½ pint	
Juices from pan		

Pour off the fat from the pan. Add the stock to the pan and scrape all the coagulated juices from the bottom with a spoon. Boil the sauce fast until it is reduced by about half. If you have no stock you can deglaze with wine, or a mixture of wine and the water green vegetables have cooked in.
About 150ml/5floz (⅔ cup)

Pan Gravy

To make a thick gravy, instead of pouring away all the fat from a roasting pan, leave enough to make a roux. Add enough flour to combine with it and stir over a moderate heat for a few minutes as for Brown Sauce. Let the roux cool, then gradually add water, vegetable cooking water, stock or wine and water, until the desired consistency is reached. Let it boil and simmer for 5–7 minutes to cook the flour. Check the seasoning.

Hollandaise Sauce

This is traditionally served with asparagus or salmon, but it is also delicious with other vegetables, such as broccoli, and other fish dishes.

	Metric/UK	US
White wine vinegar	5 Tbsp	5 Tbsp
Peppercorns	6	6
Bayleaf	1	1

Tournedos Henri IV are classically garnished with spicy Béarnaise Sauce.

Butter	175g/6oz	¾ cup
Egg yolks	3	3
Salt	⅛ tsp	⅛ tsp

Put the vinegar, peppercorns and bayleaf in a small saucepan and bring to the boil. Simmer over a moderate heat until the liquid is reduced to 1¼ tablespoons (about 10 minutes). Strain into a cup and set aside.

In a small mixing bowl, cream the butter with a wooden spoon until it is soft. In another small, heat-proof mixing bowl or the top of a double boiler, beat the egg yolks well with a wire whisk to mix them together. Beat in the salt and a heaped teaspoon of the butter. Stir in the strained vinegar, and mix well. Place the bowl or pan with the egg yolk mixture over a sauce-pan filled with warm water. Place the pan over a low heat. The water should heat slowly but never be allowed to boil. Whisk or stir the egg yolk mixture until it begins to thicken.

Add the remaining butter, a teaspoon at a time, stirring constantly. Add a little more salt if needed; if a little too sharp, add more butter. If the sauce is too thick, add a little cream. Serve warm.
About 250ml/8floz (1 cup)

39

Variations

1. Hollandaise Sauce with egg whites: 2 stiffly beaten egg whites may be folded in just before serving to lighten the sauce and make it go further.

2. Hollandaise Sauce with Herbs: 1 tablespoon of finely chopped mixed fresh herbs may be stirred into the sauce before serving. Choose from tarragon, marjoram, oregano, chives or lemon thyme.

3. Hollandaise Sauce with Orange: Add 1 teaspoon of orange juice to the initial vinegar mixture, and just before serving stir in 2 tablespoons of orange juice and 1 teaspoon of grated orange rind.

4. Hollandaise Sauce with Cream (Mousseline Sauce): Add 250ml/8floz (1 cup) of stiffly whipped double (heavy) cream to the basic Hollandaise.

Béarnaise Sauce

Béarnaise Sauce is similar to Hollandaise Sauce but is thicker and sharper. It is served with steak, other grilled (broiled) red meat such as pork chops or venison cutlets or fish and some shellfish.

	Metric/UK	US
Wine vinegar	5 Tbsp	5 Tbsp
Shallot or small onion, cut in 4 pieces	1	1
Bayleaf	1	1
Tarragon sprig	1	1
Chervil sprig	1	1
Peppercorns	4	4
Butter	100g/4oz	$\frac{1}{2}$ cup
Large egg yolks	2	2
Salt	$\frac{1}{8}$ tsp	$\frac{1}{8}$ tsp
Cayenne pepper	$\frac{1}{8}$ tsp	$\frac{1}{8}$ tsp
Chopped fresh tarragon and chervil, mixed	1 tsp	1 tsp

Put the vinegar in a small saucepan with the shallot or onion, bayleaf, tarragon sprig, chervil sprig and peppercorns. Bring to the boil and simmer until the vinegar is reduced to 1 tablespoon. Strain and set aside. Now proceed as for Hollandaise sauce. When all the butter has

Beurres Composées, or flavoured butters, make interesting accompaniments or garnishes. On the Top Right is Beurre au Citron (lemon butter) used with cold hors d'oeuvre; top Extreme Right is Beurre de Crevettes à Froid (cold shrimp butter) used with fish soups and sauces; Bottom Right is Beurre à l'Oeuf (egg yolk butter) used for sandwiches or canapés; and bottom Extreme Right Beurre de Moutarde (mustard butter) used with kidneys, steaks or grilled (broiled) fish.

been added, add the cayenne and chopped tarragon and chervil.
About 150ml/5floz ($\frac{2}{3}$ cup)

Beurre Nantais

Warm, thick and creamy, this is usually served with pike but is equally delicious with any fish.

	Metric/UK	US
White wine vinegar	75ml/3floz	$\frac{1}{3}$ cup
Dry white wine or lemon juice	75ml/3floz	$\frac{1}{3}$ cup
Shallot, finely chopped	1 Tbsp	1 Tbsp
Salt	$\frac{1}{4}$ tsp	$\frac{1}{4}$ tsp
White pepper	$\frac{3}{4}$ tsp	$\frac{3}{4}$ tsp
Chilled butter, cut into 24 pieces	350g/12oz	$1\frac{1}{2}$ cups

Boil the vinegar, wine or lemon juice, shallot, salt and pepper until reduced to 1 tablespoon as in Béarnaise Sauce. Remove from heat and slowly whisk in one piece of butter. When it has been absorbed, add another piece and whisk vigorously. Return to a very low heat and continue to add pieces of butter, whisking continuously, until it has all been absorbed and the sauce is thick and creamy. Adjust the seasoning. Serve at once.
About 350g/12oz ($1\frac{1}{2}$ cups)

Beurre Noir

	Metric/UK	US
Butter	175g/6oz	$\frac{3}{4}$ cup
Chopped parsley	3 Tbsp	3 Tbsp
Wine vinegar	4 Tbsp	4 Tbsp
Salt	$\frac{1}{4}$ tsp	$\frac{1}{4}$ tsp
Black pepper	$\frac{1}{4}$ tsp	$\frac{1}{4}$ tsp

This sauce should never be black, despite its name. To avoid this, clarify the butter first.

To clarify, melt the butter over a low heat until it foams. Skim off the foam and pour the clear butter into a bowl. Rinse out the pan and strain the butter into it. Place the pan over the heat and the butter will turn brown. Remove from the heat and stir in the parsley. Set aside. Reduce the vinegar to 1 tablespoon. Stir it into the browned butter. Add the salt and pepper. Either serve at once or keep warm until needed over warm water.
About 175g/6oz ($\frac{3}{4}$ cup)

Flavoured Butter

Butter can be transformed by beating various flavourings into it; it is sometimes known as beurre composé. *Flavoured butters can be served with grilled (broiled) fish or meat or used to fill hard-boiled (hard-cooked) eggs; they can also be stirred into sauce or soup to give added flavour and sheen.*

Various Flavoured Butters

Name	Addition to 100g/4oz ($\frac{1}{2}$ cup) softened butter	Variations in method	Name	Addition to 100g/4oz ($\frac{1}{2}$ cup) softened butter	Variations in method
Beurre d'Ail (*Garlic Butter*)	4 garlic cloves, unpeeled	Drop the garlic in boiling water. Drain, peel. Pound to a smooth paste with the butter. Chill.	Beurre d' Estragon (*Tarragon Butter*)	1 Tbsp lemon juice, 3 Tbsp chopped tarragon, $\frac{1}{4}$ tsp salt, $\frac{1}{8}$ tsp white pepper	Beat in the lemon juice then add the remaining ingredients. Chill.
Beurre au Citron (*Lemon Butter*)	Grated rind of 1 lemon, $\frac{1}{4}$ tsp salt, $\frac{1}{4}$ tsp pepper	Combine the ingredients. Strain, cover and chill.	Beurre de Moutarde (*Mustard Butter*)	1 Tbsp prepared French mustard, $\frac{1}{4}$ tsp salt, $\frac{1}{8}$ tsp pepper, 2 Tbsp chopped parsley	Combine everything. Chill.
Beurre de Crévettes à Froid (*Cold Shrimp Butter*)	100g/4oz ($\frac{2}{3}$ cup) peeled cooked shrimps. 1 Tbsp lemon juice, $\frac{1}{2}$ tsp salt	Combine the pounded shrimps, butter and lemon juice. Strain, cover and chill.	Beurre à l'Oeuf (*Egg Yolk Butter*)	4 hard-boiled (hard-cooked), strained egg yolks, salt, pepper, 2 Tbsp chopped chives	Beat in the egg yolks and seasonings. Chill.

Mayonnaise

Like Hollandaise, Mayonnaise is an emulsion made from egg yolks and fat, but while Hollandaise is served warm, Mayonnaise is served cold. Olive oil is used in it traditionally, but any good salad oil can be substituted successfully, such as corn, groundnut or soya-bean oil, or you can use half olive oil and half one of these oils. Really fresh eggs form the most stable emulsion and it is recommended that all the ingredients be at room temperature. The addition of a little cream to a finished Mayonnaise enhances the texture and flavour. Mayonnaise is used as a salad dressing, to coat cold fish and eggs and to decorate cold buffet dishes.

	Metric/UK	US
Egg yolk	1	1
Salt	$\frac{1}{4}$ tsp	$\frac{1}{4}$ tsp
Dry mustard	$\frac{3}{4}$ tsp	$\frac{3}{4}$ tsp
White pepper	$\frac{1}{8}$ tsp	$\frac{1}{8}$ tsp
Oil (olive or vegetable)	150ml/5 floz	$\frac{2}{3}$ cup
White wine vinegar or lemon juice	1 Tbsp	1 Tbsp
Castor (superfine) sugar	1 tsp	1 tsp

Place the egg yolk and dry seasonings in a medium-sized bowl. Beat with a wire whisk until thoroughly blended and slightly thickened. Place the oil in a small jug and begin adding to the egg mixture a drop at a time, whisking vigorously. When the emulsion begins to thicken—by this time about half the oil will have been added—you can begin to add the oil in a thin, steady stream still beating continuously. Do not be tempted to add the oil too quickly or the mixture will curdle. Add a few drops of vinegar or lemon juice when the mixture becomes too thick to beat easily. Continue to add the oil in a steady stream, beating well. The finished mayonnaise should be as thick as double (heavy) cream. When all the oil has been added, beat in enough vinegar or lemon juice to make the required consistency. Taste and adjust the seasoning. The addition of a little sugar can help to pull the flavours together.
About 150ml/5 floz ($\frac{2}{3}$ cup)

Curdling

If the mixture has curdled, the following steps can be taken to remedy the situation.

Firstly, try warming the bowl with a warm cloth. This can sometimes be sufficient if the curdling process has just begun. If this is not successful, then take a clean mixing bowl and put in a fresh egg yolk and seasonings. Slowly beat in the curdled mixture and a smooth mayonnaise should result. Adjust the seasoning.

Another method of rectifying curdled mayonnaise is to warm a small bowl in hot water and dry it thoroughly. Put in a tablespoon of mayonnaise and a teaspoon of dry mustard and whisk until creamy. Continue to add the sauce, teaspoon by teaspoon, whisking very well after each addition.

Blender method

Mayonnaise can be made successfully in an electric blender. The tendency of the emulsion to curdle is greatly reduced. Use whole eggs instead of egg yolks, but the ingredients and amounts remain the same. Place the eggs, seasoning and most of the vinegar (reserve a small amount for adjusting later) in the blender. Switch the blender on and add the oil in a thin, steady stream, with the blender running. Adjust the consistency of the finished mayonnaise and season to taste. Mayonnaise made with whole eggs is slightly lighter than that made with yolks only.

Jellied Mayonnaise

If the mayonnaise is required for piping and garnishing cold dishes, then a slightly jellied mayonnaise can easily be prepared.

A classic home-made mayonnaise—not at all difficult to do particularly if you have a blender. For a lighter version use vegetable or good groundnut oil instead of olive, or add a whole egg instead of just the yolk.

Sauce or dressing	To basic mayonnaise add to taste:—	Sauce or dressing	To basic mayonnaise add to taste:—
Verte	Chopped herbs, puréed spinach, chopped watercress.	Aurore	Pulped tomatoes, tabasco sauce.
Niçoise	Tomato purée (paste), peppers, chives, tarragon.	Green Goddess	Anchovy, spring onions (scallions), herbs, sour cream.
Blue Cheese	Crumbled blue cheese (Danish, Stilton), sour cream.	Thousand Island	Pickle, tabasco sauce, olives and French dressing.
Tartare	Chopped gherkins (pickles), capers, chives, chervil, parsley.	Aioli	Crushed garlic.
Rémoulade	Hard-boiled (hard-cooked) egg, chopped gherkins (pickles), capers, chives, crushed garlic.	Gribiche	Strained hard-boiled (hard-cooked) egg yolk, capers, gherkins (pickles), strips of egg white.

Prepare one quantity of mayonnaise as in the basic method. Set aside. Over a low heat dissolve 7g/¼oz (½ envelope) gelatine in 2 tablespoons lemon juice and 1 tablespoon water. Add 1 teaspoon sugar and stir gently until dissolved. Allow the gelatine mixture to cool, but not set, then stir it into the mayonnaise until well blended. Leave in a cool place until on the point of setting, then use as required.

Variations

The basic flavour of mayonnaise can be altered to taste by adding a little Worcestershire sauce, horseradish, chopped cucumber, curry powder or paprika.

There are several classic sauces derived from mayonnaise, and these are outlined in the above chart although true individuality can be achieved by experimenting with unusual additions.

Sauce Demi-Glace

Based on a brown sauce, demi-glace sauce is itself often used as a base for other sauces, although it can be used as it is as an accompaniment to roasts or steaks.

	Metric/UK	US
Brown sauce	750ml/ 1¼ pints	3 cups
Beef stock	1.2L/2 pints	5 cups
Mushroom peelings	2 Tbsp	2 Tbsp
Madeira	5 Tbsp	5 Tbsp

Put the brown sauce and the beef stock in a large saucepan with the mushroom peelings. Bring the liquid to the boil, then reduce the heat to moderate and simmer gently for 30 minutes or until reduced to one third of the original quantity. Stir in the Madeira. Strain the sauce through cheesecloth and serve in a warmed sauceboat. Once again, it is worth making a large quantity of this sauce at one time and freezing the surplus.

Two sauces based on sauce demi-glace are Sauce Bigarade—the classic accompaniment to Canard à l'Orange, the most famous of duck dishes—and the rich, creamy Sauce Ivoire, which complements eggs, chicken and liver so well.
About 600ml/1 pint (2½ cups)

Sauce Ivoire

	Metric/UK	US
Arrowroot	1 tsp	1 tsp
Sauce demi-glace	50ml/2 floz	¼ cup
Butter	50g/2oz	¼ cup
Flour	25g/1oz	¼ cup
Chicken stock	900ml/ 1½ pints	3¾ cups
Single (light) cream	250ml/8 floz	1 cup

Dissolve the arrowroot in the sauce demi-glace.

In a medium-sized saucepan, use half of the butter and the flour to make a roux. Add half the chicken stock and make a thick, creamy sauce. Gradually pour in the remaining chicken stock, stirring constantly. Increase the heat to high and bring the sauce to the boil. Continue boiling for 10 minutes or until the sauce is reduced by about half.

Place the arrowroot and sauce mixture in a small saucepan and bring to the boil. Reduce the heat to low and cook for 2–3 minutes, stirring continuously, until the mixture is very thick.

Remove the chicken stock sauce from the heat and stir in the cream. Return to the heat and cook gently for 5 minutes. Remove from the heat and add the remaining butter, a little at a time until well blended. Stir in the arrowroot mixture and cook for a further 5 minutes, stirring continuously until smooth, well-blended and hot. Pour into a warm sauceboat and serve.
About 750ml/1¼ pints (3 cups)

Sauce Bigarade

This sauce—the classic accompaniment to Canard à l'Orange—takes its name from Bigarade oranges, the bitter oranges traditionally used in it.

	Metric/UK	US
Butter	15g/½oz	1 Tbsp
Shallots, finely chopped	2	2
Red wine	125ml/4 floz	½ cup
Bayleaf	1	1
Sauce demi-glace	450ml/ ¾ pint	2 cups
Thinly pared rind and juice of 1 orange		
Redcurrant jelly	1 tsp	1 tsp

In a medium-sized saucepan, melt the butter over a moderate heat. Add the shallots and cook them, stirring occasionally, until they are soft and translucent.

Add the wine and bayleaf and cook for 5 minutes or until the liquid is reduced by about one-third. Stir in the sauce demi-glace. Add half the orange rind and the orange juice. Reduce the heat to low and simmer the sauce for 7 minutes, stirring occasionally.

Meanwhile, finely chop the remaining orange rind. Place in a small saucepan and cover with water. Place over a high heat and boil for 5 minutes. Strain the sauce into a third saucepan, stir in the softened rind and the redcurrant jelly. Bring to the boil and, stirring gently, cook for 2 minutes until the jelly has dissolved. Pour into a warm sauceboat and serve immediately.
About 450ml/¾ pint (2 cups)

Tomato Sauce

If this fresh tomato sauce is not required at once, it will keep for up to 5 days in a screw-top jar in the refrigerator.

	Metric/UK	US
Tomatoes, halved	1.35kg/3lb	3lb
Salt	2 tsp	2 tsp
Sugar	2 tsp	2 tsp
Dried basil	1 tsp	1 tsp
Lemon rind, grated	½ tsp	½ tsp

Preheat the oven to warm (170°C/325°F, Gas Mark 3). Place the tomatoes in a large ovenproof dish, cover and bake for about 45 minutes, or until they are very soft.

Remove the tomatoes from the oven and transfer them to a strainer placed over a large saucepan. Rub the tomatoes through the strainer, with the back of a wooden spoon, to press out the juice. Discard the pulp left in the strainer. Add the salt, sugar, basil and lemon rind to the tomatoes in the pan and place it over a moderate heat. Cook to reduce the sauce, stirring frequently with a wooden spoon, for 10 minutes or until the mixture is fairly thick. Remove the pan from the heat, and pour the sauce into a warm sauceboat, if you are serving it immediately. Or cool completely, pour into a screw-top jar and store in the refrigerator until required.
About 750ml/1¼ pints (3 cups)

Bread Sauce

	Metric/UK	US
Onion, studded with 2 cloves	1	1
Bayleaf	1	1
Milk	300ml/ ½ pint	1¼ cups
Fresh white breadcrumbs	50g/2oz	1 cup
Salt	½ tsp	½ tsp
Black pepper	¼ tsp	¼ tsp
Butter	1 Tbsp	1 Tbsp
Single (light) cream	1 Tbsp	1 Tbsp

Put the onion, bayleaf and milk into a medium-sized

Rich, tangy Sauce Ivoire has, as its base, demi-glace sauce and cream. It is traditionally served with eggs, chicken or thinly sliced liver.

saucepan, cover and cook for 10–15 minutes over a very low heat. The milk will become infused with the flavour of the onion and spices.

Remove the onion and bayleaf. Bring the milk to just below boiling point and add the breadcrumbs. Reduce the heat to low and simmer for 3–4 minutes, or until the sauce is thick and creamy.

Remove the pan from the heat and stir in the seasonings, butter and cream. Gently reheat the sauce over a very low heat, being careful not to let it boil. Serve at once.
4 servings

Mint Sauce

	Metric/UK	US
Finely chopped fresh mint	12 Tbsp	12 Tbsp
Sugar	1½ Tbsp	1½ Tbsp
Malt or white vinegar	90ml/3 floz	⅓ cup
Water, hot	1 Tbsp	1 Tbsp

Pound the mint and sugar together in a mortar with a pestle. Alternatively, beat them together in a small bowl with a wooden spoon. Add the vinegar and hot water and stir until the sugar has dissolved. Set the bowl aside and leave it to infuse for 1–2 hours before serving.
About 175ml/6 floz (¾ cup)

Apple Sauce

Tart apple sauce is the traditional accompaniment to roast pork, goose or duck.

	Metric/UK	US
Cooking apples	700g/1½lb	1½lb
Lemon rind, finely grated	1 Tbsp	1 Tbsp
Water	1 Tbsp	1 Tbsp
Salt	⅛ tsp	⅛ tsp
Sugar to taste		
Butter	40g/1½oz	3 Tbsp

Peel, core and slice the apples. Place them in slightly salted water while they are being prepared to prevent them from turning brown. Then drain and rinse, and put them in a pan with the lemon rind, water and salt.

Cover the pan and simmer over a low heat until the apples are soft. Add the sugar to taste a little at a time, stirring continuously. (This sauce should not be sweet however.) Allow the apples to cool, then rub them through a strainer with the back of a wooden spoon to make a fine purée. Beat in the butter. If the sauce is to be served hot, return it to a clean saucepan and simmer it over a low heat for 2–3 minutes.
About 250ml/8 floz (1 cup)

45

EGGS

The egg is used a great deal in cooking. It contains protein, fat, calcium, iron and vitamins—a balanced meal in its own right, and easily digested. Eggs have five basic functions in cooking:

Egg yolk is used as an emulsifying agent in such fat-based sauces as Mayonnaise and Hollandaise. It absorbs butter or oil to make a rich sauce. Beaten egg yolks are used to thicken sauces, custards and soups; whole eggs or egg yolks are used to bind particles of food in croquettes and fish or meat cakes; beaten egg with breadcrumbs is used to coat food before frying. This helps to stop the food from disintegrating; whisked egg whites trap air and vastly increase in size. This makes them useful as a raising (leavening) agent in baking cakes and soufflés.

Storage

Eggs should be eaten as fresh as possible, so it is advisable to buy frequently from a store where there is a large turnover. There is no real need to store them in a refrigerator, except in very hot climates, as any cool, airy place will suffice. If you do keep them in a refrigerator, take them out and let them warm to room temperature before cooking.

Eggs cannot be frozen whole, but surplus yolks *or* whites can be frozen separately and used at a later date, thus avoiding waste with certain recipes which call for either yolks alone or whites alone.

Separating eggs

You can buy small egg separators, which hold the yolk in a central depression and allow the white to drain away into a ready-waiting bowl, but they are not really necessary. The simplest method is to break the shell neatly in half over a bowl or cup and tip the yolk carefully from one half of the shell to the other, allowing the white to run off into the bowl. If the egg is fresh the yolk should be firm enough not to break; if any yolk escapes into the white, its whisking properties will be spoiled. So break each egg individually and add separately to the mixing bowl.

Beating egg whites

No yolk must be present in the white, nor should any grease particles be present in the bowl or on the beater. The inside of the bowl can be carefully rubbed over with a small piece of lemon to ensure this.

The best whisk for hand beating is a large balloon whisk made of thin wire, but the kind of beater with a handle at the top and a rotary handle at the side, which is held against the bottom of the bowl, will also give good results. Use a large bowl, china is fine, or stainless steel if you are using an electric beater.

Begin by beating slowly, and when the whites begin

to foam add a tiny pinch of salt (or cream of tartar if you are using a stainless steel bowl). Gradually increase the speed until you are beating vigorously and the whites resemble stiff snow.

When stiff, the whites will hold a peak-shape, and you should be able to turn the bowl upside down without them falling out!

Beaten egg whites should be used at once, as they begin to separate almost immediately. If sugar has been added, as in a meringue mixture, then they will remain firm for a little longer, but they should be used as soon as possible. When you are adding egg whites to other ingredients, such as a soufflé mixture, tip the whites on top of the mixture, then lightly cut and fold, using a large metal spoon; take care not to over-mix as the air will be knocked out of the whites.

COOKING METHODS

The basic methods of cooking eggs are boiling, scrambling, frying, poaching, baking, omelettes and soufflés.

1. Boiling

There are almost as many ways of boiling eggs as there are cooks. Here are two of the simplest. In the first, the egg is placed in a pan of simmering water and allowed to simmer for 3–4 minutes, according to the size of the egg. Alternatively, the egg can be placed in a pan of gently simmering water, simmered for 1 minute, then removed from the heat, covered and allowed to stand for 5 minutes. During this time it goes on cooking gently.

A small instrument can be bought for making a tiny pinhole in the shell at the round end of the egg before boiling; this stops the shell from cracking as the air inside expands. But if the egg is not too cold and the water is not boiling but simmering, then the shell should stay whole without this.

Many recipes call for hard-boiled (hard-cooked) eggs. These should be timed carefully. If an egg is boiled for too long, it becomes leathery, tough and unpleasant. The eggs should be placed in a pan of gently boiling water, and simmered for 10 minutes. Remove the eggs from the pan with a slotted spoon, and gently crack the shells, without removing them. Place the eggs under cold, running water for a few minutes, then shell when cold. This prevents a dark ring from forming around the yolk.

2. Scrambling

In a small bowl, beat 2 eggs together with ½ teaspoon

salt, $\frac{1}{4}$ teaspoon black pepper and 2 tablespoons milk or single (light) cream (optional). In a medium-sized pan, melt a piece of butter the size of small walnut over a moderate heat. Pour in the egg mixture and cook over a low heat for 3–4 minutes, stirring continuously with a wooden spoon until the mixture starts to thicken. Remove the pan from the heat before the eggs look done, and continue to stir until thick and creamy. Opinions vary on how 'done' the eggs should be, but it is easy to overcook them. Serve at once.

3. Frying

Fried eggs can be used to top many favourite dishes, adding colour and food value. They are delicious with hamburgers and grilled (broiled) and fried meat.

In a small frying-pan, heat 1 tablespoon of olive oil, butter or bacon fat. When it is sizzling, break the egg carefully into the pan. Reduce the heat to low and cook gently until the white is set and the yolk fairly firm. Remove with a spatula and serve immediately.

If you like your fried egg well done, the egg can be turned when nearly cooked, so that the top cooks firmly.

4. Poaching

Half fill a small saucepan with water. Add $\frac{1}{2}$ teaspoon salt and 1 teaspoon of vinegar. Place over a moderate heat and bring to the boil. Break an egg into a cup, and carefully tip it into the middle of the boiling water. Reduce the heat to low and simmer gently for 3 minutes. Remove the egg with a slotted spoon.

If you find this gives a ragged-edged egg, try poaching the egg in less water—just enough to cover. Another useful trick is to put a round pastry (cookie) cutter into the pan of water and break the egg into that.

To make it really easy, you can use an egg-poacher. Half fill the bottom section of the pan with water. Put a small piece of butter in each egg compartment and place the pan over the heat. When the water boils, break the eggs into the compartments. Cover and simmer for 3–5 minutes or until the eggs are lightly set. Loosen the eggs with a knife and slide on to a plate or buttered toast.

5. Baking

This is one of the oldest methods of cooking eggs.

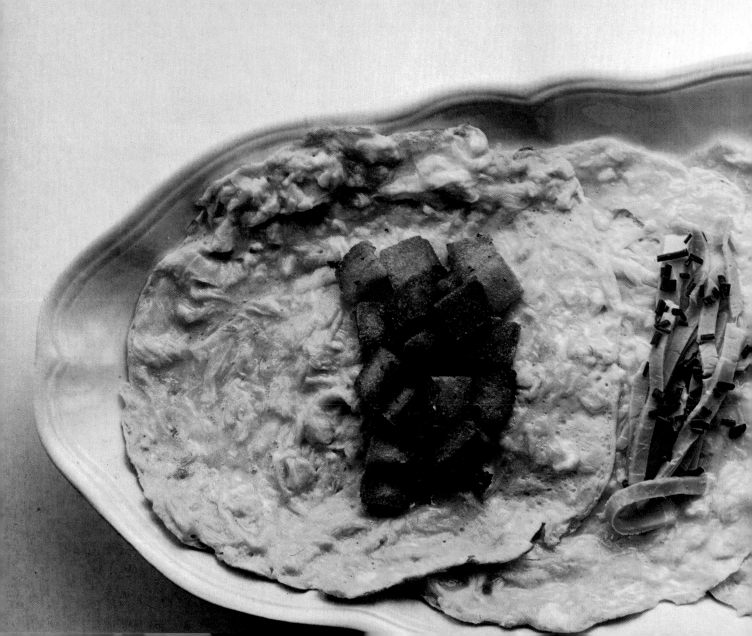

Usually they are cooked in individual cocotte dishes, although several can be cooked together in a shallow, ovenproof dish. Place the cocotte dishes on a baking sheet, put ½ teaspoon of butter in each dish, and cook in an oven preheated to fairly hot (200°C/400°F, Gas Mark 6) for 2 minutes. Break an egg into each dish, season with salt and pepper and bake in the oven for 4–5 minutes until lightly set. Serve at once.

6. Omelette

Ideally, keep a small heavy pan for cooking omelettes only. Do not wash it, but clean it out with kitchen paper towels. If it has to be washed, dry and oil it as when it was new. A classic French omelette should never be overcooked; the centre should still be soft and creamy.

BASIC RECIPE

	Metric/UK	US
Eggs	4	4
Salt	¼ tsp	¼ tsp
Black pepper	¼ tsp	¼ tsp
Cold water	2 Tbsp	2 Tbsp
Butter	25g/1oz	2 Tbsp

If the omelette has a filling, prepare this first. Set aside.

For the basic omelette mixture, beat the eggs, seasoning and water together with a fork. Heat the pan over a moderate heat for about half a minute. Melt the butter and, when it has stopped foaming, pour in the eggs.

Stir the eggs, then wait for a few seconds while the bottom sets. Lift the opposite side of the omelette with a spatula or knife and tilt the pan away from you, so that the liquid egg runs to the bottom. Put it level again. If you are using a filling, when the omelette is nearly set, spoon the filling on to one side of it. When it is just set, flip one half of the omelette over to make a semi-circle, and slide quickly on to a warmed serving dish.
2 servings

Fillings

You can use different fillings, and a few are suggested in the following chart.

Five omelette fillings, from left to right: croûtons, ham, asparagus, tuna fish and bonne femme.

A classic French omelette, here flavoured with grated Parmesan cheese and filled with cubed Gruyère and thick cream.

Name	Filling	Name	Filling
Omelette aux Champignons (Mushroom Omelette)	6 medium-sized button mushrooms, sliced and cooked for 3 minutes in 25g/1oz (2 Tbsp) butter.	Omelette aux Crevettes (Shrimp Omelette)	100g/4oz ($\frac{2}{3}$ cup) chopped, shelled shrimp and 1 Tbsp chopped parsley cooked in 25g/1oz (2 Tbsp) butter.
Omelette Lyonnaise (Onion Omelette)	2 small onions, thinly sliced and gently cooked in 25g/1oz (2 Tbsp) butter.	An Omelette aux Fines Herbes has 1½ Tbsp chopped fresh mixed herbs added to the egg mixture before cooking.	
Omelette au Jambon (Ham Omelette)	4 slices lean ham, cooked and diced then cooked until crisp in butter.	Omelette Chasseur (Mushroom, Shallots and Wine Omelette)	3 shallots, finely chopped, 6 mushrooms, sliced cooked in butter and 2 Tbsp white wine.
Omelette Bonne Femme (Bacon, Mushroom and Onion Omelette)	1 small onion thinly sliced and 2 bacon slices, chopped cooked in butter with 4 mushrooms.	Omelette à la Lorraine (Bacon, Cheese and Cream Omelette)	3 bacon slices, diced and cooked in butter. Add 2 Tbsp thick cream and 1½ Tbsp grated cheese. Garnish with chopped chives.

Butter a 1.4 L (2½ pint) soufflé dish generously. Coat with grated Parmesan cheese or dry breadcrumbs, swirling until coated and tipping out the excess. Chill.

Make a roux of butter and flour and, off the heat, gently add the liquid (usually milk), stirring continuously with a wooden spoon until the mixture becomes smooth.

Remove the sauce from the heat when thick and cool until tepid. Then stir in the filling (grated cheese in this case) and previously well beaten egg yolks.

Now beat the egg whites in a large bowl until they are very stiff and stand up in peaks (you should be able to turn the bowl upside down without the eggs falling out).

Gradually fold the cooled egg yolk mixture and the egg white mixture together until they are blended. Preheat the oven to moderate (about 180°C/350°F, Gas Mark 4 or above).

Finally pour the mixture into the soufflé dish and decorate the surface by marking a circle with a spatula or slice. Cook for 25–30 minutes or until it has risen and is golden.

Sweet omelettes

Sweet omelettes can also be delicious. They have a little icing (confectioner's) sugar added to the egg mixture.

Strawberry Omelette

This is delectable served with whipped cream. Other fruits such as raspberries or blackberries may be substituted.

Add 175g/6oz (1 cup) crushed strawberries to 2 Tbsp double (heavy) cream. Set aside. Add 40g/1½oz (⅓ cup) icing (confectioner's) sugar to the basic egg mixture. Proceed as before. Use the strawberry and cream mixture to fill the omelette. Dust with icing (confectioner's) sugar and serve.

7. Soufflé

This classic mixture of egg yolks mixed with a white sauce flavoured with vegetables, fish or fruit and lightened with stiffly beaten egg whites, may be eaten hot or cold. Savoury soufflés, however, are almost always eaten hot; sweet soufflés resemble a mousse in texture and are set by gelatine (gelatin) rather than just by the egg content.

To make a basic savoury soufflé, make a thick white sauce with butter and flour, then add the flavouring (usually in purée form) and the egg yolks. When the sauce has cooled, fold in the stiffly beaten egg whites and spoon the mixture into a well-greased soufflé dish. Bake in the oven preheated to moderate (180°C/350°F, Gas Mark 4) for 20–30 minutes, or until the soufflé has risen above the top of the dish.

RECIPES

Spanish Omelette

A Spanish omelette has a texture quite different from a French omelette. It is well cooked and weighty, and made with various fillings, such as onions and potatoes. It is cut in wedges like a cake and often eaten cold, on its own or with bread.

	Metric/UK	US
Butter	15g/$\frac{1}{2}$ oz	1 Tbsp
Olive oil	2 tsp	2 tsp
Large onion, chopped	1	1
Medium-sized potatoes, cooked and diced	4	4
Chopped parsley	1 Tbsp	1 Tbsp
Large eggs, lightly beaten	4	4
Salt and pepper to taste		

In a medium-sized frying pan, melt the butter with the oil over a moderate heat. Add the onion and fry until golden brown. Add the potatoes and cook for 2 minutes, stirring occasionally. Stir in the parsley. Combine the eggs and seasoning, and turn the heat to high.

Pour the eggs into the pan so that the bottom is evenly covered. Reduce the heat to moderate. Lift the edge of the omelette to let the liquid egg run underneath, as in a French omelette.

When the omelette is set, slide it carefully on to a plate, then turn it over as you return it to the pan, so that the other side can cook. Alternatively, the top can be browned under the grill (broiler).

Other possible fillings are garlic, tomatoes, canned pimentos, peas or Spanish sausage (chorizo). When the omelette is very bulky do not try to turn it over, but brown it under the grill (broiler).
2 servings

Oeufs Florentine (Eggs with Spinach)

Oeufs Florentine consists of poached eggs on a bed of creamy spinach sauce. If you allow one egg per person it can be served as an appetizer; with two eggs per person it makes a light main course dish.

	Metric/UK	US
Béchamel Sauce	350ml/ 12 fl oz	1$\frac{1}{2}$ cups
Grated nutmeg	$\frac{1}{4}$ tsp	$\frac{1}{4}$ tsp
Spinach purée	700g/1$\frac{1}{2}$lb	1$\frac{1}{2}$lb
Poached eggs, kept warm	8	8
Parmesan cheese, grated	50g/2oz	$\frac{1}{2}$ cup

In a medium-sized saucepan, combine one quarter of the béchamel sauce with the nutmeg and spinach. Place the pan over a moderate heat and cook, stirring continuously, for 3–4 minutes or until the sauce is smooth.

Preheat the grill (broiler) to high. Pour the spinach sauce into a shallow flameproof dish. Place the poached eggs on top. Spoon the remaining béchamel sauce over the eggs and sprinkle the top with Parmesan cheese. Place the dish under the grill (broiler) and cook for 3-4 minutes until the top is browned and bubbling. Serve at once.
4 servings

Cheese Soufflé

	Metric/UK	US
Butter	65g/2$\frac{1}{2}$oz	5 Tbsp
Gruyère and Parmesan cheese, grated	150g/5oz	1$\frac{1}{4}$ cups
Flour	4 Tbsp	4 Tbsp
Milk, scalded	300ml/ $\frac{1}{2}$ pint	1$\frac{1}{4}$ cups
Salt	1 tsp	1 tsp
White pepper	$\frac{1}{8}$ tsp	$\frac{1}{8}$ tsp
Ground mace	$\frac{1}{8}$ tsp	$\frac{1}{8}$ tsp
Paprika	$\frac{1}{8}$ tsp	$\frac{1}{8}$ tsp
Egg yolks	5	5
Egg whites	5	5
Cream of tartar	$\frac{1}{4}$ tsp	$\frac{1}{4}$ tsp

Preheat the oven to moderate (180°C/350°F, Gas Mark 4).

With 1 tablespoon of butter, grease a 1.35L/2$\frac{1}{4}$ pint (1$\frac{1}{2}$ quart) soufflé dish. Sprinkle 4 tablespoons of the grated cheese round the inside of the dish and press it on to the bottom and sides with a knife. Set the dish aside.

In a large saucepan, melt the remaining butter over a moderate heat. Stir in the flour with a wooden spoon and cook the roux, stirring continuously, for 1 minute. Do not allow it to brown.

Remove the pan from the heat. Gradually add the milk, stirring all the time. Return to the heat and cook, stirring continuously, for 1 minute or until it is thick and smooth.

Remove the pan from the heat and add $\frac{1}{2}$ teaspoon of salt, the pepper, mace and paprika. Beat the egg yolks into the hot sauce, a little at a time. Set the pan aside to allow the mixture to cool slightly.

Meanwhile, in a mixing bowl, beat the egg whites until foamy. Add the remaining salt and the cream of tartar. Continue beating until the egg whites form stiff peaks. Then stir the remaining cheese into the hot sauce. Spoon the egg whites on top and gently but quickly fold them in with a metal spoon. Stir the

Eggs Benedict, comprises poached eggs, ham and Hollandaise sauce on crumpets (muffins).

mixture at once into the prepared soufflé dish. Carefully mark a deep circle in the centre of the soufflé with a knife, place in the centre of the oven and bake for 20–30 minutes until the soufflé is lightly browned on top and has risen above the top of the dish. Serve at once or the soufflé will sink.

4–6 servings

Eggs Benedict

	Metric/UK	US
Thick slices of cooked ham	8	8
Crumpets (English muffins)	8	8
Butter	25g/1oz	2 Tbsp
Hot poached eggs	8	8
Hollandaise Sauce	250ml/ 8floz	1 cup

Preheat the oven to cool (140°C/275°F, Gas Mark 1). Preheat the grill (broiler) to high.

Place the ham slices on the grill (broiler) pan and cook them for 2–3 minutes on each side. Transfer them to an ovenproof dish and put them in the oven to keep warm.

Prepare the Hollandaise Sauce by the basic method given in Chapter 2. When it is ready, set aside and keep warm.

Quickly toast the crumpets (muffins) and spread with butter.

Arrange the crumpets (muffins) on 4 warmed serving plates.

Place a slice of ham on each crumpet (muffin), and top with a poached egg. Pour a little of the sauce over each and serve at once.

4 servings

Eggs Stuffed with Ham and Herbs

These are delicious served with a Tomato Sauce.

	Metric/UK	US
Hard-boiled (hard-cooked) eggs	4	4
Cooked ham, finely chopped	50g/2oz	$\frac{1}{3}$ cup
Butter	100g/4oz	$\frac{1}{2}$ cup
Chopped fresh chives	1 Tbsp	1 Tbsp
Dried thyme	1 tsp	1 tsp
Worcestershire sauce	1 tsp	1 tsp

Eggs (uncooked)	2	2
Salt	$\frac{1}{2}$ tsp	$\frac{1}{2}$ tsp
Black pepper	$\frac{1}{4}$ tsp	$\frac{1}{4}$ tsp
Dry white breadcrumbs	25g/1oz	$\frac{1}{3}$ cup

Cut the cooked eggs in half, lengthways. Remove the yolks and place them in a medium-sized mixing bowl. Set the whites aside. Add to the yolks the ham, half of the butter, the chives, thyme, Worcestershire sauce, one raw egg and the salt and pepper. With a wooden spoon, cream the mixture thoroughly. Spoon the the mixture back into the egg white halves. Sandwich each pair together to form a whole egg. The halves should not fit tightly together.

In a small bowl, lightly beat the second raw egg with a fork. Roll each cooked 'egg' in the beaten egg and then in the breadcrumbs. In a medium-sized frying-pan, melt the remaining butter over a moderate heat. Place the stuffed eggs in the pan and fry them for 5 minutes, or until they are golden brown all over.

With a slotted spoon, carefully transfer the stuffed eggs to a warmed serving dish and serve at once.

4 servings

Egg and Bacon Scramble

	Metric/UK	US
Vegetable oil	1 Tbsp	1 Tbsp
Medium-sized onion, finely chopped	1	1
Streaky (fatty) bacon slices, coarsely chopped	8	8
Courgettes (zucchini), chopped	4	4
Large tomatoes, peeled and chopped	2	2
Button mushrooms, halved	100g/4oz	1 cup
Salt	$\frac{1}{2}$ tsp	$\frac{1}{2}$ tsp
Black pepper	$\frac{1}{4}$ tsp	$\frac{1}{4}$ tsp
Eggs	6	6
Milk	4 Tbsp	4 Tbsp
Grated nutmeg	$\frac{1}{8}$ tsp	$\frac{1}{8}$ tsp
Coarse fresh white breadcrumbs	50g/2oz	1 cup
Butter, cut into small pieces	15g/$\frac{1}{2}$oz	1 Tbsp

In a shallow flameproof casserole, heat the oil over a moderate heat. Add the onion and bacon and cook, stirring occasionally, until the onion is soft and translucent and the bacon has rendered its fat.

Add the courgettes (zucchini), tomatoes, mushrooms, salt and pepper to the casserole. Reduce the heat to low and cook for about 15 minutes, or until the courgettes (zucchini) are tender. Preheat the grill (broiler) to high.

Beat together the eggs, milk and nutmeg and stir into the casserole. Cook gently until the eggs are scrambled.

Eggs Stuffed with Ham and Herbs can be served as a snack, as an hors d'oeuvre or, with salad, as a light lunch or supper.

Above, Eggs Essen,
a family casserole; and
Right, Omelette Soufflé, an
elegant dessert.

Remove from the heat. Sprinkle the breadcrumbs on top and dot with the pieces of butter. Place the casserole under the grill (broiler) and cook until the top is lightly browned. Remove from the heat and serve immediately.

4 servings

Eggs Essen

	Metric/UK	US
Olive oil	4 Tbsp	4 Tbsp
Medium-sized onion, finely chopped	1	1
Medium-sized potatoes, sliced	2	2
Cooked ham, diced	50g/2oz	⅓ cup
Small green pepper, seeded and finely chopped	1	1
Canned tomatoes, drained and chopped	225g/8oz	½ lb
Frankfurters, cut into 1cm/½in slices	8	8
Dried basil	¼ tsp	¼ tsp
Eggs	6	6
Salt	1 tsp	1 tsp
Black pepper	½ tsp	½ tsp

Preheat the oven to very hot (230°C/450°F, Gas Mark 8).

In a large frying-pan, heat the oil over a moderate heat. Add the onion and potatoes and cook, stirring occasionally, for 5 minutes. Add the ham, green pepper, tomatoes, frankfurters and basil. Cook for about 15 minutes.

Remove from the heat and turn the mixture into a medium-sized ovenproof dish. Smooth the top with a knife. Break the eggs on top and sprinkle them with salt and pepper. Place in the upper part of the oven and bake for 8–10 minutes, or until the eggs whites are set. Serve at once.

4 servings

Omelette Soufflé

This omelette is cooked in the oven, rather than on top of the stove, and the eggs are separated and beaten to make it light and foamy. It can be served plain or with whipped cream, or flavoured with a little liqueur. It makes an elegant dessert.

	Metric/UK	US
Butter	1 tsp	1 tsp
Icing (confectioner's) sugar	1 Tbsp	1 Tbsp
Sugar	100g/4oz	½ cup
Egg yolks	6	6
Finely grated lemon rind	1 Tbsp	1 Tbsp
Egg whites	8	8

Preheat the oven to hot (220°C/425°F, Gas Mark 7). With a teaspoon of butter, lightly grease a 23cm × 30cm (9in × 12in) baking dish. Sprinkle over the icing (confectioner's) sugar and shake out any excess. Set aside.

In a large mixing bowl, beat the sugar, egg yolks and lemon rind together with a fork until well blended. In another large mixing bowl, beat the whites with a wire whisk until they form stiff peaks. Fold carefully, with a metal spoon, into the yolk mixture.

Pour the mixture into the prepared dish, shaping it to a gentle dome with a flat knife. Place in the oven and bake for 8–10 minutes until lightly browned. Serve at once.

4-6 servings

Oeufs Provençales (Eggs with Tomatoes and Olives)

	Metric/UK	US
Vegetable oil	3 Tbsp	3 Tbsp
Onions, sliced in rings	2	2
Garlic clove, chopped	1	1
Green peppers, seeded and sliced	2	2
Tomatoes, peeled and sliced	6	6
Black olives, stoned (pitted)	4	4
Salt	½ tsp	½ tsp
Black pepper	¼ tsp	¼ tsp
Fried eggs, kept hot	4	4

In a medium-sized frying-pan, heat the oil over a moderate heat. Add the onions, garlic and green peppers and fry, stirring occasionally, until the onions are soft and translucent. Add the tomatoes, olives and seasoning and cook for a further 5 minutes, stirring frequently. Remove the pan from the heat, turn the mixture into a warmed dish and place the eggs decoratively on top.

Serve at once.

4 servings

FISH

Fish is the alternative to meat as the basis for most savoury dishes. It is, in fact, almost a perfect food, being easily digested and high in proteins, vitamins and minerals. It can be cooked whole, (in which case it is usually cleaned and gutted—the head can be left or removed according to taste), or filleted, something which will be done by the fish merchant if the fish is not sold ready filleted. In either case, it is quick to cook, for the basic principle in fish cooking is to cook it gently until it is just done, not overdone. High heat and long cooking make fish tough and tasteless.

Buying fish

Buy fish as fresh as possible, refrigerate it until you cook it, and cook it on the day it is bought. Fish freshly caught from sea or river and eaten the same day is best of all. When buying fish, make sure it has clear shining eyes, firm flesh—pressing with a finger should not leave a dent—and an appetizing smell. Good frozen fish is as fresh as fish bought from a fish merchant or supermarket, in fact often fresher, as it is quick-frozen soon after being caught. As well as fresh or frozen, fish is sold dried, salted, smoked, pickled and canned.

Types of fish

Fish can be divided into groups in a number of ways: wet fish (what one thinks of as fish) and shellfish; freshwater or saltwater; white [sole, plaice (flounder), cod, halibut, hake] or oily (mackerel, herrings, sardines, pilchards, eel, trout, salmon); flat [plaice (flounder), sole, turbot, whiting] or round (cod, haddock, trout, hake, mackerel, salmon). Oily fish are a good source of vitamin D, which is needed for making strong bones and teeth, so they are often given to children and pregnant mothers. Vitamin D is also found in the livers of non-oily fish, such as cod—hence cod liver oil. Flat fish are sold whole or filleted; round fish, whole or cut across into steaks.

PREPARATION

Fish merchants usually clean and fillet fish for you. But preparing whole fish is not difficult. There are four stages: scaling, gutting or cleaning, skinning and filleting.

1. Scaling

You can cook fish with the scales on and skin it before

serving. To scale when raw, dip the fish in cold water and lay it on a wooden board or some newspaper. Hold it by the tail and, with the blunt edge of a knife, scrape away the scales from the tail towards the head. Rinse the fish under cold water and pat dry with kitchen paper towels. Very small round fish cooked whole, such as sardines, do not need scaling.

2. Gutting or cleaning

In round fish the entrails are in the belly; in flat fish, they are in a cavity behind the head.

To gut round fish, cut the head off just below the gills and make a deep cut down the underside to just above the tail. Scrape out the entrails and wash the cavity in cold running water. Cut off the tail and all the fins. If the fish is to be cooked with head and tail on, you can gut it with a similar slit in the belly, or you can remove the intestines through the gills; cut out the gills with a sharp knife and part of the gut will come

Gutting Flat Fish

1

2

3

Lay the fish on a board, head facing you. Cut off the head and tail and trim fins. (1) Now insert the knife, blade facing away from you, at the head end and push under the flesh. (2) Work along the backbone, towards the edge. (3).

Gutting Round Fish

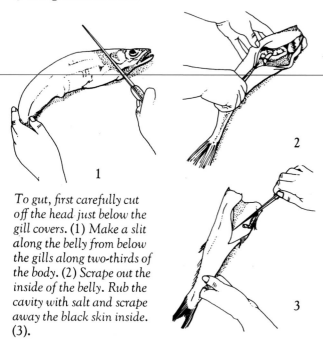

1

2

3

To gut, first carefully cut off the head just below the gill covers. (1) Make a slit along the belly from below the gills along two-thirds of the body. (2) Scrape out the inside of the belly. Rub the cavity with salt and scrape away the black skin inside. (3).

with it. The rest can then be removed with your fingers. When leaving the head and tail on, still cut off the fins and gills.

To gut small round fish, simply cut off the heads and squeeze out the entrails. You can leave the tails on sardines and other small fish.

To gut flat fish, make a semi-circular slit behind the head, on the side with dark skin. Scrape out the entrails and wash the cavity in cold running water. If cooking the fish whole, cut off the fins and gills.

3. Skinning

Not all fish needs to be skinned. Round fish can be cooked with the skin on and the skin can be removed after cooking. Cutlets or steaks from large round fish such as cod should not be skinned before cooking, and the central bone should also be left in to help keep its shape. With flat fish, the dark skin is usually removed before cooking, and the white skin on the other side can be removed also, though it is often left on.

When skinning, rub your fingers in salt to get a good grip. To skin round fish, slit the skin along the belly and back, and loosen the skin round the head with a sharp knife. Then draw the skin down towards the tail. Repeat on the other side. To skin flat fish, slit the skin just above the tail. Holding the fish by the tail, pull the skin firmly towards the head.

If you are filleting the fish it is easiest to fillet first and then skin each fillet. Put the fillet on a board skin side down, and ease the flesh off the skin with a sharp knife, cutting away from you and taking care not to break the fillet.

4. Filleting and boning

Round fish provide two fillets, flat fish four. Use a very sharp but pliable knife for filleting. Cut the fish down its backbone—down the middle of a flat fish, along the back of a round fish—and carefully ease the fillets away from the bones with short, sharp cuts. When filleting flat fish, also make a semi-circular cut just below the head. Turn the fish over and fillet the back in the same way.

Small round fish such as herrings and mackerel can be filleted, but are more often boned and then cooked whole or stuffed. To bone, cut off the head, tail and fins. Slit the fish along the belly, open it out and spread it flat, skin side up. Press along the backbone to loosen it. Turn the fish over and with a knife ease out the backbone and as many small bones as will come with it, starting from the head end.

Fish need not be filleted or boned until after cooking, though it must be cleaned and gutted. When the fish is cooked, follow the same method for filleting; slit down the backbone and lift off the fillets. The process is much easier with cooked fish.

COOKING METHODS

Fish can be fried, poached, steamed, grilled (broiled), baked or stewed. When it is done, the flesh is opaque, comes away from the bone and is just on the point of flaking. If the flakes fall apart it is overdone. Test for doneness by gently prodding with a fork.

1. Frying

This a very popular and quick method of cooking fish. It may be shallow or deep fried.

Filleting Round Fish

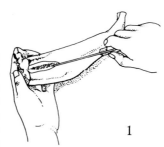

1

2

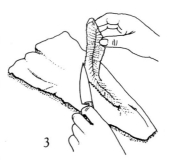

3

To fillet, cut along the backbone to the tail end, cutting into flesh not just through the skin. (1) Open out the flesh flat by easing the belly cavity open. (2) Lift out the backbone from the head end. Ease out the flesh and cut fillets in half. (3).

Shallow frying Suitable for small whole fish such as herrings, mackerel, mullet, plaice (flounder), sole, trout and for very small ones such as sardines and whitebait; also for fillets or steaks of cod, coley, haddock, hake and eel. Coat the prepared fish with seasoned flour and/or an egg and breadcrumb coating. Heat a little vegetable oil and butter in a frying-pan over a moderate heat. Put in the fish, fry until brown on one side, then turn over carefully with a fish slice or spatula and brown the other side. It will take 8–10 minutes, depending on the thickness of the fish.

Deep frying Suitable for fillets such as plaice (flounder), cod, rock salmon, sole, haddock, and for very small whole fish such as sardines and whitebait. The fish must have a thick coating, either batter or egg and breadcrumbs, to protect it from the high temperature of the fat. A deep saucepan (deep fat fryer) is essential; a wire frying basket which fits into it is useful. Olive oil, good vegetable oil, dripping or vegetable fat may be used.

Fill the pan one-third full with fat. Heat slowly to 190°C/375°F, a temperature which will brown a cube of day-old bread in 50 seconds. The thinner the fish, the higher the temperature can be; the fish will be cooked inside before the outside can overcook. If using a basket, heat it in the pan with the oil so the fish will not stick to it. Put the coated fish into the basket and lower it into the fat. Depending on the size of the pieces, they will take 3–7 minutes to cook. The breadcrumbs or batter will turn golden brown. When cooking whole fish the tail turns up when the fish is done. Remove the fish and drain on kitchen paper towels. Do not over-crowd the basket or pan; if all the fish will not fit in, cook it in batches and keep warm in a cool oven.

Coating with egg and breadcrumbs

Have a dish of seasoned flour on your left, a bowl of lightly beaten egg in front of you, a sheet of grease-proof or waxed paper heaped with dried breadcrumbs on your right, and a plate to receive the coated pieces. Dip each piece of fish in the flour and shake off the excess; coat it completely with egg, and drain for a few seconds; toss it lightly in the breadcrumbs, pressing them on well with a pliable knife.

Coating with batter

The simplest batter is made from 50g/2oz self-raising (½ cup self-rising) flour and a pinch of salt, mixed to a smooth cream with 3–4 tablespoons water.

A richer batter can be made from 100g/4oz plain (1 cup all-purpose) flour, 1 egg and about 150ml/5 floz (⅔ cup) milk. Sift the flour into a bowl, add the salt, make a well in the centre and break the egg into it. Beat together with a wooden spoon, then gradually add the milk. Beat until smooth.

Put the batter in a small, deep bowl and have the hot fat ready. With two skewers, dip a piece of fish deeply into the batter, hold it over the bowl for a few seconds to drain, then carefully drop it into the fat without splashing. Repeat with the other pieces.

Filleting Flat Fish

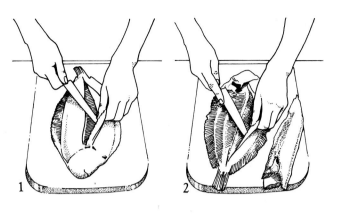

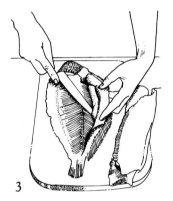

To fillet flat fish, make an incision down the backbone and ease the flesh away. (1) Turn round so that the head faces you and remove the other fillet in the same way. (2) Turn over on its front and remove the black-skinned fillets with any roes. (3).

2. Poaching

Poaching—very slow simmering in just enough liquid to cover—is ideal for all kinds of fish. It can be done on top of the stove or in the oven. The liquid can be milk, fish stock, wine, water or Court Bouillon. If the fish is large and difficult to handle, wrap it in cheesecloth and leave the ends hanging out of the pan. Chopped onion, parsley, lemon slices, mushroom stalks, sliced carrots, celery, a bayleaf and a few peppercorns may be added to the liquid to give more flavour.

To poach in the oven, preheat the oven to moderate (180°C/350°F, Gas Mark 4). Lay the fish in a shallow baking dish. Heat the poaching liquid to nearly boiling, pour it over the fish and cover the dish with foil. If cooking on top of the stove, cover the fish with the liquid and bring to a gentle boil. Lower the heat to a simmer. When the fish is cooked, lift it out with a slotted spoon or by the ends of the cheesecloth. If wrapped, unwrap it before serving.

Allow 8–10 minutes per ½kg/1lb for whole fish, and 15–20 minutes in all for small whole plaice, flounder or sole. Give fillets 8–12 minutes and allow 15 minutes for steaks. Test the fish with a fork at the thickest part; if it comes away from the bone it is done.

Strain the poaching liquid and use it in a sauce; those good with fish are Parsley, Cheese, Anchovy and Shrimp.

Court Bouillon

This classic acidulated stock is used for poaching fish, especially salmon, trout and salmon trout.

	Metric/UK	US
Carrots, sliced	2	2
Onion, sliced	1	1
Celery stalks, chopped	2	2
Shallots, chopped	2	2
Bayleaf	1	1
Parsley stalks	3	3
Thyme sprigs	2	2
Lemon juice	2 Tbsp	2 Tbsp
Dry white wine	300ml/ $\frac{1}{2}$ pint	1$\frac{1}{4}$ cups
Salt and black pepper to taste		
Water	900ml/ 1$\frac{1}{2}$ pints	3$\frac{3}{4}$ cups

Put all the ingredients in a saucepan and bring to the boil. Cover and simmer for 15 minutes. Set aside, cool for a few minutes, then strain and use. Refrigerate the stock if it is not to be used immediately.

3. Steaming

This method retains the flavour in thin fillets of delicate white fish, and is ideal to serve to young children and invalids. Put the filleted fish in a steamer, season with salt and pepper and place over a pan of boiling water. Put the lid on. If you have no steamer, steaks or fillets may be cooked in a heatproof soup plate or deep dish over a pan of boiling water, using the lid of the pan to cover the fish. Times are the same as for poaching.

4. Grilling (Broiling)

This useful, quick method can be used for small whole fish, flat or round, and fillets and steaks. Score whole fish on both sides with a sharp knife to prevent curling and allow the heat to penetrate.

Preheat the grill (broiler) to high. Brush white fish such as plaice (flounder) or sole with melted butter or oil; oily fish such as mackerel need no extra fat, though it can be added. Add a squeeze of lemon juice. Turn the grill (broiler) down to moderate, and place the fish under the heat. Cook for 5–15 minutes, depending on the thickness of the fish. Thick steaks and whole fish must be turned over to cook right through; thin steaks, fillets, or boned fish that have been opened out need not be turned. Cook the latter skin side down.

5. Baking

Small or medium-sized whole fish or steaks or fillets can all be baked, either in a shallow ovenproof dish or wrapped in foil.

To bake in a dish, butter the dish and put in the prepared fish. Dot with more butter and season with salt, pepper and lemon juice, and chopped parsley if liked. You can score whole fish as for grilling (broiling). Place in an oven preheated to moderate (180°C/350°F, Gas Mark 4). Allow 30–40 minutes for thick whole fish such as trout, 25–30 minutes for very thick steaks and small whole fish, and 10–20 for small steaks and fillets. Cover the fish if you like it moist; if you leave the lid off, the top will brown slightly. If it is uncovered it will cook more quickly.

This basic method can be varied by adding a little cider, apple juice or wine, with or without the butter; or by laying the fish on very thinly sliced vegetables such as tomatoes, mushrooms or onions and topping it with more of the same. The slices must be thin because most vegetables cook more slowly than fish. This will add a few minutes to the cooking time. Another variation is to coat the fish before baking with a thick sauce such as Cheese, Tomato, Parsley or Anchovy and sprinkle the top with browned breadcrumbs and dots of butter. This is cooked without a lid to brown the top.

To bake in foil, preheat the oven to cool (150°C/300°F, Gas Mark 2). Lay the whole fish or steaks on a large piece of foil. If whole, put a bayleaf, salt, pepper and thin slices of onion inside the fish. Dot with butter, wrap in the foil like a parcel, leaving room for air to circulate, and seal the edges. Place in the oven. A 1–1½kg/2–3lb fish will take about 1 hour, steaks about 40 minutes. Remove from the foil while still hot and gently take off the skin with a knife.

6. Stewing

This is a good method for thick fillets such as cod. If using cod, cut the fish in 5cm/2in pieces, sprinkle with salt and leave for 30 minutes before cooking. This makes the flesh firmer. Drain well. The basis of a stew is usually a tasty vegetable, such as onions or leeks, which are fried first until brown in a little fat. The fish is added, with a little stock or wine, and the stew is cooked over a low heat, below boiling point, until the fish is tender. It can be served with the cooking liquid; thicken the liquid if necessary, by one of the methods for thickening given in chapter 2.

Fish roes

Roes—the eggs of fish—can be either hard or soft. Try to remove them whole from the fish, keeping intact the membrane that holds them in shape. Small roes such as herring can be dipped in flour or egg and

Put the smoked fish, head first, into a jug large enough to immerse it completely.

Pour in enough boiling court bouillon to cover the fish and leave aside for 5–10 minutes.

Remove the fish gently from the jug by the tail, lay flat and pat dry with paper towels.

breadcrumbs, then shallow fried until light brown. Serve on toast with slices of lemon.

Roes can also be grilled (broiled) or poached. Cod roe should be poached for about 30 minutes in a thin cloth to keep the shape. Leave in the cloth until cold, then cut in thick slices, coat with flour and fry until brown in hot fat.

Smoked and pickled fish

There are two methods of smoking—hot smoking and cold smoking. Hot-smoked fish is already cooked and does not need further cooking. Smoked cod roe, eel, buckling, mackerel, salmon and trout are all hot-smoked. All are served cold as an hors d'oeuvre or main course, with lemon wedges and brown bread and butter or toast, or with a sharp dressing or sauce and new potatoes.

Cold-smoking flavours but does not cook the fish, so it needs cooking. This group includes smoked cod, haddock, bloaters, kippers (kippered herring) and sprats. Smoked cod and haddock can be poached in milk, or milk and water, allowing 8 minutes per ½kg/ 1lb. Or put in an ovenproof dish with dots of butter and a little milk and bake for 15 minutes in an oven preheated to moderate (180°C/350°F, Gas Mark 4). Haddock can also be grilled (broiled). Whole kippers (kippered herring) and Arbroath Smokies (small haddock or whiting) are grilled (broiled) for 3 minutes on each side. Bloaters (kippered herring) are grilled (broiled) in the same way but need cleaning first as they are sold ungutted.

Herring fillets pickled in vinegar—available as rollmops, curled around a stuffing of onions and gherkins (pickles), or flat—are served cold as an hors d'oeuvre.

Canned fish

This will keep a long time if the cans are kept dry.

After opening, treat as cooked fresh fish and use within a day or two. The most widely available canned fish are crab, pilchards, oysters, mussels, clams, prawns (shrimp), salmon, tuna, anchovies and sardines. Sardines and pilchards are good heated up on toast under the grill (broiler); crab, pilchards, prawns (shrimp), tuna, sardines and salmon can be used in salads—tuna is an ingredient in Salade Niçoise; oysters, anchovies, mussels and clams can be eaten as an hors d'oeuvre. Canned mussels or clams can be made into a sauce for fish or spaghetti. Pilchards, salmon and sardines also make good fishcakes if no fresh fish are available; mix with mashed potatoes and an egg, season well, form into patties and coat with egg and bread-crumbs before frying.

SHELLFISH

Small shellfish are used in soups and sauces or eaten as an appetizer. Crab, lobster and crayfish can make a main course or a first course. Shellfish deteriorate rapidly and should be bought very fresh. If bought alive they must, in most cases, be cooked, usually in boiling water, before being dressed or used in a recipe. Oysters, which are usually eaten raw, are an exception.

Preparation and cooking

Live shellfish can be put straight into boiling water, or placed in cold water and slowly brought to the boil. The second method is supposed to be less painful. Small live bivalves such as mussels and cockles hold the two halves of their shells tightly together; if the shell stays open when tapped or put in water, the flesh should be discarded. They should open when cooked; if any stay closed, discard them.

Clams

All clams are sandy, so they must be scrubbed, washed

in several changes of water and then soaked in salted water. Sold in the shell or shucked, they may be eaten raw or cooked, in chowders, fritters, etc. (See also **mussels on page 71 for further information on cleaning, etc.).**

Crab

Crabs should show movement when bought alive, and feel heavy. Light crabs will be full of water and stale. The male has larger claws and therefore more flesh. Both claws must be on; if one is missing or comes off, water will get in during cooking and dampen the meat.

Cook a live crab for 15–20 minutes, or 10–15 minutes per ½kg/1lb. Allow to cool in the cooking water. To remove the meat from a cooked crab first pull off the legs and claws. Crack the claws with a hammer or nutcrackers and pick out the flesh. If the legs are large, do the same to them; if small, keep them for decoration. The claws and legs contain the white meat. Turn the crab on its back to remove the body meat. Discard the stomach bag, the grey gills or spongy 'dead man's fingers' and the green intestine, but keep the yellow liver. Use a spoon to remove the creamy soft brown meat from the shell.

Crab meat can be chopped and dressed with mayonnaise, vinaigrette, lemon juice, or white wine vinegar seasoned with salt, black pepper and cayenne, and then piled back into the washed trimmed shell. Garnish with slices of lemon, strained hard-boiled (hard-cooked) egg yolk or finely chopped parsley to add the finishing touch to a delicious summer meal.

Lobster

The tail of a fresh lobster should turn under the body, not hang down, when it is picked up. The shell should be hard and the meat firm. Live lobsters are dark blue; the shell goes bright red when cooked. The smell should be fresh and pleasant.

Cook a live lobster as for crab, simmering for 20 minutes. To remove the meat, first twist off the large claws. Crack them with a small hammer through the centre and at the joint. Use small claws for garnishing. Use a large, pointed knife to split the lobster in two from head to tail down to the middle. Remove the flesh, discarding the stomach (in the head), the dark intestinal vein and the gills. The green liver is a delicacy and should be kept. If there is any spawn 'coral' under the tail, keep it for garnishing.

Preparing Fresh Crab

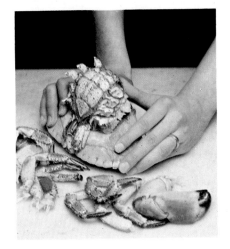 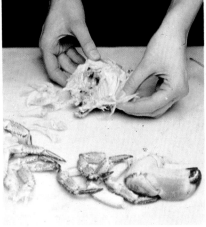 

To prepare crab for serving, first remove the legs and pincers. Then, holding the shell firmly with your hands, pull the body away from the shell.

Discard the stomach bag and any spongy matter from the shell. Pull off the gills and discard them. Then very carefully scoop out all the meat from the claws.

Finally, using a skewer or a two-pronged fork, carefully scoop out all the flesh from the shell and add it to the claw meat, so that you can serve together.

Mussels

Mussels should be bought alive. Scrub hard and scrape off the beards. Soak for 1 hour in a large bowl of cold water. Discard any that stay open or that have broken shells, and any that float to the surface. If you can leave them a few hours, put a little oatmeal or flour in the water. They will feed on it and excrete dirt.

They can be eaten raw with lemon juice, boiled, steamed, baked, smoked or fried. If they are over-cooked—as in soups and stews—they become rubbery and unpleasant. To steam 1L/1quart of mussels, add them to enough water to make a 1cm/½in layer in the pan. Add a pinch of bicarbonate of soda (baking soda), a bouquet garni and salt and pepper. Cover and simmer for 6–10 minutes, or until they are all open. Keep the cooking liquid, it can be made into a good hot sauce for the mussels by adding 25g/1oz (2 Tbsp) of butter, 1 tablespoon lemon juice and 1 teaspoon Worcestershire sauce. Discard one shell from each mussel before serving.

Oysters

Oysters are always bought alive, and usually served raw in their shells as an hors d'oeuvre. Six per person is about right. The shells should be tightly closed and should close hard on the knife when you put it in to open them. To open, hold the oyster over a bowl to catch the juice. Slide the knife into the hinge with a see-saw movement. Prise open and cut the two muscles above and below the oyster. Discard the rounded shell and loosen the oyster with a knife from its flat shell. Slightly season with salt and pepper and pour any spilled juice back into the shells. Put the oysters in their flat shells on a bed of cracked ice, and chill for

1 hour before serving with lemon juice, pepper and brown bread and butter. Oysters are sometimes added to other dishes, such as steak and kidney pie.

Scallops

These ribbed shellfish have a fluted edge and white flesh with a small red coral lip. The shells of live scallops should be tightly closed and they should smell sweet and fresh. Sometimes they are sold raw but already opened and cleaned; these must be very fresh.

If the scallops have not been prepared, scrub the shells in cold water. Put them on a baking sheet, round shell uppermost, in an oven preheated to cool (150°C/ 300°F, Gas Mark 2). Cook until the shells open— about 5 minutes. Cut through and remove the hinge muscles and take off the rounded shell. These are beautiful; keep them for serving the scallops, or for any hors d'oeuvre. The beard-like fringe round the scallop must be scraped off and the black intestinal thread removed. Ease the white and orange flesh from the shell with a sharp knife. The scallops are now ready to cook.

Shrimps and prawns

When live, both prawns and shrimps should have a mild sweet sea odour with firm meat and a tight-fitting transparent shell. The tails should be stiffly turned inwards. If stale they smell strongly and will be difficult to shell when cooked. They are usually bought cooked; if live they are boiled for 7–8 minutes. The shell turns pink when cooked.

Dublin Bay prawns (jumbo Gulf shrimp or langoustines) are large and need boiling for 10–15 minutes if bought alive.

RECIPES

Fish Kebabs

These look especially attractive served on a bed of water-cress and garnished with black olives and slices of lemon.

	Metric/UK	US
Mackerel, cleaned, gutted, opened out and backbones removed	4	4
Pickling (pearl) onions	6	6
Small tomatoes	4	4
Button mushrooms	4	4
Large green pepper, seeded and cut into 1cm/½in strips	1	1
White wine vinegar	50ml/2floz	¼ cup
Olive oil	50ml/2floz	¼ cup
Salt	½ tsp	½ tsp
Black pepper	¼ tsp	¼ tsp
Dried oregano	1 tsp	1 tsp

Cut each mackerel into 4 or 5 slices. Thread the slices of fish on to skewers, alternating with onions, tomatoes, mushrooms and green pepper strips. In a large shallow dish, combine the vinegar, oil, salt, pepper and oregano. Lay the prepared skewers in the dish and leave to marinate at room temperature for about 2 hours, turning occasionally.

Preheat the grill (broiler) to high. Cook the kebabs for 8–10 minutes, basting frequently with the marinade and turning occasionally until the fish is cooked. Serve immediately on a warm serving dish.

4 servings

Baked Fish Fillets with Wine and Mushrooms

	Metric/UK	US
Shallot, very finely chopped	1	1
Mushrooms, sliced	225g/8oz	2 cups
White fish fillets, skinned (cod, haddock or turbot)	1kg/2lb	2lb
Lemon juice	1 Tbsp	1 Tbsp
White pepper	¼ tsp	¼ tsp
Salt	½ tsp	½ tsp
Dry white wine	350ml/12floz	1½ cups
Beurre Manié	50g/2oz	¼ cup
Chopped parsley	1 Tbsp	1 Tbsp

Preheat the oven to moderate (180°C/350°F, Gas Mark 4). Put the shallot and mushrooms in a large, shallow ovenproof dish. Place the fish fillets on top and sprinkle over the lemon juice, pepper and salt. Pour in the wine. Tightly cover the dish with buttered greaseproof or waxed paper or foil, then with the lid. Put into the oven and bake for 20–30 minutes, depending on the thickness of the fillets.

Remove the dish from the oven and transfer the fillets to a warm dish. Keep hot. Pour the cooking liquid and vegetables into a small saucepan. Place over a moderate heat and stir in the beurre manié, a little at a time, until the sauce is thick and smooth. Pour the sauce over the fish and sprinkle with chopped parsley before serving.

6 servings

Fish and Chips

If well prepared, homemade fish and chips is a delicious dish.

	Metric/UK	US
FISH		
White fish fillets, skinned (cod, haddock, plaice or flounder)	1kg/2lb	2lb
BATTER		
Flour	100g/4oz	1 cup
Salt	⅛ tsp	⅛ tsp
Egg	1	1
Egg yolk	1	1
Vegetable oil	1 Tbsp	1 Tbsp
Milk	150ml/5floz	⅔ cup
CHIPS		
Potatoes, cut into strips	1kg/2lb	2lb
Vegetable oil for deep frying		
Salt	1 tsp	1 tsp

First prepare the batter. Sift the flour and salt into a medium-sized mixing bowl. Make a well in the centre and add the egg, egg yolk and oil. Use a wooden spoon to mix the eggs and oil together, slowly incorporating the flour. Gradually stir in the milk. Mix to a smooth batter and beat well. Preheat the oven to very cool (120°C/250°F, Gas Mark ½).

Dry the potato strips on kitchen paper towels. In a deep frying pan (deep fat fryer), heat the oil to 190°C/375°F. Put a third of the potatoes in the frying basket and fry for 2–3 minutes or until crisp and golden. Transfer to kitchen paper towels to drain, then keep warm in the oven until the remainder are cooked in the same way. Sprinkle with salt and keep in the oven while you fry the fish.

Dry the fish fillets with kitchen paper towels. Coat with the batter and fry in the oil until golden brown as described on page 64. Serve the fish and chips at once on a warmed serving dish.
4-6 servings

Fried Trout in Sour Cream Sauce

	Metric/UK	US
Medium-sized trout, cleaned through the gills	6	6
Seasoned flour	75g/3oz	¾ cup
Butter	100g/4oz	½ cup
Vegetable oil	2 Tbsp	2 Tbsp
Small button mushrooms, halved	350g/12oz	3 cups
Salt	½ tsp	½ tsp
Black pepper	¼ tsp	¼ tsp
Lemon juice	1 tsp	1 tsp
Paprika	1 tsp	1 tsp
Sour cream	300ml/ ½ pint	1¼ cups
Finely chopped parsley	1 Tbsp	1 Tbsp

Coat the fish with seasoned flour, shaking off any excess. In a frying-pan, melt half of the butter. Add the fish and fry for 5 minutes on each side or until lightly browned and cooked. Transfer to a warm serving dish and keep hot. Pour off and discard the cooking juices, but do not wash the pan. Place the remaining butter and the oil in the pan and stir in any sediment. Add the mushrooms and cook for 3 minutes. Add the salt, pepper, lemon juice, paprika and sour cream. Stirring constantly, cook for 2–3 minutes or until hot but not boiling. Pour the sauce over the fish and sprinkle with parsley. Serve at once.
6 servings

Devilled Large Prawns (Large Gulf Shrimps)

	Metric/UK	US
SAUCE		
Dark brown sugar	4 tsp	4 tsp
Black pepper	½ tsp	½ tsp
Salt	¼ tsp	¼ tsp
Ground ginger	½ tsp	½ tsp
Soy sauce	2 tsp	2 tsp
Worcestershire sauce	1 tsp	1 tsp
Dry white wine	250ml/8floz plus 1 Tbsp	1 cup plus 1 Tbsp
Garlic clove, finely chopped	1	1
Cornflour (cornstarch)	1 Tbsp	1 Tbsp
RICE		
Long-grain rice, washed, soaked for 30 minutes and drained	225g/8oz	1⅓ cups
Cold water	600ml/ 1 pint	2½ cups
Salt	1 tsp	1 tsp
PRAWNS (Shrimp)		
Dublin Bay prawns (jumbo Gulf shrimp), cooked, shelled and deveined	1kg/2lb	2lb

A superb sauce based on sour cream and mushrooms adds piquancy to Fried Trout in Sour Cream Sauce.

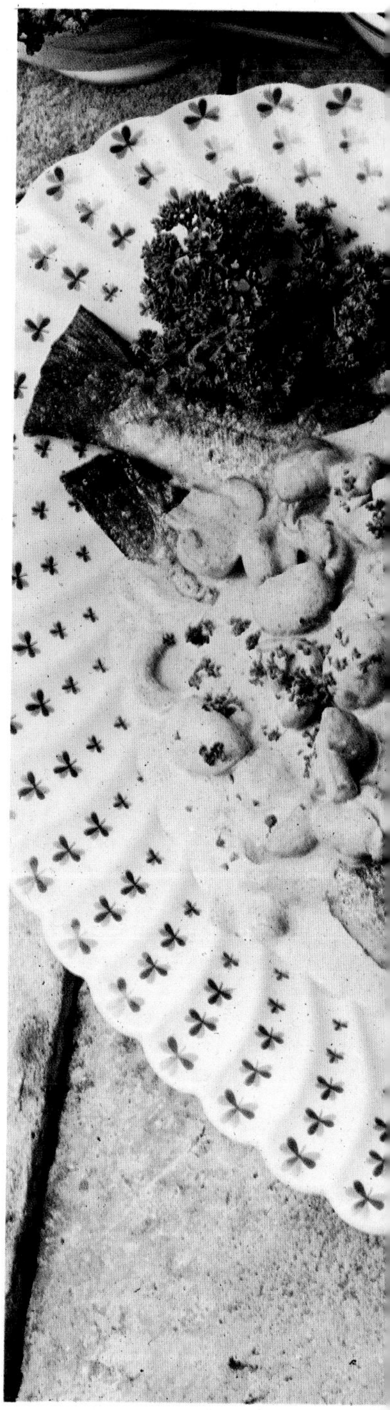

Cayenne pepper	¼ tsp	¼ tsp
Olive oil	3 Tbsp	3 Tbsp
Large red pepper, seeded and cut into 1cm/½in lengths	1	1

To make the sauce, combine the sugar, pepper, salt and ginger in a saucepan. Add the soy sauce, Worcestershire sauce and the 250ml/8floz (1 cup) of wine and mix thoroughly. Add the garlic. Place over a high heat and bring to the boil. Reduce the heat to low, cover and simmer for 20 minutes.

Dissolve the cornflour (cornstarch) in the remaining wine and stir into the sauce. Bring to the boil. Simmer for 5 minutes or until the sauce has thickened. Remove from the heat and set aside.

Put the rice, water and salt in a large saucepan. Bring to the boil, then reduce the heat and simmer for 15–20 minutes or until the rice is tender and the liquid absorbed. Transfer to a serving dish and keep warm.

Sprinkle the prawns (shrimp) with the cayenne. In a large frying-pan heat the oil over a moderate heat. Add the prawns (shrimp) and red pepper and cook, turning frequently, for 6–8 minutes. Reheat the sauce. Arrange the prawns (shrimp) and pepper on top of the rice and pour over the hot sauce.

6 servings

Baking is a neglected art where fish fillets is concerned—so try Baked Fish, Greek Style.

Baked Fish, Greek-Style

	Metric/UK	US
Olive oil	4 Tbsp	4 Tbsp
Large onions, sliced	2	2
Tomatoes, sliced	4	4
White fish fillets, skinned	1kg/2lb	2lb
Salt	1 tsp	1 tsp
Black pepper	$\frac{1}{2}$ tsp	$\frac{1}{2}$ tsp
Lemon, thinly sliced	1	1
Black olives, stoned (pitted)	6	6
Finely chopped parsley	1 Tbsp	1 Tbsp
Dry white wine	150ml/5floz	$\frac{2}{3}$ cup

Preheat the oven to moderate (180°C/350°F, Gas Mark 4). In a medium-sized frying-pan, heat the oil over a moderate heat. Add the onions and fry, stirring occasionally until they are soft and translucent. Add the tomatoes and fry for 5 minutes.

Put half the mixture in a medium-sized casserole. Place the fish fillets on top and sprinkle with the salt and pepper. Spoon the remaining tomato and onion mixture over the fish. Arrange the lemon slices and olives on top and sprinkle over the parsley. Pour in the wine. Cover tightly, and cook for 30–40 minutes. Serve at once.
6 servings

Coquilles Saint-Jacques à l'Ail (Scallops with Garlic)

	Metric/UK	US
Scallops	700g/1$\frac{1}{2}$lb	1$\frac{1}{2}$lb
Juice of $\frac{1}{2}$ lemon		
Seasoned flour	75g/3oz	$\frac{3}{4}$ cup
Vegetable oil	6 Tbsp	6 Tbsp
Shallots, finely chopped	3	3
Garlic cloves, crushed	3	3
Dried basil	$\frac{1}{4}$ tsp	$\frac{1}{4}$ tsp
Butter	25g/1oz	2 Tbsp
Chopped parsley	1 Tbsp	1 Tbsp

Take the scallops out of their shells and dry them on

kitchen paper towels. Cut them into 1cm/½in pieces and sprinkle with lemon juice. Coat with the seasoned flour, shaking off any excess.

In a large frying-pan, heat the oil over a moderate heat. Add the scallops and cook for 5 minutes, stirring and turning occasionally, or until they are lightly browned. Add the shallots, garlic and basil and cook for a further 2 minutes. Remove from the heat, stir in the butter and parsley and transfer to 4 individual warm serving dishes or scallop shells. Serve at once.

4 servings

Mussels Baked with Basil and Tomato Sauce

	Metric/UK	US
Butter	15g/½oz	1 Tbsp
Olive oil	3 Tbsp	3 Tbsp
Large onion, finely chopped	1	1
Garlic cloves, crushed	3	3
Canned tomatoes, chopped	700g/1½lb	1½lb
Salt	½ tsp	½ tsp
Black pepper	¼ tsp	¼ tsp
Chopped fresh basil	3 Tbsp	3 Tbsp
Mussels, scrubbed, steamed and removed from their shells (weight before shelling)	3L/2 quarts	2½ quarts
Fresh breadcrumbs	2 Tbsp	2 Tbsp
Parmesan cheese, grated	50g/2oz	½ cup

Preheat the oven to moderate (180°C/350°F, Gas Mark 4). In a frying-pan melt the butter with the oil over a moderate heat. Add the onion and garlic and cook, stirring occasionally, for 5–7 minutes or until the onion is soft and translucent. Stir in the tomatoes with their juice, salt, pepper and basil. Reduce the heat to low and simmer for 15 minutes. Remove from the heat and stir in the mussels. Pour into a greased baking dish. Combine the breadcrumbs and cheese and sprinkle over the mussel mixture. Put into the oven and bake for 20 minutes or until the top is golden brown. Serve at once.

4 servings

Fish Grilled (Broiled) with Cheese

This is simple but delicious, served with tomato salad and potatoes.

	Metric/UK	US
Thick cod or haddock steaks, boned	4	4
Butter, melted	25g/1oz	2 Tbsp
Small onion, grated	1	1
Cheddar cheese, grated	100g/4oz	1 cup
Prepared mustard	1 tsp	1 tsp
Tomato ketchup	2 tsp	2 tsp
Salt	½ tsp	½ tsp
Black pepper	¼ tsp	¼ tsp
Cayenne pepper	⅛ tsp	⅛ tsp

Classic French cooking at its best, Coquilles St. Jacques à L'Ail.

Preheat the grill (broiler) to high. Place the fish steaks on the rack and brush with the melted butter. Place them under the heat, reduce the heat to moderate and grill (broil) for 5–6 minutes on each side or until done.

Meanwhile, in a small mixing bowl combine the onion, cheese, mustard, ketchup, salt, pepper and cayenne. Mash the mixture well. Remove the steaks from the heat and spread a little of the cheese mixture over each one, pressing it on well. Return the steaks to the heat and grill (broil) for a further 3–5 minutes or until the cheese mixture is brown and bubbling. Serve at once.

4 servings

The richness of crab combines with the creaminess of a quiche mixture and the crispness of shortcrust to make this Crab meat Flan.

Crab meat Flan

	Metric/UK	US
Fresh crab meat	½kg/1lb	1lb
Lemon juice	1 tsp	1 tsp
Chopped fresh fennel leaves	1 Tbsp	1 Tbsp
Small onion, finely chopped	1	1
Chopped parsley	2 Tbsp	2 Tbsp
Dry sherry	2 Tbsp	2 Tbsp
Shortcrust Pastry	175g/6oz	1½ cups
Eggs, lightly beaten	4	4
Single (light) cream	350ml/12 floz	1½ cups
Ground cinnamon	¼ tsp	¼ tsp
Salt	½ tsp	½ tsp
White pepper	¼ tsp	¼ tsp

Combine the crab meat with the lemon juice, fennel, onion, parsley and sherry. Chill for 1 hour.

Preheat the oven to hot (220°C/425°F, Gas Mark 7). Roll out the pastry dough to 5mm/¼in thick and use to line a 23cm/9in flan ring or pie pan. Trim the edges with a sharp knife and bake blind for 15 minutes.

Remove the pastry case from the oven and spoon in the crab mixture. Combine the eggs, cream, cinnamon, salt and pepper and strain over the crab mixture. Return to the oven and bake for 10 minutes. Reduce the heat to moderate (180°C/350°F, Gas Mark 4) and continue baking for 20–30 minutes, or until a knife inserted into the centre of the flan comes out clean.

Serve hot or cold.

6 servings

Salmon Mousse

	Metric/UK	US
Salmon steaks	700g/1½lb	1½lb
Dry white wine	250ml/8 floz	1 cup
Small shallots, thinly sliced	2	2
Lemon, thinly sliced	1	1
Salt	1 tsp	1 tsp
Black peppercorns, coarsely crushed	4	4
Large bayleaf, crumbled	1	1
Liquid aspic	300ml/½ pint	1¼ cups
Gelatine (gelatin)	15g/½oz	1 envelope
Hot water	4 Tbsp	4 Tbsp
Béchamel Sauce, cold	250ml/8 floz	1 cup
Cayenne pepper	¼ tsp	¼ tsp
Tomato purée (paste)	2 tsp	2 tsp
Madeira	2 Tbsp	2 Tbsp
Lemon juice	2 Tbsp	2 Tbsp
Double (heavy) cream, whipped until thick	250ml/8 floz	1 cup
GARNISH		
Large lettuce leaves	6	6
Mayonnaise	250ml/8 floz	1 cup
Hard-boiled (hard-cooked) eggs, thinly sliced	6	6

Very small tomatoes, thinly sliced	6	6
Black olives, stoned (pitted)	11	11

Salmon Mousse can be made (as here) with salmon steaks or good-quality canned salmon.

Poach the salmon steaks in the wine, with the shallots, lemon, salt, peppercorns and bayleaf, for 10–15 minutes. Drain the fish and transfer to a chopping board. Remove any skin or bones. Cut it into chunks with a sharp knife, then mince (grind) or blend it and set aside.

Pour 200ml/7floz (scant 1 cup) of the aspic into a 1.2L/2 pint (2½ pint) fish-shaped mould. Tip and rotate over a bowl of crushed ice until the aspic has set evenly over the sides and bottom of the mould. Place in the refrigerator to chill for 30 minutes.

Dissolve the gelatine in the hot water. In a medium-sized mixing bowl, combine the salmon, béchamel sauce and gelatine mixture, stirring thoroughly. Beat in the cayenne, tomato purée (paste), Madeira, lemon juice and cream. Adjust the seasoning. Spoon the salmon mixture into the chilled mould and smooth it flat with a knife. Chill for 2 hours or until set. Pour over the remaining aspic to cover the top. Chill for a further 4 hours.

Cover a large, chilled serving dish with overlapping lettuce leaves. Remove the mould from the refrigerator and loosen the mousse with a sharp knife. Invert the mould over the dish and run a hot cloth over it. Give a sharp shake to loosen the mousse and it will slide out easily.

Pipe the mayonnaise around the mousse and use the egg and tomato slices and olives to garnish. Chill for 30 minutes before serving.

6–8 servings

79

Fish Balls with Almonds is made here from a combination of cod and smoked haddock—but you can try your own variations on the theme, if you prefer.

Fish Balls with Almonds

Serve with a hot Tomato Sauce.

	Metric/UK	US
Butter	15g/½oz	1 Tbsp
Onion, finely chopped	1	1
Green pepper, seeded and finely chopped	½	½
Cod fillets, cooked, skinned and flaked	225g/8oz	½lb
Smoked haddock, cooked, skinned and flaked	225g/8oz	½lb
Large slices white bread, crumbled	2	2
Salt	½ tsp	½ tsp
Black pepper	¼ tsp	¼ tsp
Paprika	1 tsp	1 tsp
Cayenne pepper	¼ tsp	¼ tsp
Dried oregano	¼ tsp	¼ tsp
Finely chopped fresh chives	1 tsp	1 tsp
Egg yolks	2	2
Milk	3 Tbsp	3 Tbsp
Flour	2 Tbsp	2 Tbsp
Egg, lightly beaten	1	1
Blanched almonds, finely chopped	150g/5oz	1¼ cups
Vegetable oil	90ml/3 floz	⅓ cup

In a small frying-pan, melt the butter over a moderate heat. Add the onion and green pepper and cook, stirring occasionally until the onion is soft and translucent. Remove the pan from the heat and drain off any excess fat. Transfer the vegetables to a large mixing bowl and stir in the fish, crumbled bread, salt, pepper, paprika, cayenne, oregano and chives. Add the egg yolks to the milk and beat lightly, then add to the fish mixture. Add the flour and mix well. The mixture should be thick enough to form balls, so add more flour if necessary.

With floured hands, roll the mixture into about 20 small balls, about 2.5cm/1in. in diameter. Coat the balls in the beaten egg, then in chopped almonds. Chill for 15–20 minutes.

In a large frying-pan, heat the oil over a moderate heat. Add the fish balls and fry for 7–10 minutes, turning occasionally, until golden brown on all sides. Drain on kitchen paper towels. Transfer to a warm serving dish and serve hot.

4 servings

Lobster in Brandy Sauce

	Metric/UK	US
Lobster	1 large	1 large
Butter	40g/1½oz	3 Tbsp
Olive oil	2 tsp	2 tsp
Salt	½ tsp	½ tsp
Black pepper	¼ tsp	¼ tsp
Cayenne pepper	¼ tsp	¼ tsp
Brandy	175ml/6 fl oz	¾ cup
Beurre Manié	15g/½oz	1 Tbsp

Remove the meat from the shell of the cooked lobster, cut into small pieces and set aside. Wipe the shell halves clean, brush with a little oil and place in a flame-proof dish with the claws. In a frying-pan melt the butter with the oil over a moderate heat. Add the lobster meat, salt, pepper and cayenne and fry for 3–4 minutes or until lightly browned. Preheat the grill (broiler) to moderate.

In a small saucepan, heat the brandy over a moderate heat until hot but not boiling. Remove from the heat and pour over the lobster meat in the frying-pan. Ignite with a match and leave until the flames have died down.

Take the meat out of the pan and put it in the shell halves. Bring the liquid in the pan to the boil. Reduce the heat to low and stir in the beurre manié a little at a time until the sauce has thickened and is smooth. Pour the sauce over the lobster meat. Place under the grill (broiler) and cook for 5 minutes or until golden brown.

2–4 servings

Usually the lobster in Lobster in Brandy Sauce can be bought already cooked from a fish merchant –but if you can find your own fresh one, it can be cooked by simmering in boiling water for 20 minutes.

MEAT

Meat remains the heart of most meals, despite its cost and despite periodic attempts to woo us away from what is a very uneconomic form of protein. Meat can be a rare fillet steak and a cheap but nourishing stew, a delicate veal escalope (scallop) or a rich leg of lamb. It is better fresh than frozen, and is more expensive when fresh. The prime cuts, of which there are only a small quantity on each animal, cost much more than the less tender. Meat is a good body-building protein food with iron and vitamins.

Storage

Frozen meat is usually sold thawed. If still frozen, it should be allowed to thaw before cooking. Unwrap both fresh and frozen meat as soon as you get it home, and wipe it clean. You can store fresh meat in the refrigerator for up to three days before cooking; use thawed frozen meat the same day. When storing meat in the refrigerator, put it in a dish and cover it with foil or plastic (cling) wrap.

Buying meat

Freshness is important with all meat. Beef should be red, tinged lightly with brown. However, if it is bright pinky-red, it has not hung for long enough and will be tough and tasteless. There should be a little fat marbled through the meat, as this keeps it juicy and moist while cooking, and there should be some fat around the meat.

Signs of freshness in lamb are a meat with a light colour, fine grain and firm texture, and soft, creamy white fat. Yellow fat indicates age, and brittle white fat means the lamb has been frozen for too long. Legs and shoulders should be plump and covered with a layer of fresh fat.

Pork should be fine-textured, firm and pink. The flesh should be marbled with specks of fat and the fat under the skin should be firm and white. Coarse thick skin is the sign of an older animal.

Good veal is not always easy to find. Always buy from a reliable source, and use it immediately, as it does not keep well. The flesh should be fresh, soft, moist and pale pink. Darker flesh indicates age, and a blue or brown tinge means the meat is stale.

Types of meat

The most common types of meat are beef, the meat of the young ox or bullock; lamb, the meat of young sheep under 1 to $1\frac{1}{2}$ years old (over this age it is mutton); pork, the fresh meat from the pig; and veal, the flesh of young calves, usually no older than 10 months, which have been either milk-fed or grass-fed.

Cuts of meat

It is useful to understand where in the animal each cut comes from. The shape of the bones makes more sense and this is a help when preparing and carving.

COOKING METHODS

The various cuts of meat require different methods of cooking. Make sure you buy the right meat for your recipe, or use an appropriate method for a particular cut of meat. The principle behind the choice of method is that the tender cuts are roasted or grilled (broiled), while tougher cuts are better pot-roasted, boiled,

braised, fried or stewed. Various things make meat tender; long, slow cooking is one of the most effective. Others are beating (as with small steaks) and marinating or cooking in an acid liquid such as wine, cider, beer, vinegar or lemon juice. Both these techniques help break down the tough fibres. Cooking meat with tenderizing liquids and/or vegetables also helps to give flavour to meat that is bland.

It is important to note that pork should never be undercooked, as it can contain parasites that are harmful to human beings. If present, these are killed by thorough cooking. Frozen pork should always be well thawed, preferably overnight in a refrigerator, before cooking. This reduces the likelihood of an underdone dish. Veal should also be well done. Beef, on the other hand, is often served underdone—'rare', with the outside cooked and the inside bloody, or 'medium rare', with the inside pink but not bloody. Some people prefer it well done, that is, brown right through. Roast lamb is also sometimes served underdone.

1. Roasting

This is the traditional method of cooking large cuts of meat by radiant heat. Small cuts under 1.35kg/3lb are not suitable for roasting, as they shrink too much; pot roast them instead. The basic method for roasting is as follows: preheat the oven to the required temperature (see Roasting Times and Temperatures below). Put a little fat in the roasting pan, rub the outside of the meat with salt and pepper and put it in the pan. After a few minutes cooking, turn the meat to seal it all over. After 15–20 minutes, reduce the heat (except for pork); baste frequently with the hot fat. There are variations on this method—very good cuts can be roasted on a high heat for the whole cooking time, and some cuts can be slow cooked without sealing first at a high heat—but the basic method is reliable if no instructions to the contrary are given in a recipe.

The meat for roasting should have some fat on it to keep it juicy, preferably in a layer over the top. Pork

can be roasted with a section of the skin on to make crackling. The skin must be deeply scored several times right through to the meat, in the direction of the grain of the meat. Rub the skin with olive or vegetable oil and coarse salt for a really crisp finish. Veal is rather dry and needs either to be rubbed with dripping and basted frequently, or larded by threading short lengths of fat through the top of the meat. This is also done for beef fillet when roasting, as it has no fat of its own.

A roasting cut can be covered in foil; this makes a moist heat and half steams the meat, and helps tenderize rather tough cuts. It also saves on oven-cleaner. The foil should be removed for the last half hour of cooking to brown the meat. Foil deflects heat, so the temperature should be higher than shown in the *Roasting Times* chart below. Another form of covered roasting is the transparent plastic roasting bag, which has all the virtues of foil and also allows the meat to brown. The bag need not be removed until the meat is done.

Preparing meat for roasting

Some cuts are roasted just as they are, others are boned and rolled, and can be stuffed. This is often done by the butcher but is quite simple to do at home. If you ask the butcher to bone a meat cut but intend to stuff it and roll it at home, make sure he gives you the bones and trimmings for stock. Suitable cuts are sirloin and rib of beef; best end of neck or rack, shoulder, loin, leg or breast of lamb; leg, fore-end, loin or hand (picnic shoulder) of pork; and shoulder, rib or breast of veal. Using a very sharp knife, ease the meat carefully off the bone, following the bones as a guide. Keep the meat in one piece if possible. Put the bones aside for stock. Lay the meat out flat, and spread on the stuffing if you are using it. Roll up tightly, tucking in ends or ragged small pieces as you go, and tie with string. Remove the string before serving.

Best end of neck or rack of lamb or pork can be shaped into a Crown Roast. A butcher will do this, but again it is quite easy to do yourself. Two pieces of best end or rack are needed, each containing seven to eight ribs or cutlets (chops). The excess fat is trimmed from the thick part of each piece, and then 3.5–5cm (1½–2in) of meat is removed from the thin end of the bones. Scrape the bone ends clean. The two pieces of meat are sewn or tied together with string so that they form a circle or crown, with the thick ends of the

cutlets (chops) as the base, and the bones pointing upwards. Slit the crown vertically on the outside between each bone and the next, half separating the cutlets (chops). The cavity in the middle can be filled with stuffing or vegetables. To serve, you can put a paper frill on the end of each bone. To carve, simply cut between each cutlet (chop) and the next.

Roasting times and temperatures

Cuts on the bone cook more quickly than boned meat, as the bone conducts heat into the meat. Large cuts

SUITABLE METHODS OF COOKING DIFFERENT CUTS OF MEAT

Method of cooking	Beef	Lamb	Pork	Veal and Mutton
Roasting	Rib cuts, sirloin whole fillet also topside rump	Shoulder, leg, rib, saddle, breast (boned and rolled), double or single loin, best end (rack) of neck	Leg, loin, rib, shoulder, fillet (tenderloin), hand and spring (picnic shoulder), spare ribs, chops, head; fore-end and hand (picnic shoulder) are often boned and rolled	Leg, fillet, loin and saddle, stuffed breast or shoulder
Grilling (broiling), frying	All steaks— fillets (or tenderloin), sirloin, rump (UK only), porterhouse, club (US only) T-bone; hamburgers minced (ground) beef	Loin or chump (rib), chops, cutlets from best end of neck, noisettes, (slices from boned and rolled best end (rack)	All chops, (snip fat with scissors to prevent curling)	Chops, cutlets, escalopes (scallops)
Braising, pot-roasting	Brisket, silverside, topside (bottom round), flank, rump, chuck	Leg, shoulder, breast (boned, rolled and stuffed), shanks or trotters	Not ideal, as pork is a fatty meat; spare ribs, cutlets, or neck chops	Breast, shoulder, leg, knuckle (shank), rump
Stewing, Casseroling	Topside (bottom round), chuck, flank, leg, oxtail, shin, skirt, silverside, salt brisket (corned beef), shoulder	Breast, rib, scrag, middle neck	As for braising, plus fillet (tenderloin)	As for braising
Boiling	Fresh, salted or pickled (corned) silverside or brisket, shin (shank)	Scrag or neck, breast, mature leg (mutton)	Fresh or salted hand (picnic shoulder), salted leg or knuckle end (hock), salted belly (bacon), often served cold	Boned and rolled breast

Meta	Oven temperature	Reduced oven temperature	Time needed per ½kg/1lb	Meat thermometer readings
Beef	220°C/425°F, Gas Mark 7	180°C/350°F, Gas Mark 4	Rare: 15min+15min over	60°/140°
			Medium: 20min+20min over	70°C/160°
			Well done: 25min+25min over	75°C/170°
Lamb	200°C/400°F, Gas Mark 6	170°C/325°F, Gas Mark 3	20min+20min over	80°C/180°
Pork	190°C/375°F, Gas Mark 5	Maintain initial temperature	30min+30min over	87°C/190°
Veal	200°C/400°F, Gas Mark 6	170°C/325°F, Gas Mark 3	20min+20min over	80°C/180°

These times are for meat on the bone. For boned, rolled cuts with or without stuffing add an extra 5–10 mins per ½kg/1lb cooking time.

need less roasting time per pound than small ones. A meat thermometer, which indicates when the meat is cooked, is very useful. Before cooking, insert the thermometer into the thickest part of the meat, making sure it does not touch the bone or fat. Thermometer readings indicating 'done' meat are shown in the chart.

Carving

Quick, neat carving is a skill acquired by practice. but a few practical points help. Put the roast on a board or a stainless steel dish with protruding spikes. This stops the meat sliding around while you are carving. Use a long, thin, sharp carving knife kept for that purpose only, and a long-handled two-pronged fork with a thumb guard. Remove any skewers or trussing thread.

Boned and rolled cuts are simply carved in neat slices. For meat on the bone, in general, carve across the grain of the meat, except for loin of veal. Aim for large thin slices. Beef should be cut into very thin slices, pork and veal into slightly thicker slices, and lamb fairly thick.

2. Grilling (Broiling)

Trim excess fat from steaks and chops. Brush the meat with oil or melted butter, and add salt and pepper. Do not put salt on ham, or bacon—it is already salty enough—or on beef, as it draws out the juice. Grease the grill (broiler) rack on which you put the meat, to stop it from sticking. Preheat the grill (broiler) to high and cook both sides of the meat for 2 minutes, to brown and seal in the juices. The heat can then be lowered to cook the meat through. Time taken varies with the thickness of the meat. Prick with a skewer to test; steaks can be served rare or medium, lamb medium or well done, but pork and veal must be thoroughly cooked through.

Carving a Wing Rib of Beef

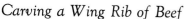

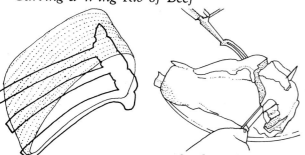

Cut down along the length of the backbone, along its entire length, to remove the chine bone. Use a carving fork to anchor the meat.

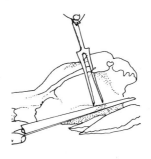

Carefully carve down the meat in slices towards the ribs. Loosen the meat from the ribs and remove the slices.

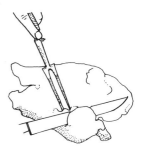

When almost all of the meat has been carved, lay the meat flat on the platter and carve the final few slices horizontally.

Carving a Leg of Lamb

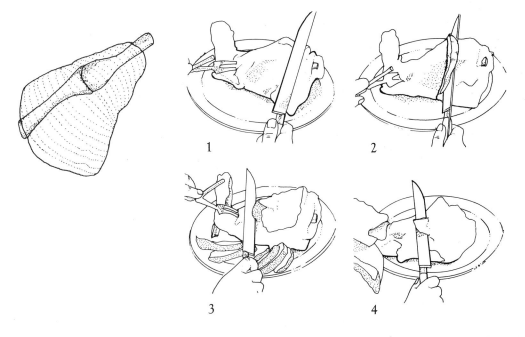

Set the leg firmly on the dish with the round side uppermost. Insert the carving fork near the knuckle and tilt the meat towards you. (1) Make a cut in the centre, through to the bone. Slant the knife a little and make a second cut to the bone so that you remove a thin slice. (2) Continue slicing from either side of the first cut, angling the knife to obtain long slices. (3) Turn the joint over and cut off surplus fat. Hold firmly with your free hand and cut thin horizontal slices along the length of the leg. (4).

Carving a Shoulder of Lamb

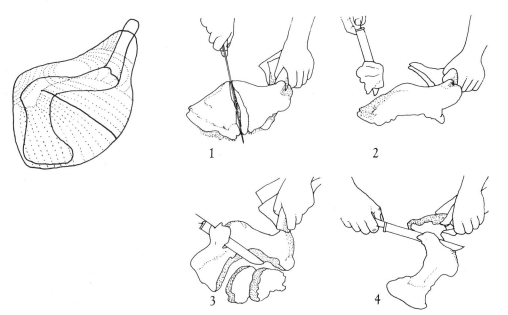

Carve a thin slice from the centre of the meat, cutting it right through to the bone. (1) Continue carving slices from either side of the first cut until the bone finally gets in the way. (2) Cut small horizontal slices from the shank bone until all the meat has been cut from the top. (3) Finally, turn the meat over and remove any surplus fat. Carve off the meat in thin slices as far as you can. (4).

3. Frying

Use butter or oil or a mixture of both, melted in a heavy frying-pan. Heat it quickly and put in the meat. Fry over a high heat for 2 minutes on each side, then reduce the heat to moderate and continue cooking until the meat is done. Again, pork and veal must be cooked through, lamb can be medium or well done, while steaks can be rare.

A good gravy can be made from the pan juices. Take out the meat, pour off the fat and put in a little stock or wine. Stir and bring to the boil, scraping the sediment from the bottom of the pan. Check seasoning and pour over the meat.

To prepare lamb cutlets (chops) for frying, you can coat with egg and breadcrumbs. Best end of neck (rack) can be made into noisettes for frying; bone, trim and roll up tightly. Tie in several places with string. Cut into rounds. Coat with egg and breadcrumbs if liked.

4. Braising

This method is used for small cuts of meat and chops and steaks, if they are not tender enough for grilling (broiling) or frying. The meat must still be lean and succulent. Coat with seasoned flour and brown all over in hot fat. Put in a casserole on a bed of vegetables such as root vegetables, peppers, onions or mushrooms, which have been lightly fried. Add enough water, stock, or wine to cover the vegetables, and tomato purée (paste), herbs and seasonings. Cover with a tight-fitting lid and cook either on top of the stove for 2–3 hours on a low heat, or in the centre of an oven preheated to warm (170°C/325°F, Gas Mark 3). Add more liquid if the meat seems too dry during cooking. The liquid and vegetables are served with the meat.

When braising a breast of lamb, usually boned, stuffed and rolled, make sure most of the fat has been trimmed off, as lamb is a very fatty meat.

5. Pot-roasting

This slow method of cooking, usually with less liquid than in braising, is good for less tender and small cuts of meat. The meat is left whole and browned in fat over a high heat in a flameproof casserole. The lid is put on tightly and the heat lowered. You can add

a bed of root vegetables to provide flavour and succulence, or put the meat on a low wire rack. Pot-roasting is usually done on top of the stove on a low heat, but it can be done in the centre of an oven preheated to warm (170°C/325°F, Gas Mark 3); allow about 45 minutes per ½kg/1lb. Turn the meat frequently with either method. When done, take it out, pour off the fat and use the juices as the basis for a sauce; or serve the vegetables with the meat. As with braising, make sure lamb is not too fatty.

6. Stewing

This long, slow method with plenty of liquid added produces a tender, succulent result from cheaper, tougher cuts of meat. The liquid turns into a flavoursome gravy or sauce and the meat is served in the sauce. The meat is cut up into 2.5cm/1in cubes and vegetables are usually added. The liquid can be water or stock, and wine, vinegar, cider, beer or tomato purée (paste) are often added to help tenderize and make it tasty.

Step-by-Step to Fry-Start Brown Casserole

First, coat the cubed meat in plenty of flour seasoned with salt and pepper (or any herb or seasoning) (a plastic bag does this job well).

Heat fat in a saucepan. Now add the cubes, a few at a time so that they don't crowd the pan, and cook and turn until they are browned all over.

When all of the meat is browned, remove the cubes from the pan with a slotted spoon. Keep hot. Add vegetables to the pan and brown them.

Stir in a little of the seasoned flour, until it forms a roux with the vegetables and fat. It should be nut brown in colour.

Add liquid and stir until it blends with the roux. Bring to the boil until smooth and add seasonings and herbs and return the meat to the pan.

Cover and cook for 1 hour. Add root vegetables, stir to blend and simmer, covered, for a further 1–1½ hours or until the meat is tender.

Most stews require the meat cubes to be coated in seasoned flour and browned in fat first. The vegetables are also fried until golden and flour is sprinkled over them to absorb the fat and form a roux. This is fried until the mixture is pale brown; the meat is put back in, the liquid added and brought to the boil, then the stew is covered tightly and simmered slowly on top of the stove or in an oven preheated to warm (170°C/ 325°F, Gas Mark 3) for 1½–3 hours. If the meat is not then tender, cook it a bit longer.

There are other ways of starting a stew; the meat and vegetables can be fried together, and the flour sprinkled on; or they can simply be put in a casserole with the liquid, with no addition of flour, for a thinner, lighter sauce. If you are putting quick-cooking vegetables (such as sliced green peppers or leeks) in your stew, add them near the end of the cooking time. New potatoes, scrubbed and skinned, can be added 30 minutes before the end of the cooking time. Or some chopped potatoes can be added at the beginning—these will disintegrate and thicken the gravy—and some small whole ones added about 30 minutes before the end of the cooking time.

Minced (ground) meat

Minced (ground) beef, veal, pork or lamb can be used in all sorts of dishes such as shepherd's pie, chili con carne or moussaka, as well as in rissoles and stuffings. Minced (ground) meat does not keep well—use it the day you buy it. Ready-minced (ground) meat can be of poor quality, with little bits of bone and gristle which spoil the texture; it is better to choose a bit of meat you can see is good and ask the butcher to mince (grind) it there and then, or mince (grind) it yourself.

Cured meats

Bacon, gammon (ham) and ham are made from pork, cured or smoked by various methods. They usually still need cooking and can be boiled, baked, roasted grilled (broiled) or fried.

Whole cuts which have not been processed should be soaked in cold water overnight before cooking to remove excess salt. Discard the water. They can be boiled, or parboiled and then roasted or baked. To boil, put the meat in a large pan, cover with cold water

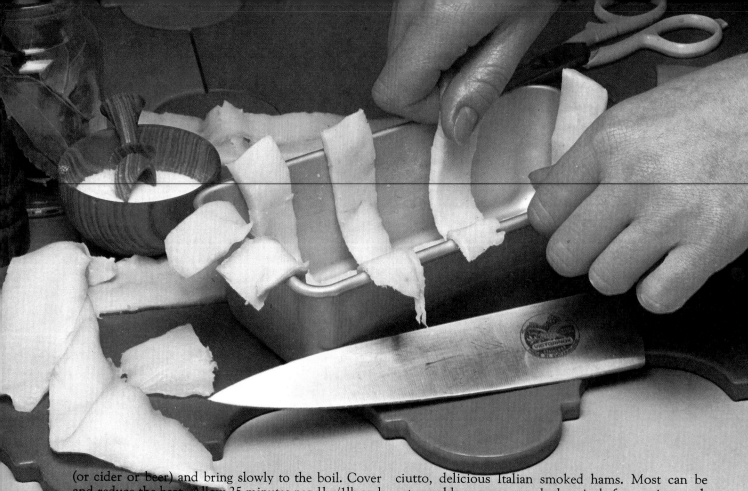

(or cider or beer) and bring slowly to the boil. Cover and reduce the heat. Allow 25 minutes per ½kg/1lb and 25 minutes extra—this weight refers to the weight of the meat *after* soaking and draining. Lift out the meat when done, peel off the skin and serve hot. To serve ham or bacon cold, leave it to cool in the liquid in which it has cooked, peel off the skin and cover with toasted breadcrumbs.

To roast, simmer first as above for half the cooking time. Then roast in an oven preheated to moderate (180°C/350°F, Gas Mark 4) for the rest of the cooking time. The meat can be glazed in the following way. Thirty minutes before the end of the cooking time, peel off the skin and make a diamond pattern in the fat with a knife. Insert whole cloves at the intersections, heads outward, and cover the top of the meat with brown sugar, clear honey, marmalade or golden (light corn) syrup. Return the meat to the oven and turn the heat up to hot (220°C/425°F, Gas Mark 7). Cook for 30 minutes.

Rashers (slices) or steaks of gammon (ham), ham or bacon can be fried or grilled (broiled). Bacon needs little or no extra fat for frying. Cut off any rind from bacon with scissors and carefully remove any gristle or bone.

Cooked meats

Some methods of curing produce cooked meats—sausages like salami, or ham such as the many German cooked, smoked varieties. Some are flavoured heavily with spices and garlic. Every country has its own specialities. Some of the best are German cervelat, a non-garlic pork sausage; chorizo, the Spanish garlic sausage; mortadella, a large mild Italian sausage with garlic and peppercorns; and coppa, Parma and pros-

ciutto, delicious Italian smoked hams. Most can be eaten cold, some are cooked again before eating, such as black or white pudding which is sliced thinly and then fried.

Pâtés and terrines

Meat that might lack flavour if cooked in an ordinary way can be minced (ground) and made into a pâté with lots of herbs and seasonings. The variety is almost infinite but the principle is the same; the meat is either minced (ground), seasoned and baked (a meat loaf) or fried or boiled and then minced (ground) with flavourings (chicken liver pâté is a good example). A layer of melted fat can be poured on to the top to preserve the pâté. The meat can be bound together with aspic or gelatine or a good jellified stock and shaped in a mould. It is then known as a terrine. Brawn [see pig's head on the offal (variety meat) chart below] is an example. Both pâtés and terrines are eaten with crisp toast or crusty bread or Melba toast as an appetizer or a light main course.

Offal (variety meat)

Although usually—as here—dealt with last in chapters on meat, offal (variety meat) can be delicious and is just as nourishing as more expensive meat. The category includes any edible internal organs of meat animals, and is also used of marrow bones, pigs' heads and feet, oxtail and sausages. The same cooking methods are employed as for meat; kidneys and liver are grilled (broiled) or fried quickly, while most other offal (variety meat) benefits from long, slow cooking.

Offal (variety meat) must be carefully prepared, and it must be fresh.

Liver Pâté

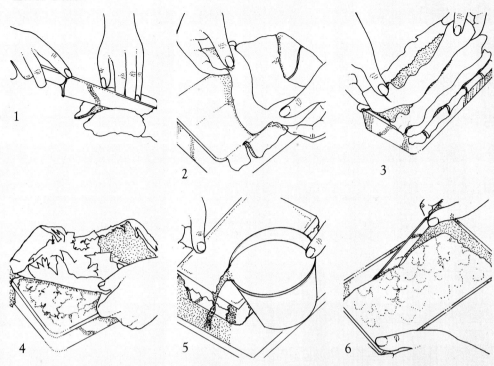

Chop all ingredients for the pâté. (1) Lay barding strips across a greased tin. (2) Mix the mixture then spoon into the tin. Cover with more barding strips. (3) Either cover with foil or cover surface with fat. (4) Put dish into a roasting pan and pour water around. (5) Bake until the juices run clear.(6)

Type	Preparation	Method of cooking	Type	Preparation	Method of cooking
Brains	Allow 1 set per person. Soak in lightly salted water for a few minutes to remove blood. Snip off bone fragments and fibres.	Poach in stock for 20 minutes, drain and press out water. Cut in slices, egg and breadcrumb and fry until golden.	Marrow bones (ox thigh and shoulder bones)	Have bones sawn into short lengths. Wash and scrub. Seal ends with flour and water paste. Tie each in a cloth.	Simmer in Court Bouillon for about 2 hours. Unwrap, spoon out marrow. Eat on toast.
Hearts	Allow 1 calf (veal) or lamb heart per person. Snip out tendons and artery stumps. Leave fleshy flaps. Soak for 10 minutes in cold water to remove blood.	Keep calf (veal) and lamb hearts whole, stuff and pot-roast or braise for 1½–2 hours. Slice and casserole ox heart.	Oxtail	Divide into joints. Trim off fat. Coat in seasoned flour.	Stew over very low heat with onions, carrots, garlic and celery, using brown stock as the liquid. Add bouquet garni. Takes 2–3 hours.
Kidneys	Allow 2 or 3 per person. Remove fat and skin. Cut in half length-ways and cut out core with scissors. Keep fat for frying. Fat from ox (beef) kidneys makes good suet crust pastry.	Fry, grill (broil) or braise calf (veal), lamb and pig (pork) kidneys. Chop ox (beef) kidneys and use in pies, puddings and casseroles. Do not overcook. Fry in butter, grill (broil) with butter; season.	Pig's head and feet (feet are also used with calf's head)	Soak in salted water for 24 hours. Wash, remove gristle and soft nostrils. Rinse well.	To make brawn; simmer in water with bayleaves, lemon rind, bouquet garni and onions for 2 hours or until meat is tender. Skim every hour. Cool. Cut off meat, reduce liquid with bones to 450ml/¾pint (2 cups), strain over meat in mould. Allow to set. Serve cold.
Liver	Soak ox (beef) liver in cold water for 1 hour. Wash and dry all liver. Cut off gristle, core, or blood vessels with scissors. Cut into 5mm/¼in slices.	Grill (broil) or fry calf (veal), lamb or pig (pork) liver, as for kidneys. Do not overcook. Braise ox (beef) or pig (pork) liver. Pig (pork) liver is also used in pâtés. When frying, coat in flour.	Sausages (intestines stuffed with meat, fat and bread)	Prick with a fork (unnecessary if cooked slowly).	Fry, grill (broil) or bake.

Type	Preparation	Method of cooking	Type	Preparation	Method of cooking
Sweetbreads (glands)	Soak in cold water for 1–2 hours. Drain. Cover with cold water, bring to the boil, drain and rinse. Repeat with salted water. Remove black veins, fat and membranes.	Poach in stock for 20 minutes. Cool. Drain. Egg and breadcrumb, fry until golden in butter or bacon fat. Can also be stewed.	Tongue	Soak salted ox (beef) tongue overnight in cold water. Cover with fresh water, bring to the boil, drain. Soak fresh ox (beef) tongues for 1–2 hours in lightly salted water; also lamb tongues. Salted (pickled) tongues have better colour and flavour.	Cover with fresh cold water, add bouquet garni, onion and peppercorns. Simmer, covered, for 2–3 hours [5–6 hours for fresh ox (beef) tongues]. Lamb tongues take only 2 hours. Plunge in cold water, peel, trim off gristle and bones. When cooked, curl ox (beef) tongue in a cake tin, pour on reduced stock, weight and chill. Serve cold. Peel and trim lamb tongues and serve hot with Parsley Sauce.
Tripe, ox (beef) (intestinal membranes)	This is sold blanched or parboiled. Check with the butcher how long it has been cooked.	Total cooking time should be $2\frac{1}{4}$ hours. Stew slowly in milk with chopped onions, tightly covered. Drain and use some of the liquid in a White Sauce to cover.			

RECIPES

Dijon Kidneys

	Metric/UK	SU
Lamb kidneys	700g/1½lb	1½lb
Butter	15g/½oz	1 Tbsp
Cooking oil	1 Tbsp	1 Tbsp
Flour	2 Tbsp	2 Tbsp
Milk	300ml/½ pint	1¼ cups
French mustard	2–3 Tbsp	2–3 Tbsp
Salt	½ tsp	½ tsp
Black pepper	½ tsp	½ tsp
Chopped parsley	6 Tbsp	6 Tbsp

Prepare the kidneys as in the offal (variety meat) chart. Cut into large pieces. In a large saucepan, melt the butter with the oil over a moderate heat. Add the kidneys and cook for 8–10 minutes, turning occasionally. Lift them out with a slotted spoon and keep warm.

Add the flour to the fat in the pan to make a roux. Gradually stir in the milk and bring to the boil. Simmer until thickened. Stir in the mustard, salt, pepper and parsley. Return the kidneys to the pan and stir into the sauce. Reheat gently. Spoon on to a warm serving dish and surround with a ring of boiled rice.

4 servings

Crown Roast of Pork with Peaches

	Metric/UK	US
Crown roast of pork, consisting of 16 chops		
Salt	1 tsp	1 tsp
Black pepper	1 tsp	1 tsp
STUFFING		
Butter	50g/2oz	¼ cup
Pearl onions, blanched and drained	100g/4oz	1 cup
Cucumber, cut into 5mm/¼in cubes	100g/4oz	1 cup
Peach, peeled, stoned (pitted) and cut into 5mm/¼in cubes	1	1
Dark treacle (molasses)	4 Tbsp	4 Tbsp

Crown Roast of Pork with Peaches is easy to cook and elegant to serve for a special meal.

GARNISH

Peaches, peeled, halved and stoned (pitted)	6	6
Paper frills	16	16

Preheat the oven to hot (220°C/425°F, Gas Mark 7). Rub the inside and outside of the crown with salt and pepper. Fill the cavity with crumpled foil, and wrap a strip of foil around the chop bone ends to keep them from burning. Place the crown in a roasting pan and roast for 20 minutes. Reduce the heat to fairly hot (200°C/400°F, Gas Mark 6) and continue roasting for 40 minutes.

Meanwhile prepare the stuffing. In a medium-sized pan, melt the butter. Add the onions and fry until they are soft and translucent. Add the cucumber and peach and fry gently for 5 minutes or until soft. Set aside.

Remove the meat from the oven and discard the foil from the cavity. Spoon in the stuffing and, using a pastry brush, brush half of the treacle (molasses), over the meat. Place the halved peaches on an ovenproof dish and brush with the remaining treacle (molasses). Place both in the oven and continue to roast for a further 1 hour or until the pork is cooked through.

Place the crown roast on a warm serving dish. Surround with the peach halves. Discard the foil from the bone ends, replace with the paper frills and serve at once.

8 servings

Stuffed Shoulder of Lamb

	Metric/UK	US
Boned shoulder of lamb, trimmed of excess fat	1.35kg/3lb	3lb
Salt	½ tsp	½ tsp
Black pepper	½ tsp	½ tsp
STUFFING		
Raisins	100g/4oz	⅔ cup
Orange juice	4 Tbsp	4 Tbsp
Butter	25g/1oz	2 Tbsp
Small onion, finely chopped	1	1
Small carrot, finely chopped	1	1
Chopped parsley	1 Tbsp	1 Tbsp
Fresh breadcrumbs	50g/2oz	1 cup
Grated lemon rind	1 tsp	1 tsp
Ground cinnamon	¼ tsp	¼ tsp

Preheat the oven to moderate (180°C/350°F, Gas Mark 4). Place the meat flat on a board. Rub in the salt and pepper. Set aside. Put the raisins to soak in the orange juice for 20 minutes.

In a small frying-pan, melt the butter over a moderate heat. Add the onion and carrot and fry until soft and translucent. Place them in a mixing bowl and add the raisins with the orange juice, parsley, breadcrumbs, lemon rind and cinnamon. Mix until thoroughly combined and spread the stuffing over the meat. Roll up and secure with string. Place in a roasting pan and cook for 2–2½ hours, or until the juices run clear when the meat is pierced deeply with a skewer.

Carve and serve with the cooking juices.

4–6 servings

Lamb Chops with Cucumber and Onion

	Metric/UK	US
Lamb chops	8	8
Seasoned flour	40g/1½oz	6 Tbsp
Egg, lightly beaten	1	1
Dry white breadcrumbs	100g/4oz	1⅓ cups
Cucumbers, peeled and cut into chunks	1½	1½
Spring onions (scallions) with 5cm/2in of green tops	18	18
Butter	50g/2oz	¼ cup
Salt	¼ tsp	¼ tsp
Black pepper	⅛ tsp	⅛ tsp
Chopped fresh mint	1 tsp	1 tsp
Vegetable oil	75ml/3floz	⅓ cup
Mousseline Sauce	300ml/½ pint	1¼ cups

Coat the chops in seasoned flour, then egg and breadcrumbs (see p. 65 for an easy method).

Put the cucumbers and spring onions (scallions) in a large bowl and cover with boiling water. Leave for 1 minute, then drain well in a colander. Melt the butter in a saucepan over a moderate heat. Add the spring onions (scallions), cucumber, salt and pepper. Cover and simmer for 6 minutes or until tender. Remove from the heat and stir in the mint.

In a large frying-pan, heat the oil over a moderate heat. Add the chops and fry gently for 4–5 minutes on each side or until tender. Remove from the heat. Heat the Mousseline Sauce gently over warm water and transfer to a warm sauceboat. Stand the chops upright on a warmed dish, or overlapping one another down the centre of a serving dish. Pile the cucumber and onion mixture in and around the chops. Decorate the bones with paper frills. Serve with the sauce.

4 servings

Right: Lamb Chops with Cucumber and Onion, glamorously presented with spring onions (scallions). Extreme Right: Lambs' Tongues in Red Wine, a delicious way to cook a very underused type of meat.

Lambs' Tongues in Red Wine

	Metric/UK	US
Lambs' tongues	4	4
Water, salted	600ml/ 1 pint	2½ cups
Salt	1½ tsp	1½ tsp
Bouquet garni	1	1
Butter	25g/1oz	2 Tbsp
Large onion, finely chopped	1	1
Flour	1 Tbsp	1 Tbsp
Tomato purée (paste)	4 Tbsp	4 Tbsp
Worcestershire Sauce	1 Tbsp	1 Tbsp
Red wine	150ml/5 floz	⅔ cup
Black pepper	½ tsp	½ tsp
Sugar	1 tsp	1 tsp
Chopped fresh parsley	1 Tbsp	1 Tbsp

Put the tongues in a saucepan with the salted water and bouquet garni. Bring to the boil, then reduce the heat and simmer for 1½ hours or until tender when pierced with a knife. Drain in a colander. When they are cool enough to handle, skin the tongues with a sharp knife and cut into 2.5cm/1in slices.

In a frying-pan melt the butter over a moderate heat. Add the onion and fry until it is soft and translucent. Stir in the flour, tomato purée (paste), Worcestershire sauce, red wine, pepper and sugar. Add the sliced tongues. Bring to the boil, stirring continuously. Cover the pan, reduce the heat to low and simmer for 15 minutes, stirring occasionally.

Remove from the heat. Make a bed of buttered noodles on a warm serving dish and spoon the tongue mixture on top. Sprinkle with parsley and serve at once.

4 servings

Brains in Butter

	Metric/UK	US
Calves' brains	3 sets	3 sets
Beef stock	250ml/8 floz	1 cup
Celery stalks, sliced	2	2
Onion, halved	1	1
Bayleaf	1	1
Dried sage	¼ tsp	¼ tsp
Peppercorns	10	10
Butter	100g/4oz	½ cup

Boeuf Stroganoff (Beef Strips in Sour Cream) is the invention of a French chef in the employ of a Russian nobleman–hence the name. It is served with rice. Fresh herbs (dill particularly) can be sprinkled over for effect.

White wine vinegar	2 tsp	2 tsp
Capers	1 Tbsp	1 Tbsp

Prepare the brains as in the offal (variety meat) chart. Bring the stock to the boil in a large saucepan. Add the brains, celery, onion, bayleaf, sage and peppercorns. Reduce the heat to low and simmer for 25 minutes.

Meanwhile, put the butter in a small saucepan and cook it until nut-brown, but do not let it burn. Stir in the vinegar and capers. Remove the brains from the saucepan with a slotted spoon and place on a warm serving dish. Pour over the browned butter mixture, and serve at once.
3 servings

Boeuf Stroganoff (Beef in Sour Cream)

	Metric/UK	US
Butter	75g/3oz	6 Tbsp
Onions, thinly sliced	2	2
Button mushrooms, sliced or quartered	225g/8oz	2 cups
Fillet of beef, cut into strips	700g/1½lb	1½lb
Sour cream	250ml/8floz	1 cup
French mustard	2 tsp	2 tsp
Salt	1 tsp	1 tsp
Black pepper	½ tsp	½ tsp

In a large, deep frying-pan melt two thirds of the butter over a high heat. Add the onions and cook gently, stirring occasionally, until they are just brown. Add the mushrooms and cook for 3 minutes. Remove the vegetables from the pan with a slotted spoon and set aside on a plate.

In the frying-pan melt the remaining butter over a high heat. Add the beef strips and sauté for 4 minutes, turning the meat constantly. Return the mushrooms and onions to the pan and season. Simmer for 1 minute.

In a small bowl beat the sour cream and mustard together. Stir into the beef, a little at a time. Raise the heat to moderately high and cook for 1 minute or until the sauce is hot but not boiling. Serve at once.

4 servings

Pot Roast with Brandy

	Metric/UK	US
Top rump (bottom round) of beef, boned and rolled	1 × 1.75kg/ 4lb	1 × 4lb
Salt	1 tsp	1 tsp
Black pepper	½ tsp	½ tsp
Vegetable oil	1 Tbsp	1 Tbsp
Shallots	1kg/2lb	2lb
Beef stock	900ml/ 1½ pints	3¾ cups
Bayleaves	2	2
Pared rind of 1 lemon		
Button mushrooms	350g/12oz	3 cups
Butter	50g/2oz	¼ cup
Brandy	90ml/3 floz	⅓ cup
Very finely grated rind of ¼ lemon		
Buerre Manié	15g/½oz	1 Tbsp

Rub the meat all over with salt and pepper. In a large flameproof casserole or pot, heat the oil. Add the beef and cook for 10–12 minutes, turning occasionally. Put half the shallots around the meat and cook until they are soft and translucent. Add the stock, bayleaves and pared lemon rind. Bring the liquid to the boil. Cover, reduce the heat to low and cook for 2½–3 hours or until the meat is very tender.

Transfer the meat to a warm dish and keep hot. Lift out the bayleaves, shallots and lemon rind and discard. Skim off any fat from the liquid. Add the remaining shallots and boil the liquid for 20–30 minutes, or until it has reduced by about half. Meanwhile, cook the mushrooms in the butter gently for 3 minutes. Remove them from the pan and keep them warm.

Remove the shallots from the liquid and place them on the dish with the meat. Strain the liquid into a medium-sized saucepan. Add the brandy and finely grated lemon rind. Bring to the boil, then reduce the heat and add the beurre manié in small pieces, stirring until the sauce is thick and smooth.

Place the meat on a carving board and carve into thick slices. Put on a warm serving dish. Arrange the mushrooms and shallots around the meat, pour over half of the sauce and serve the remainder separately with the meat.

8 servings

Pot Roast with Brandy makes a warming and sustaining dinner main dish. Serve with boiled or mashed potatoes and a green vegetable.

Grilled (Broiled) Porterhouse Steaks with Watercress Butter

	Metric/UK	US
Porterhouse steaks, on the bone and 2.5cm/1in thick	2 × ½kg/1lb	2 × 1lb
Tabasco sauce	1 Tbsp	1 Tbsp
Salt	½ tsp	½ tsp
Black pepper	¼ tsp	¼ tsp
Butter	50g/2oz	¼ cup
Finely chopped watercress	2 Tbsp	2 Tbsp

Preheat the grill (broiler) to high and line the grill (broiler) pan with foil to reflect the heat. Use a sharp knife to cut each steak across in half. Rub each steak with Tabasco sauce, and season with salt and pepper. Place the steaks on the rack and grill (broil) each side for 2 minutes. Reduce the heat and continue cooking for 2–4 minutes on each side, depending on how rare you want the steaks to be.

Meanwhile, soften the butter and mash with the watercress. Transfer the steaks to a warm serving dish and put a little of the watercress butter on top of each. Serve at once.

4 servings

Pork Chops in Tomato and Green Pepper Sauce

	Metric/UK	US
Salt	1 tsp	1 tsp
Pepper	1 tsp	1 tsp
Pork loin chops, 2cm/¾in thick	6	6
Vegetable oil	4 Tbsp	4 Tbsp
Garlic cloves, crushed	2	2
Dried basil	1 tsp	1 tsp
Dried thyme	1 tsp	1 tsp
Bayleaf	1	1
Dry red wine	90ml/3 floz	⅓ cup
Canned tomatoes, drained and finely chopped	450g/1lb	1lb
Tomato purée (paste)	2 Tbsp	2 Tbsp
Butter	40g/1½oz	3 Tbsp
Medium-sized green peppers, seeded and finely chopped	3	3
Onion, chopped	1	1
Button mushrooms, quartered	225g/8oz	2 cups
Cornflour (cornstarch)	2 Tbsp	2 Tbsp
Water	1 Tbsp	1 Tbsp
Chopped parsley	1 Tbsp	1 Tbsp

Rub salt and pepper into the chops. In a frying-pan heat the oil. Add the chops and brown for 3 minutes on each side. Transfer to a warm dish. Pour off most of the fat from the pan and add the garlic, basil, thyme and bayleaf. Stir in the wine and bring to the boil. Add the tomatoes and tomato purée (paste). Return the pork chops to the pan and baste thoroughly. Cook, covered, for 30–40 minutes or until cooked through, basting regularly.

Ten minutes before the end of the cooking time, melt the butter in another frying-pan. Add the green peppers and onion and cook for 5 minutes. Add the mushrooms and cook for 2–3 minutes. Transfer the vegetables to the chops in the frying-pan and cook everything, uncovered, for a further 15 minutes. Transfer the chops to a warm serving dish.

Dissolve the cornflour (cornstarch) in the water and stir into the mixture in the pan. Simmer for 3–5 minutes or until thickened. Remove the bayleaf. Pour the vegetables and sauce over the pork chops. Sprinkle with parsley and serve with buttered noodles.

6 servings

Veal Ragoût

	Metric/UK	US
Boned veal shoulder, cut into 5cm/2in cubes	1kg/2lb	2lb
Seasoned flour	25g/1oz	¼ cup
Butter	50g/2oz	¼ cup
Medium-sized onions, finely chopped	2	2
Caraway seeds	2 tsp	2 tsp
Stock	250ml/8 floz	1 cup
Paprika	2 tsp	2 tsp
Cayenne pepper	⅛ tsp	⅛ tsp
Mushrooms, sliced	175g/6oz	1½ cups
Sour cream	150ml/5 floz	⅔ cup
Chopped parsley	1 Tbsp	1 Tbsp

Coat the cubes of meat in the seasoned flour, shaking off any excess. Set aside. In a saucepan melt the butter. Add the onions and cook until they are soft and translucent. Add the meat and caraway seeds and cook for 5 minutes, turning to brown the meat cubes. Gradually add the stock to the pan, stirring continuously, and bring to the boil. Reduce the heat to low and mix in the paprika, cayenne and mushrooms. Cover and simmer for at least 1 hour or until the meat is tender. Stir in the sour cream just before serving and sprinkle with the chopped parsley.

4 servings

Grilled (Broiled) Porterhouse Steaks with Watercress Butter are so very easy to cook—and they're even easier to eat! Serve with baked potatoes and a tossed green salad for a special meal to remember.

Using up leftover meat needn't mean dull meals—try Shepherd's Pie and see!

Shepherd's Pie

Leftovers from a roast can be transformed into a hearty supper dish.

	Metric/UK	US
Butter	75g/3oz	6 Tbsp
Onions, finely chopped	2	2
Cooked lamb, minced (ground)	1kg/2lb	2lb
Salt	2 tsp	2 tsp
Black pepper	1 tsp	1 tsp
Dried mixed herbs	1 tsp	1 tsp
Worcestershire sauce	2 tsp	2 tsp
Beef stock	50ml/ 2 floz	¼ cup
Potatoes, mashed and kept warm	1.35kg/3lb	3lb
Milk, hot	50ml/2 floz	¼ cup

Preheat the oven to fairly hot (200°C/400°F, Gas Mark 6). In a large saucepan melt 25g/1oz (2 tablespoons) of butter over a moderate heat. Add the onions and cook, stirring occasionally, until they are soft and translucent. Stir in the meat, half the salt, the pepper, herbs and Worcestershire sauce and cook for 5 minutes, stirring frequently. Add the stock and remove the pan from the heat. Transfer the mixture to a shallow ovenproof dish and set aside.

Place the mashed potatoes in a mixing bowl and beat in half the remaining butter, salt and pepper and hot milk. Spoon the potatoes over the meat in an even layer. Cut the remaining butter into small dice and scatter over the top.

Bake the pie in the oven for 25–35 minutes or until the potatoes are golden brown. Serve immediately.
4–6 servings

Country Pâté

	Metric/UK	US
Butter	50g/2oz	¼ cup
Shallot, grated	1	1
Garlic clove, chopped	1	1
Belly (bacon) of pork, minced (ground)	½kg/1lb	1lb
Lean pork, minced (ground)	½kg/1lb	1lb
Stewing veal, minced (ground)	½kg/1lb	1lb
Pig (pork) liver, chopped	700g/1½lb	1½lb
Chicken livers, chopped	225g/8oz	½lb
Brandy	3 Tbsp	3 Tbsp
Double (heavy) cream	2 Tbsp	2 Tbsp
Lemon juice	1 tsp	1 tsp
Egg	1	1
Ground mace	⅛ tsp	⅛ tsp
Ground allspice	⅛ tsp	⅛ tsp
Salt and pepper to taste		
Pork fat, sliced evenly	700g/1½lb	1½lb
Bayleaves	3	3

In a shallow frying-pan, melt half the butter over a moderate heat. Add the shallot and garlic and fry, stirring occasionally, until they are soft and translucent. Transfer to a bowl and beat in the minced (ground) meats and the chopped pig (pork) liver.

Melt the remaining butter in the same frying-pan. Add the chicken livers and fry, turning them over occasionally, until they are brown on the outside but still pink inside. Remove the livers from the pan and set aside.

Meanwhile, preheat the oven to moderate (180°C/350°F, Gas Mark 4).

Pour the brandy into the frying-pan and bring it to the boil, stirring in any remaining oil and sediment left from the chicken livers. Pour the hot liquid over the meat mixture and beat in the cream, lemon juice, egg, and seasonings. Mix together then pound with a pestle until the ingredients are well blended but not too smooth.

Grease a 3L/5 pint (3 quart) terrine or deep ovenproof dish, then line with strips of pork fat, overlapping them slightly. Keep enough aside to cover the dish. Arrange half the meat in the dish, then arrange the chopped chicken livers in an even layer on top. Cover with the remaining meat mixture and top with the remaining pork fat. Arrange the bayleaves in a pattern on top. Cover with foil, then with a lid, if possible and stand in a roasting pan half filled with boiling water. Bake in the oven for 2¼ hours.

Remove the lid and foil and bake for a further 15–30 minutes to brown the top layer of fat slightly. Remove the dish from the oven and run a skewer into the centre; if the pâté is cooked through, the skewer will come out clean.

Cover the top of the pâté and place a weight over the cover. Leave in a pan of cold water to cool completely, then remove the weight and cover. Wrap in foil and chill in the refrigerator for 24 hours before serving.
About 2.5kg/5½lb pâté

Goulasch

This dish is of Hungarian origin and is flavoured with the traditional paprika and sour cream.

	Metric/UK	US
Butter	40g/1½oz	3 Tbsp
Vegetable oil	2 Tbsp	2 Tbsp
Stewing (chuck) steak, cubed	1kg/2lb	2lb
Onions, sliced	½kg/1lb	1lb
Garlic clove, crushed	1	1
Salt	1 tsp	1 tsp
Black pepper	½ tsp	½ tsp
Paprika	2 Tbsp	2 Tbsp
Water	150ml/5floz	⅔ cup
Bayleaf	1	1
Potatoes, sliced	½kg/1lb	1lb
Sour cream	150ml/5floz	⅔ cup

In a large saucepan, melt the butter with the oil over a moderate heat. Add the beef, a few pieces at a time, and fry quickly, stirring frequently until they are brown on all sides. Transfer the beef on to a plate and set aside.

Place the onions in the fat and fry, stirring occasionally until they are golden brown. Stir in the garlic, salt, pepper, paprika, water and bayleaf. Return the meat to the pan. Bring to the boil, cover, reduce the heat to low and simmer for 1 hour. Add the potatoes and simmer for a further 1 hour.

Remove the pan from the heat. Taste the goulasch and add more seasoning if necessary. Remove the bayleaf and transfer the stew into a warm serving dish. Spoon over the sour cream and serve at once.
4 servings

Irish Stew

This traditional stew uses the most economical cuts of lamb and so requires a long slow cooking.

	Metric/UK	US
Lamb, neck or scrag end	1.35kg/3lb	3lb
Potatoes, sliced	1.35kg/3lb	3lb
Onions, thinly sliced	½kg/1lb	1lb
Salt	1 tsp	1 tsp
Black pepper	½ tsp	½ tsp
Dried thyme	1 tsp	1 tsp
Cold water	450ml/¾ pint	2 cups

Classic Beef with Olives.

Divide the lamb into cutlets. Arrange a layer of potato slices on the bottom of a large, heavy-bottomed sauce-pan. Cover with a layer of onions, then a layer of cutlets. Sprinkle each layer with a little salt, pepper and thyme. Continue making layers in this way until all the ingredients are used up, ending with a layer of potatoes.

Pour in the water and place the pan over a moderately high heat. Bring to the boil, then reduce the heat to low and cover the pan tightly. Simmer gently for 2–2½ hours or until the cutlets are tender. Shake the pan occasionally to ensure that the potatoes do not stick to the bottom. Serve immediately.

6 servings

Beef with Olives

	Metric/UK	US
Butter	15g/½oz	1 Tbsp
Olive oil	1 Tbsp	1 Tbsp
Sirloin steak, in one piece	1.35kg/3lb	3lb
Green olives, stoned (pitted)	350g/12oz	2 cups
Salt	½ tsp	½ tsp
Black pepper	⅛ tsp	⅛ tsp

In a large frying-pan, melt the butter with the oil over a moderate heat. Add the meat, fat side up. Reduce the heat to moderate and cook for 7 minutes on each side.

Leave the meat fat side down for the rest of the cooking. Add the olives, salt and pepper and cover the pan with a lid. Cook for 15–20 minutes, depending on how rare you wish the meat to be. Cut the steak into thick, diagonal slices and serve immediately with the green olives.

6–8 servings

Chili Con Carne

Almost a national dish from the western states of the US, Chili con Carne is a combination of beef and red kidney beans, flavoured with cayenne and chili seasoning.

	Metric/UK	US
Olive oil	2 Tbsp	2 Tbsp
Onions, finely sliced	2	2
Garlic cloves, chopped	2	2
Beef, minced (ground)	700g/1½lb	1½lb
Canned tomatoes	225g/8oz	1 cup
Tomato purée (paste)	75g/3oz	6 Tbsp
Bayleaf	1	1
Ground cumin	1 tsp	1 tsp
Dried oregano	1 tsp	1 tsp
Cayenne pepper	1 tsp	1 tsp
Chili seasoning (mild)	2 Tbsp	2 Tbsp
Salt	2 tsp	2 tsp
Beef stock	350ml/12 floz	1½ cups
Canned red kidney beans	400g/14oz	14oz

In a large saucepan, heat the oil over a moderate heat. Add the onions and garlic and fry, stirring occasionally until they are soft and translucent. Add the meat and fry, stirring occasionally, until it browns.

Add the tomatoes and the juice, tomato purée (paste), bayleaf, cumin, oregano, cayenne, chili seasoning, salt and stock. Cover the pan and bring to the boil over a moderate heat. Reduce the heat to low and simmer, stirring occasionally, for 1 hour. Stir in the beans, then re-cover and simmer for a further 30 minutes. Remove the bayleaf and serve at once.

4–6 servings

Moussaka

	Metric/UK	US
Aubergines (eggplants), sliced	½kg/1lb	1lb
Salt	4 tsp	4 tsp
Butter	25g/1oz	2 Tbsp
Onion, finely chopped	1	1
Garlic clove, crushed	1	1
Lamb or mutton, minced (ground)	½kg/1lb	1lb
Tomatoes, peeled and coarsely chopped	4	4
Tomato purée (paste)	2 Tbsp	2 Tbsp
Dried thyme	¾ tsp	¾ tsp
Black pepper	½ tsp	½ tsp
Flour	3 Tbsp	3 Tbsp
Vegetable oil	125ml/4 floz	½ cup
Béchamel Sauce	300ml/ ½ pint	1¼ cups
Egg yolks	2	2
Kefalotiri or Parmesan cheese, finely grated	25g/1oz	¼ cup

Preheat the oven to hot (190°C/375°F, Gas Mark 5).

Place the aubergine (eggplant) slices in a colander and sprinkle with 3 teaspoons of salt. Set aside for 30 minutes to dégorge (reduce their water content).

Meanwhile, in a frying-pan melt the butter over a moderate heat. Add the onion and garlic and fry, stirring occasionally, until the onion is soft and translucent. Add the meat and fry for about 8 minutes, stirring frequently, until it is thoroughly browned. Add the tomatoes, tomato purée (paste), thyme, pepper and remaining salt and cook, stirring occasionally, for 4 minutes. Remove the pan from the heat and set aside.

Pat dry the aubergine (eggplant) slices on kitchen paper towels then dip them in the flour, coating them thoroughly and shaking off any excess. Set aside.

In a frying-pan, heat half the oil over a moderate heat. Add about half the aubergine (eggplant) slices and fry them for 3–4 minutes on each side or until they are lightly browned. Drain on kitchen paper towels and fry the remaining slices in the remaining oil.

Arrange half the aubergine (eggplant) slices on the bottom of a baking dish. Spoon over the meat mixture and cover with the remaining aubergine (eggplant) slices.

In a small mixing bowl, beat the béchamel sauce and egg yolks together. Pour over the top of the moussaka, then sprinkle over the cheese. Bake in the oven for 35–40 minutes or until the top is lightly browned.

4 servings

Moussaka is a classic Greek recipe which can be made either from lamb or beef—or leftover meat.

POULTRY AND GAME

Poultry is the word used for all domestic birds reared for the table—chicken, duck, goose and turkey. Game refers to wild animals and birds which are hunted for sport and then eaten; it includes wild goose, duck and turkey, grouse, partridge, pheasant, wild pigeon, quail, woodcock and other small birds, known as 'feathered' game; and also hare, rabbit, venison (deer) and boar known as 'ground' game or 'furred' game.

Poultry is the word used for all domestic birds reared for the table—chicken, duck, goose and turkey. Game refers to wild animals and birds which are hunted for sport and then eaten; it includes wild goose, duck and turkey, grouse, partridge, pheasant, wild pigeon, quail, woodcock and other small birds, known as 'feathered' game, and also hare, rabbit, venison (deer) and boar, known as 'ground' or 'furred' game.

Buying birds

Frozen poultry and game birds are now available all the year round, but fresh birds taste better; free-range poultry has more flavour than that raised in intensive farming. When buying fresh birds, choose an unmarked bird with firm flesh, no discoloration of the skin, and pliable feet. When using frozen poultry or game, make sure it is completely thawed before you cook it. This makes undercooking less likely, and reduces the risk of food poisoning by bacteria, which would be killed with thorough cooking. Let the bird thaw slowly in a refrigerator and, when thawed, use as soon as possible.

When buying game, try to get it from a reliable source where it is hung, plucked and cleaned for you. Make sure the bird looks plump, has no skin infections or abrasions and has pliable feet. Carefully remove all shot from the flesh.

Types of poultry

Chicken, once a luxury dish, is now an economical buy and a good value protein dish of great versatility. It can be roasted, fried, grilled (broiled), boiled, braised or stewed. It comes in various sizes.

Poussins, very small chickens, 6 weeks old, weighing ½kg–575g/1–1¼lb. Allow one per person.

Spring chickens (broilers), about 3 months old, weighing 1–1.25kg/2–2½lb. (Fryers weigh 1.25–1.6kg/ 2½–3½lb. One serves 2–3 people.)

Roasting chickens, larger birds up to 8 months or 1 year old, weighing 1.35–1.75kg/3–4lb (1.6–2.25kg/3½–5lb in the USA). One serves 3–4 people.

Boiling fowls (stewing chicken), larger, older and slightly tougher birds needing long, slow cooking. Weighing 1.75kg–2.75kg/4–6lb. One serves 4–6 people.

Capons, young castrated cocks which have been

specially fattened, weighing 2.75–4.5kg/6–10lb. One serves 8–10 people.

Duck, which has rich, fatty flesh, is very tasty and succulent. But it has a large, heavy carcass and little meat, so a 1.75kg/4lb duck will only serve two people amply, while a 2.75kg/6lb duck will serve four, or five at most.

Goose is specially fattened and can reach 10kg/24lb in weight. But younger, smaller geese are more succulent and tender. Choose one not more than a year old, with yellow pliable feet. Allow 350g/¾lb uncooked weight per person.

Turkeys are big birds suitable for a special occasion, and are usually cooked at Thanksgiving and Christmas, though the traditional Christmas bird once was a goose. Allow ½kg/1lb uncooked weight per person

PREPARATION OF BIRDS

Poultry and game birds are usually made ready for cooking before you buy them, but if you have a freshly killed bird which has not been prepared, it is quite easy to do it yourself. The first three stages are plucking, hanging and drawing.

1. Plucking

Poultry is plucked just after killing, as the feathers come out easily when the bird is still warm. Begin plucking in the breast area, and pull out two or three feathers at a time, pulling in the direction of the head. Take care not to tear the skin. When all the feathers are out, use a lighted taper or wooden spill to singe the downy stubble and hairs from the bird.

Game birds are not plucked until after they have been hung. When the breast feathers come away easily, the bird has hung long enough. It is then plucked in the same way as poultry.

2. Hanging

Both game and poultry, when freshly killed, are hung up in a cool, well-ventilated place for a few days before cooking for the flavour to develop. If the bird is not hung, the meat will be tough and disagreeable. The first stages of decomposition make it tender and tastier.

Poultry is hung up by the feet, game birds are hung by the head. The length of time for hanging depends on the weather, and the age and size of the birds. In warm wet weather the birds will be ready sooner than in cold dry weather; old birds need longer hanging than younger birds, and large birds need longer than small birds. Chicken, is hung for 1 day, geese and ducks for 1 to 2, turkeys for 3 to 5. Game birds can be hung for between 4 and 10 days, depending on the size of the bird, and on whether you like their much-prized 'high' flavour. Wild duck should be hung for 3 days at most, usually less.

3. Drawing

When the bird is ready to cook, the entrails are drawn out. Lay it on its back, and cut off the head with a sharp cleaver. With long-necked birds, cut the neck 7.5cm/3in from the body. Slit the neck skin and loosen it, and cut off the skinned neck close to the body. Take out the crop and windpipe.

Game birds are cooked with their feet left on. To remove the feet of poultry, cut nearly through the leg, grasp the foot and with a twisting, pulling movement pull out the sinews from the legs.

Put the right hand into the neck opening, palm down, with the fingers up under the breastbone. Dislodge the entrails; do not try to take them out. Now enlarge the vent at the other end of the bird and remove the entrails through it. Keep the heart, neck, liver and gizzard for making stock. Discard the gall bladder which is attached to the liver. Wipe the bird well with a damp cloth and wipe the cavity clean.

The birds are now ready for cooking, but further preparation is usually needed. Birds for roasting are usually stuffed; poultry is trussed after stuffing to help it keep its shape, and most birds have their breasts barded with bacon. Poultry can also be cut up for stewing, braising and frying, or boned for a galantine, while smallish birds can be cut in half or quartered.

Stuffing

Stuffing the cavity of a roasting bird helps to keep the flesh moist and give it flavour. The stuffing is served with the bird and makes the meat go further. Stuffing expands during cooking, so the cavity should not be tightly filled. 100g/4oz (2 cups) stuffing is enough for a 1.75kg/4lb roasting chicken. Chicken is stuffed from the neck end, duck and goose from either end, turkey from both ends, often with two different stuffings.

If you have no stuffing, slices of lemon or orange, sliced onion or herbs can be put in the cavity to give flavour. But a stuffing containing butter, or suet, or fat meat such as sausagemeat, has better moistening properties.

Stuffing

	Metric/UK	US
Butter, melted	25g/1oz	2 Tbsp
Fresh white breadcrumbs	100g/4oz	2 cups
Small onion, finely chopped	1	1
Salt	½ tsp	½ tsp
Pepper	½ tsp	½ tsp
Egg, lightly beaten	1	1
Stock or water to moisten		

In a bowl, pour the melted butter over the breadcrumbs. Stir in the onion, salt, pepper and egg and add enough stock or water to moisten.

You can add chopped herbs such as parsley or sage to this basic mixture, or chopped mushrooms or celery, fried gently in a little butter.

To make sausage stuffing for turkey, add 225g/8oz (1 cup) sausagemeat to the Basic Stuffing. A medium-sized turkey needs at least 1kg/2lb stuffing altogether (about ½ cup per ½kg/1lb of meat). A second stuffing often used for turkey is chestnut stuffing; add 50g/2oz (⅓ cup) diced bacon, fried crisp, 225g/8oz canned chestnut purée and 2 tablespoons chopped parsley to the Basic Stuffing.

Trussing

After stuffing, large birds such as chickens are usually trussed to keep their shape during cooking and make them easier to carve. There are two simple ways to truss a bird.

Using a skewer and a piece of string

1. Lay the bird on its breast. Fold the neck skin over the back, covering the neck opening, and fold the wings over the body to hold the skin in place.
2. Now lay the bird on its back. Pushing the legs upwards towards the neck, push the skewer through the bird from side to side, just below the thigh bone.
3. Turn the bird on its breast again. Pass the string under the ends of the skewer, catching in the wing tips to hold them against the body. Cross the string over the back of the bird.
4. Turn the bird on its back again, loop the string round the drumsticks and tail (parson's or pope's nose) and tie the ends together securely.

Perfect poultry demands perfect care in preparation. The two methods of trussing given above right will ensure a perfect roast bird if followed carefully. The rest depends on the quality of the flesh–its succulence and freshness; always buy fresh birds if possible.

Trussing Method 1

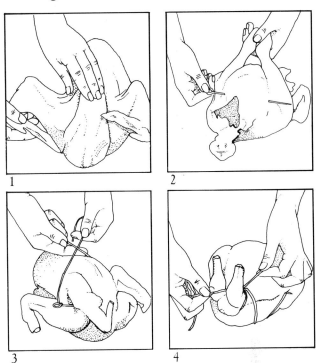

Trussing Method 2

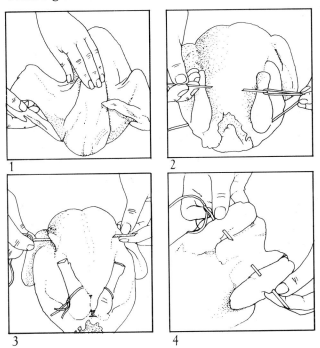

Using a long trussing needle and string

1 Same as in the first method.
2. Lay the bird on its back. Make a slit in the skin above the vent and put the tail through it to hold it in place.
3. To truss the legs, first press them well into the sides to plump the breast. Push the threaded needle through the body from side to side, under the legs. Bring the string up over one folded leg, push the needle through the tip of the breastbone and tie the ends of the string

Portioning a Chicken

Cut through the pink moist part of the joint to sever the leg completely. (1) To sever the wing, cut through the joint and fold into a neat shape with the breast underneath. (2) To remove the breast, separate from the back by cutting through the rib bones along the side. (3).

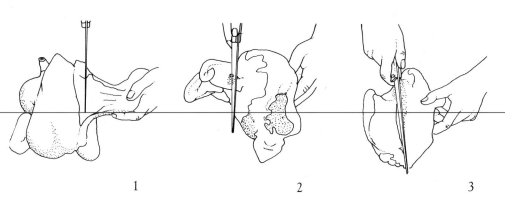

1　　　　　2　　　　　3

firmly over the other leg.

4. To truss the wings, thread the needle again. Push it through the carcass from side to side above the wings. Turn the bird on its breast again, and push the needle through one wing, the neck flap and backbone, and the other wing. Tie the ends firmly together.

Barding

If the trussed bird is to be roasted, the dry breast flesh may be protected with strips of fat bacon to keep it moist. This is known as barding. The bacon can be tied on, or simply laid on. It should be removed 20 minutes before the end of cooking time to brown the meat. Duck and goose do not need barding, as they are fatty birds. For other birds, if you have no bacon, rub butter generously over the breast before roasting and baste frequently.

Jointing (Cutting up)

Chicken pieces are needed for many recipes, and chickens and turkeys can be bought cut up into portions, either fresh or frozen. But it is easy to cut up your own chicken. First remove the legs, cutting where they join the carcass. The legs can be further divided into drumstick and thigh. Next make a sharp, deep cut near the tip of the breastbone, cutting off the wing with some of the breast meat. Cut off the other wing. The breasts can be removed by cutting the flesh away from the bone on either side in two whole pieces. Cut the breast meat into two or three pieces. Keep the carcass for making stock.

A smaller bird such as spring chicken (broiler) or duck can be halved by placing it on its back and cutting down through the breastbone and backbone. Each half can be further divided in half.

Boning

Some recipes call for boned birds, and it is easiest to get your butcher to do this. But it is not so difficult, and can be done at home with a little time and patience. Use a sharp knife. Cut down the length of the breastbone, then ease away the flesh from the bones of the carcass all down one side. Cut the sinews at each joint as you go along, and ease wing and leg bones from the

flesh so that the flesh turns inside out. You will be left with a large, flat parcel of flesh without any bones.

METHODS OF COOKING

1. Roasting

This is the most popular method of cooking whole chicken, duck, goose and turkey and also game birds. Rub the outside of the bird with salt, pepper and butter. Except for duck and goose, all birds should be barded or generously rubbed with butter or fat before cooking. Small game birds are often very dry and need special care. Baste frequently if not using bacon. If the breast becomes too brown, protect it with a piece of greaseproof or waxed paper or foil.

As with meat, there are various methods of roasting. A successful and widely used method for poultry, as for meat, is to start the bird at a high heat and turn the heat down after 15 minutes. The bird can also be covered in foil and cooked at a fairly high heat, and the foil removed for the last half hour of cooking. Or it can be cooked at a lower heat for a longer time, without sealing first; the heat can be turned up at the end to brown. Smaller birds are best cooked at a higher heat; this applies to most game birds. The temperatures and times given for poultry in the chart below are for the first method.

When a bird is done, the juices run clear, not pink, when the thick thigh meat or lower breast is pierced deeply with a skewer, and the skin is crisp, brown and aromatic.

When roasting duck and goose, first pierce the skin with a skewer in several places to let the fat run out. If a lot of fat collects in the pan, pour most of it off from time to time. The fat is wonderful to cook in, makes good pastry and can be used in potting; and goose-grease used to be rubbed on the chest for a cold! Goose is usually stuffed with a fruit stuffing, such as Basic Stuffing with dried apricots added.

When roasting game, the bird need not be stuffed

The perfect meal every time—crisply roasted chickens, served with green vegetables, such as peas, as in the picture right.

114

POULTRY	ROASTING TIMES AND TEMPERATURES			
	Initial oven temperature	Reduced oven temperature	Time needed per ½kg/1lb	Meat thermometer readings
Chicken	220°C/425°F, Gas Mark 7	180°C/350°F, Gas Mark 4	25–30min up to 1kg/2lb. For each additional ½kg/1lb add 10–15 min	80°C/180°F
Duck	,,	,,	20–25min	80–85°C/180–185°F
Goose	,,	,,	20–25 min	85°C/185°F
Turkey	,,	,,	15min	80–85°C/180–185°F

These times are for unstuffed birds. For stuffed chicken, add 10–20 minutes to total time; for stuffed duck, goose and turkey, add 5 minutes to the basic time per ½kg/1lb.

GAME		
	Preheat oven to	Total cooking time
Grouse	200°C/400°F, Gas Mark 6	30–45min
Partridge	,,	,,
Pheasant	220°C/425°F, Gas Mark 7	Allow 20min per ½kg/1lb
Pigeon	,,	,,
Quail	,,	20min
Snipe	,,	,,
Woodcock	,,	,,
Wild duck	220°C/425°F, Gas Mark 7	25min or more
Wild turkey	,,	30min or more

or trussed. Put a knob of butter inside the bird, if not using stuffing, add salt and pepper, and bard the breast with fat bacon. Put each bird on a piece of bread or toast in the roasting pan; this browns and absorbs the juices, and the bird should be served on it. With small birds—grouse, partridge, quail, snipe, woodcock—allow one per person; larger birds such as pheasant or pigeon can be split in half for serving, allowing half a bird per person.

When roasting wild duck or turkey, experts disagree about whether they should be well done. Some like the birds just heated through, with the juices still running red; some cook them through until the juices are clear.

Pheasant and grouse particularly are superb if roasted and accompanied by the traditional garnishes of game chips, chopped watercress, roasted chestnuts and a thin gravy.

Carving

Use a sharp knife and two-pronged fork with a thumb guard. Remove the legs and wings first, each in one piece unless the bird is very large, when the leg can make two portions—thigh and drumstick. On a turkey, cut the drumstick off first, hold it in one hand by the knuckle and carve slices from it, then cut slices from the thigh still attached to the body.

Next cut meat from the breast in thin slices, carving parallel to the breastbone. With turkey, give each person a serving of some white breast meat and dark leg meat.

Small game birds are served whole or simply cut in half.

2. Braising

Goose is not suitable for braising. Whole roasting chicken, chicken pieces and whole, halved or jointed (cut up) ducks and game birds can be braised. Both braising and stewing are good methods for older birds and birds of uncertain age.

Fry the bird or pieces in a little oil or butter over a high heat until golden all over. Then put them on a bed of lightly fried vegetables in a flameproof casserole dish, add a little liquid such as stock or wine, cover tightly and cook on a low heat, either on top of the stove or in the oven. This is a slow method of cooking; timing depends on the size and age of the bird. When braising a whole bird, the roasting times given above are a useful guide.

3. Stewing

Stewing is similar to braising but uses a larger amount of cooking liquid such as wine, stock or a mixture of the two. Chicken pieces and whole, halved or jointed (cut up) game birds are suitable. As there is a liquid to turn into sauce, the pieces can be coated in flour before frying, to make a thicker sauce. Add lightly fried chopped vegetables at the beginning or halfway through cooking, depending on how long the vegetables take to cook. This method is not as slow as braising.

4. Sautéing

This method of cooking in butter is only suitable for tender young chicken and turkey pieces. Brown the pieces in butter over a high heat for 8–10 minutes, then cover and cook for 20–25 minutes or until tender. Pour off the fat, put aside the pieces to keep warm and make the juices into a sauce; varying the ingredients of the sauce can produce a wide variety of different recipes.

5. Boiling

This method is only used for chickens; it is suitable for older birds and pieces. Often the cooked flesh is used in other dishes, but it can also be drained and served as it is with a good white sauce, plain or flavoured.

To boil, put the chicken in a pan, just cover with water and add a bouquet garni, carrot and onion, and ½ teaspoon salt for every ½kg/1lb of chicken. Bring to the boil, then cover and simmer the bird slowly until done; a whole bird takes 2–3 hours, jointed pieces 15–20 minutes.

Save the cooking liquid; it is always good as chicken stock and it can be used in soups and sauces, or as

Carving a Chicken

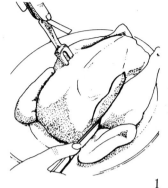

1

To carve a chicken, first anchor the fork in the bird to hold firmly; then carve off the right leg and thigh. (1) Now carve each of the wing joints (served with a little breast meat they can make two more portions). (2) Finally, with the front end of the carcass facing you, carve the breast into thin slices. (3).

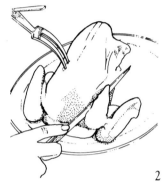 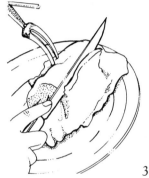

2   3

gravy.

6. Grilling (Broiling)

Chicken pieces, or halved spring chickens (broilers), or poussins, or fryers can be grilled (broiled), as can turkey pieces and small tender game birds such as grouse, quail and partridge, halved and flattened. All should be seasoned and well buttered, and basted often. Preheat the grill (broiler) to high. After 2–3 minutes reduce the heat to moderate and cook, turning frequently, until done. Chicken pieces take 20–30 minutes altogether—slightly less for breasts. Halved birds take 25–30 minutes.

7. Frying

Chicken pieces can be fried. You can coat them with seasoned flour or egg and breadcrumbs first to keep the flesh juicy inside a crisp coating. They can either be shallow fried—brown the pieces quickly and then fry over a moderate heat until tender, about 15–20 minutes—or deep fried. Directions for deep frying fish apply to chicken pieces. They take about 10–15 minutes.

Cold poultry: All cooked poultry is delicious served cold. Use it in salads, sandwiches, pies, croquettes and savoury dishes of all kinds.

RABBIT AND HARE

Rabbit sold in the shops is bred specially for the table and tastes much like chicken. Wild rabbit has a more gamey flavour. Rabbit is eaten when about 3 months old. Hare has more flavour than rabbit but needs long slow cooking to make it tender. European hare is all dark meat, while American domestic hare is all white.

Preparation

Rabbit and hare are usually sold skinned and paunched (drawn), but these processes can be carried out at home with a freshly killed animal. Rabbit is never hung, but prepared for cooking as soon as it is killed. Hare is hung by the back feet for a week to 10 days, with a bowl beneath it to catch any blood, which can be used to thicken the gravy. A drop of vinegar in the bowl stops the blood coagulating.

Skinning and paunching

The skin is peeled off in one piece, as if undressing the animal. Cut off the feet at the first joint, slit the belly skin lengthways and ease it off the flesh. Pull the skin away as far as the hind legs, turning the leg skin inside out to free it. Now pull the skin off the lower back and towards the head and off the forelegs and head. Open the belly with scissors and take out all the entrails. Discard all except the kidneys, liver and heart, which can be used for the sauce.

Hare and rabbit are usually braised or stewed. For this you need pieces. To joint (cut up) a skinned animal, cut off the flaps below the ribcage, split the carcass in two lengthways, remove the hind legs of the first joint and the forelegs where they join the body, and cut the remaining carcass in half.

COOKING METHODS

1. Braising

Coat the pieces in seasoned flour and brown them in hot fat in a casserole. Add red wine or game stock to cover, put the lid on tightly and cook in an oven preheated to warm (170°C/325°F, Gas Mark 3) for about 2 hours. Before serving, the juice can be thickened with a little of the blood (for hare) or with beurre manié or sour cream. Do not heat again if using blood.

2. Roasting

Young hares can be roasted whole; the saddle of older ones can be roasted. A whole hare serves 4–6, a whole rabbit 3 people.

To truss a whole animal for roasting, cut the thigh sinews of the hind legs, push them forward and fasten them to the body with skewers, or trussing needle and string. Fasten the forelegs close to the body in the same way. Fill the body with Basic Stuffing. Bard the back with fat bacon, add butter or fat and roast in an oven preheated to moderate (180°C/350°F, Gas Mark 4) for 1½–2 hours, basting often.

VENISON

Venison, the strong but delectable meat of antlered animals such as deer, moose and elk, is sold in joints (roasting cuts).

COOKING METHODS

The leg and saddle are roasted; the shoulder meat, neck cutlets and loin chops are tougher and best stewed. Chops and cutlets can also be fried. For stews, the meat is often marinated to make it more tender.

1. Roasting

Brush the meat generously with oil and wrap in foil. Roast in an oven preheated to fairly hot (190°C/375°F, Gas Mark 5) for 35 minutes per ½kg/1lb. Redcurrant jelly is usually served with roast venison.

2. Stewing

Leave the meat, cut into cubes, in a marinade for 4 hours, then lift out, drain and dry. Brown it with onions and bacon fat, add flour to make a roux, pour on a liquid, such as red wine, to cover and stir to make a sauce. Season and simmer for about 1 hour. Strain the marinade and add it. Cook for a further 30 minutes or until tender. There are several variations in this basic method.

3. Frying

Thin chops, cutlets and 5cm/2in fillet slices for frying should be flattened slightly with a meat cleaver. Season and fry over a high heat in oil or butter until tender, turning once only. For the fillet, brown on each side over a high heat without fat, add butter and cook about 8 minutes more on a low heat, turning once.

RECIPES

Turkey with Cherry Stuffing

	Metric/UK	US
Turkey, oven-ready	1 × 5.4kg/ 12lb	1 × 12lb
Salt	1 tsp	1 tsp
Black pepper	1 tsp	1 tsp
Butter, melted	100g/4oz	½ cup

STUFFING

Large egg, well beaten	1	1
Canned stoned Morello (Bing) cherries, drained and chopped (reserve 125ml/4floz (½ cup) can juice)	450g/1lb	1lb
Cherry brandy	4 Tbsp	4 Tbsp
Fresh white breadcrumbs	175g/6oz	3 cups
Butter	50g/2oz	¼ cup
Spring onions (scallions), finely chopped	4	4
Pork sausagemeat	1kg/2lb	2lb
Lean veal, finely minced (ground)	½kg/1lb	1lb
Finely grated rind and juice of 2 lemons		
Ground allspice	½ tsp	½ tsp
Salt	1 tsp	1 tsp
Black pepper	1 tsp	1 tsp
Dried basil	1 tsp	1 tsp

Preheat the oven to warm (170°C/325°F, Gas Mark 3). Rub the turkey inside and out with salt and pepper. Set aside.

In a large mixing bowl, combine the egg, cherry can juice and cherry brandy with the breadcrumbs. Allow to soak for 10 minutes. Beat until smooth. Set aside. In a large saucepan melt the butter over a moderate heat. Add the spring onions (scallions) and fry, stirring occasionally until they are soft and translucent. Add the sausagemeat and cook, stirring, until it has lost its pinkness. Beat in the breadcrumb mixture, veal, cherries, lemon rind and juice, allspice, salt, pepper and basil. Remove from the heat and allow to cool. Spoon the mixture into the cavities of the turkey and sew up with a trussing needle. Place in a large roasting pan and brush with the melted butter. Place in the oven.

Roast for 3¾ hours, basting occasionally and turning

Turkey with Cherry Stuffing gives any celebration a special touch.

over after 1½ hours.

Increase the heat to hot (230°C/450°F, Gas Mark 8). Turn the turkey breast up and roast for a further 30 minutes or until the turkey is cooked and the skin deep golden brown.

Remove the trussing string and serve at once.

12 servings

Poussins au Gingembre (Baby Chickens with Ginger)

	Metric/UK	US
Poussins, spring chickens (broilers), split through the breastbone	4	4
Salt	½ tsp	½ tsp
Black pepper	½ tsp	½ tsp
Butter, melted	75g/3oz	⅓ cup

SAUCE

Butter	25g/1oz	2 Tbsp
Fresh root (green) ginger, peeled and finely chopped	7.5cm/3in piece	3in piece
Garlic clove, crushed	1	1
Tomato purée (paste)	1 Tbsp	1 Tbsp
White wine vinegar	1 Tbsp	1 Tbsp
Salt	½ tsp	½ tsp
Black pepper	½ tsp	½ tsp
Soft brown sugar	1 tsp	1 tsp
Dry white wine	300ml/ ½ pint	1¼ cups
Chicken stock	250ml/8floz	1 cup
Flour mixed to a paste with 3 Tbsp water	2 Tbsp	2 Tbsp
Lemon juice	2 tsp	2 tsp

First make the sauce. In a saucepan, melt the butter over a moderate heat. Add the ginger and garlic and fry for 3 minutes, stirring continuously. Stir in the tomato purée (paste), vinegar, salt, pepper, sugar, wine and stock. Bring to the boil. Reduce the heat to low and simmer for 20 minutes. Strain and return to the saucepan. Set aside.

Place the poussins or broilers on a working surface and, grasping each cut edge of breast with your hands, pull them apart until the ribs break. Rub all over with salt and pepper.

Preheat the grill (broiler) to high. Pour the melted butter into the grill (broiler) pan. Place the poussins, skin side up in the pan and turn to baste them with the butter. Grill (broil) for 8 minutes, basting occasionally, then turn over and cook the other side for 8 minutes,

still basting. Cook until tender and golden.

Stir the flour and lemon juice into the sauce. Bring back to boil, reduce the heat and simmer, stirring, for 3 minutes. Serve the poussins at once on a warm serving dish and accompany them with the sauce.

4 servings

Poulet aux Crevettes (Chicken with Shrimp and Wine)

	Metric/UK	US
Salt	1 tsp	1 tsp
Black pepper	½ tsp	½ tsp
Chicken, cut into serving pieces	1 × 1.75kg/ 4lb	1 × 4lb
Olive oil	4 Tbsp	4 Tbsp
Garlic cloves, crushed	2	2
Fresh root (green) ginger, peeled and finely chopped	2.5cm/1in piece	1in piece
Shallots, finely chopped	3	3
White wine	300ml/½ pint	1¼ cups
Chopped fresh marjoram	2 tsp	2 tsp
Prawns (shrimp), shelled	300g/10oz	1⅔ cups
Lemon juice	1 tsp	1 tsp
Cornflour (cornstarch) dissolved in 1 Tbsp white wine	1 tsp	1 tsp

Rub salt and pepper into the chicken pieces. In a large flameproof casserole heat the oil over a moderate heat. Add the chicken pieces and brown for 8–10 minutes. Transfer them to a plate and set aside. Add the garlic, ginger and shallots to the casserole and cook for 3–4 minutes.

Return the chicken to the casserole. Pour over the wine, add the marjoram and bring to the boil. Reduce the heat to low, cover the casserole and simmer for 45–60 minutes or until the chicken pieces are cooked and tender. Add the prawns (shrimp) and cook for a further 5 minutes. Transfer the chicken pieces to a warm serving dish and arrange the prawns (shrimp) around them. Keep hot.

Bring the liquid in the casserole back to the boil. Reduce the heat to low, add the lemon juice and cook for 2 minutes. Stir in the cornflour (cornstarch) mixture and simmer, stirring, until the sauce thickens. Pour over the chicken and serve immediately.

4 servings

Poulet Sauté à l'Archduc (Sautéed Chicken in Madeira Flavoured Cream Sauce)

	Metric/UK	US
Salt	1 tsp	1 tsp
Paprika	1 tsp	1 tsp
Chicken, cut into serving pieces	1 × 1.75kg/ 4lb	1 × 4lb
Butter	100g/4oz	½ cup
Lemon juice	2 tsp	2 tsp
Small onions, coarsely chopped	2	2
White wine	125ml/4 floz	½ cup
Single (light) cream	175ml/6 floz	¾ cup
Madeira	2 Tbsp	2 Tbsp
Beurre Manié	15g/½oz	1 Tbsp
Parsley sprigs	4	4

Sprinkle salt and paprika over the chicken pieces. In a flameproof casserole, melt the butter over a moderate heat. Add the chicken pieces and cook for 8–10 minutes or until they are brown. Sprinkle over the lemon juice, add the onions and reduce the heat to low. Cook for 20–25 minutes or until the chicken is tender. Remove the chicken pieces and keep warm.

Skim off any fat from the cooking liquid, then stir in the white wine. Increase the heat to high and boil for 10 minutes or until it has reduced by half. Strain the liquid into a small saucepan. Gradually stir in the cream and cook over a low heat, without boiling, for 3 minutes. Stir in the Madeira. Stir in the beurre manié, a little at a time until the sauce is thick and smooth. Pour the sauce over the chicken. Garnish with parsley and serve immediately.

4 servings

Chicken Florentine

	Metric/UK	US
Parmesan cheese, grated	100g/4oz	1 cup
Dry white breadcrumbs	100g/4oz	1⅓ cups
Seasoned flour	3 Tbsp	3 Tbsp
Egg beaten with 1 Tbsp water	1	1
Chicken breasts, skinned and boned	6	6
Butter	175g/6oz	¾ cup
Large packages frozen spinach	2	2
Salt	1 tsp	1 tsp
Lemon juice	1½ Tbsp	1½ Tbsp
Mushrooms, sliced	700g/1½lb	1½lb
Lemon, sliced	1	1

Small furred game such as rabbit and hare are not used nearly enough in cooking– yet they're both delicious and economical. Hare in Sweet and Sour Sauce, for instance, is special enough to serve for guests, inexpensive enough to afford for a family supper.

Mix the cheese and breadcrumbs together. Use the seasoned flour, then egg and then the breadcrumb mixture to coat the chicken breasts. Place in the refrigerator to chill for 1 hour.

In a large frying-pan, melt two thirds of the butter over a moderate heat. Add the chicken breasts and cook for about 20 minutes or until they are tender, turning occasionally. While the chicken is cooking, cook the spinach as directed on the packages. Squeeze between two plates to remove excess moisture, then chop coarsely. Arrange on a warm flat serving dish and sprinkle with salt and lemon juice. Place the chicken breasts on top of the spinach. Cover and keep hot.

Fry the mushrooms for 4–5 minutes in half of the remaining butter. Remove with a slotted spoon and arrange around the chicken. Cook the remaining butter over high heat until brown. Strain over the chicken breasts and garnish with lemon slices.
6 servings

Hare in Sweet and Sour Sauce

	Metric/UK	US
Hare, cut into serving pieces and skinned	1 × 2.25kg/ 5lb	1 × 5lb
Seasoned flour	50g/2oz	½ cup
Butter	50g/2oz	¼ cup
Olive oil	1 Tbsp	1 Tbsp
Onions, finely chopped	2	2
Carrots, sliced	2	2
Bouquet garni	1	1
Beef stock	900ml/ 1½ pints	3¾ cups
Canned cranberry sauce	100g/4oz	4oz
Red wine	175ml/6floz	¾ cup
Salt	½ tsp	½ tsp
Black pepper	¼ tsp	¼ tsp

Soak the hare pieces in cold salted water for 1 hour. Drain in a colander and dry with kitchen paper towels. Coat the pieces in the seasoned flour. Preheat the oven to warm (170°C/325°F, Gas Mark 3). In a large flame-proof casserole, melt the butter with the oil over a moderate heat. Add the hare and brown quickly for 3–5 minutes. Remove the meat and set aside. Add the onions and carrots to the casserole and cook gently until the onions are soft and translucent. Replace the hare in the casserole and add the bouquet garni, salt and pepper. Pour in the stock and bring to the boil. Cover and transfer to the oven. Braise for 2½ hours or until the meat is very tender.

Transfer the hare pieces to a warm dish. Strain the juices from the casserole into a measuring jug. Pour 450ml/¾ pint (2 cups) into a saucepan and reserve the rest. (It is not needed in this recipe, but should be kept and added to soup or stock). Add the cranberry sauce and wine to the saucepan and simmer for 5 minutes, stirring occasionally. Return the hare to the casserole and pour over the sauce. Return to the oven and cook for a further 20 minutes. Serve immediately.
6 servings

Venison can be difficult to obtain, but if you can the rich taste and succulence more than repays the effort— as in Venison Chops with Sour Cream and Horseradish Sauce.

Venison Chops with Sour Cream and Horse-radish Sauce

	Metric/UK	US
Venison chops	4	4
Salt	1 tsp	1 tsp
Black pepper	1 tsp	1 tsp
Garlic cloves, halved	2	2
Vegetable oil	4 Tbsp	4 Tbsp
Sour cream	175ml/6 floz	¾ cup
Grated horseradish	1 tsp	1 tsp
MARINADE		
Dry white wine	125ml/4 floz	½ cup
Olive oil	4 Tbsp	4 Tbsp
Onion, thinly sliced	1	1
Garlic clove, crushed	1	1
Black peppercorns	12	12
Dried thyme	1 tsp	1 tsp

Combine all the marinade ingredients in a dish and add the venison chops. Leave to marinate at room temperature for 2–4 hours, turning occasionally. Remove the chops and dry on kitchen paper towels. Rub with the salt, pepper and garlic cloves.

In a large frying-pan, heat the oil over a moderate heat. Add the chops and cook for 5 minutes on each side or until they are brown. Pour in the marinade and bring to the boil. Cover and simmer for 20 minutes or until tender. Remove from the heat and allow to cool in the marinade. Leave for 24 hours.

Return the pan to the heat and bring to the boil. Reduce the heat to low and simmer for 15 minutes. Transfer the chops to a warm serving dish. Strain the pan liquid into a saucepan. Bring to the boil, then reduce to a low heat. Stir in the sour cream and horseradish and cook gently for 2 minutes until hot but not boiling. Remove the pan from the heat and pour the sauce over the chops. Serve at once.

4 servings

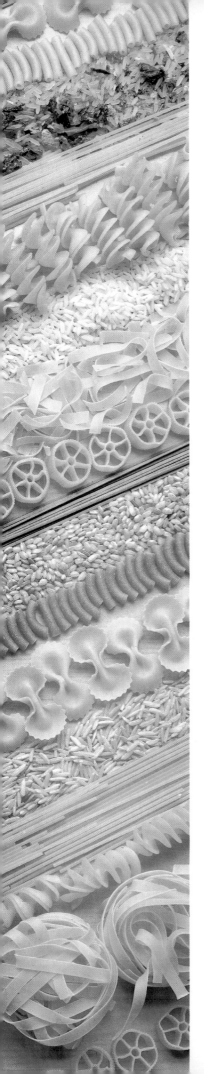

RICE
AND PASTA

Rice and pasta are both cereals; both are used to make a little protein—meat or fish—go a long way. They are mild in flavour, and filling, so they go well with tasty sauces and strong flavoured meat and fish dishes. Boiled rice is the classic accompaniment to curry, and is the basis for risotto and pilaff dishes.

Rice

Many different kinds of rice are grown all over the world. Both white (polished) rice and brown (unpolished) rice come in three grain sizes, long, medium and short. Brown rice is more nutritious and provides essential roughage.

For plain boiled rice to accompany meat, fish, stews and curries, look for a long, thinnish grain, which absorbs less liquid than a short thick grain. For risotto or pilaff, where the rice is cooked together with other ingredients, Italian rice (Avorio), which is husked but not polished, is ideal, though long grain is also suitable. Brown rice, which is nutty in taste, is delicious as a plain boiled rice but not suitable for risottos and pilaffs. For sweet dishes use white rice from Carolina, which has a short round grain.

Keep rice in an airtight jar in a cool dry place. Do not store it for too long.

Preparation

If rice is bought in sealed packets already washed and polished, it does not need washing again. Loose or brown rice needs washing before you use it: put the measured quantity in a conical strainer and hold it under a running tap until all cloudiness disappears from the water. This washes away the surface starch.

COOKING METHODS

Rice can be boiled on its own, cooked slowly with other ingredients as in risotto, fried or baked as in rice pudding. 175g/6oz (1 cup) of uncooked rice will serve three people; or allow 40g/1½oz (¼ cup) to 50g/2oz (⅓ cup) per person

1. Boiling

There are two ways of boiling rice—the fast boiling and the absorption method. Both have their devotees. Use whichever you find easier.

Fast boiling

For each 50g/2oz (⅓ cup) rice use 600ml/1 pint (2½ cups) water and 1 teaspoon salt. Bring the water to a boil in a large pan. Add the salt, and the juice of ½ lemon if you are using white rice, to keep it white. Sprinkle the rice into the fast boiling water and stir until it reaches full boil. Put the lid on. Cooking time varies between 8 and 12 minutes, depending on the thickness of the grain. Begin to test after 8 minutes cooking. A grain should be soft right through but not mushy. Drain thoroughly and put the rice back in the pan, in which you have melted a knob of butter to stop it sticking. Cover and keep warm on the top of the stove, shaking from time to time until dry and fluffy. Or you can dry the drained rice in the oven. Put it in a shallow, buttered dish, cover it tightly, and put it in the centre of an oven preheated to warm (170°C/325°F, Gas Mark 3) for 10 minutes.

Absorbtion method

For 100g/4oz (⅔ cup) rice allow 300ml/½ pint (1¼ cups) water; or for 1 cup of rice use 2 cups of water or stock. Bring the water to the boil, add the rice and turn the

1   2   3   4

heat down to simmer once it has boiled again. Cover with a folded teacloth or dish towel, put on the lid and weight it to stop steam escaping. After 15 minutes all the liquid should have been absorbed. Turn the rice on to a serving dish and fluff it up with a fork.

Brown rice

Brown rice takes longer to cook than white rice. For fast boiling allow about 25 minutes, for the absorption method about 45 minutes.

Parboiled rice

This semi-cooked rice needs a shorter cooking time. Follow the instructions on the package.

Instant rice

Instant rice is fully cooked, then dehydrated. Follow the instructions on the package.

Wild rice

This is not a cereal but a form of grass seed. It is rare and expensive but very good. It goes well with game. Boil as for ordinary rice.

2. Frying

Either cooked or raw rice can be used. Either boil the rice until just tender, then drain well and fry gently until lightly coloured, stirring occasionally. Or fry the raw rice very gently in butter and bacon fat until transparent, add 300ml/½ pint (1¼ cups) stock [for 100g/4oz (⅔ cup) rice] and cook over a moderate heat until all the liquid is absorbed, adding more stock as needed until the rice is tender.

Cold rice

Cold rice is a delicious ingredient in a salad. Toss in Vinaigrette when cold, or while still warm. Add finely chopped cooked peppers or onions, or small cooked peas (fresh or canned), or fruit such as pineapple or apricot, to make a delightful accompaniment to ham or poultry.

Cold rice is also used in stuffings.

Different types of rice, from left to right : patna, which is long grain and available in white or brown. (1) Wild rice—not a rice at all but a wild grass. (2) Basmati, a long grain rice used in curries. (3) prefluffed or easy-cook rice. (4) Minute rice which, as the name suggests, can be reconstituted quickly. (5) Boil-in-bag rice is also easy to cook. (6) Rice with flavourings—there are many on the market with both vegetables and meat. (7) Italian rice, short grain and with a nutty taste when cooked. Used in risottos. (8) .

5   6   7   8

Pork Fried Rice makes a very tasty, substantial supper dish with a slightly Eastern taste.

Pork Fried Rice

	Metric/UK	US
Vegetable oil	3 Tbsp	3 Tbsp
Small onion, finely chopped	1	1
Celery stalks, finely chopped	2	2
Small carrots, finely chopped	2	2
Cooked roast pork, cut into 2.5cm/1in strips	225g/8oz	$1\frac{1}{3}$ cups
Small cabbage, finely shredded	$\frac{1}{2}$	$\frac{1}{2}$
Black pepper	$\frac{1}{2}$ tsp	$\frac{1}{2}$ tsp
Soy sauce	2 Tbsp	2 Tbsp
Cooked long grain rice	225g/8oz	3 cups
Eggs, lightly beaten	2	2
Salt	$\frac{1}{4}$ tsp	$\frac{1}{4}$ tsp

In a large frying-pan, heat 2 tablespoons of the oil over a moderate heat. Add the onion, celery and carrots and cook for 5 minutes. Add the pork, cabbage, pepper, soy sauce and rice. Cook, stirring continuously, until hot—about 2–3 minutes. Mix the beaten eggs and salt and fry in the remaining oil to make a flat omelette. Cut into thin strips and use to garnish the fried rice.
4 servings

Rise e Bisi
(Rice with Peas)

	Metric/UK	US
Olive oil	1 Tbsp	1 Tbsp
Lean bacon, chopped	175g/6oz	6oz
Butter	50g/2oz	$\frac{1}{4}$ cup
Onion, thinly sliced	1	1
Peas, weighed or measured after shelling	450g/1lb	3 cups
Italian rice	450g/1lb	$2\frac{2}{3}$ cups
Dry white wine	90ml/3floz	$\frac{1}{3}$ cup
Homemade chicken stock	1.2L/ 2 pints	5 cups
Salt	1 tsp	1 tsp
Black pepper	$\frac{1}{2}$ tsp	$\frac{1}{2}$ tsp
Parmesan cheese, grated	100g/4oz	1 cup

This Italian dish is an example of the risotto method of cooking rice. In a large saucepan, heat the oil. Add the bacon and fry until it is crisp. Remove. Add 25g/1oz (2 Tbsp) of the butter and cook the onion until it is soft and translucent. Add the peas and rice, reduce the heat to low and cook, stirring for 5 minutes. Add the wine and one third of the stock and bring to the boil. Keep the rice bubbling gently and stir occasionally with a fork. When the liquid has been absorbed, add another one third of the stock. Continue in this way until the rice is cooked and tender, but still firm. Stir in the bacon, remaining butter, the salt, pepper and half the cheese. Simmer for 1 minute. Serve hot, with the remaining cheese.

4–6 servings

Walnut and Rice Salad

	Metric/UK	US
Large firm tomatoes	6	6
Walnuts, halved	175g/6oz	$1\frac{1}{2}$ cups
Cooked long grain rice	200g/7oz	$2\frac{1}{2}$ cups
Cooked ham, diced	350g/12oz	2 cups
French (green) beans, cooked and drained	225g/8oz	1 cup
Sultanas (raisins)	100g/4oz	$\frac{2}{3}$ cup
Canned sweetcorn, drained	400g/14oz	14oz
Chopped fresh sage	1 tsp	1 tsp
Chopped fresh basil	2 tsp	2 tsp
French Dressing	4 Tbsp	4 Tbsp
GARNISH		
Walnut halves	12	12
Chopped parsley	1 Tbsp	1 Tbsp

Cut the tops off the tomatoes, spoon out the seeds and discard them. Mix all the remaining ingredients together, except the dressing. Toss in the dressing until well coated. Fill the tomatoes with the mixture and garnish with walnut halves and parsley.

6 servings

Rice Pudding

	Metric/UK	US
Butter	25g/1oz	2 Tbsp
Short round grain rice (Carolina rice)	100g/4oz	$\frac{2}{3}$ cup
Milk	1.8L/ 3 pints	$7\frac{1}{2}$ cups
Salt	$\frac{1}{4}$ tsp	$\frac{1}{4}$ tsp

131

Castor (superfine) sugar	2 tsp	2 tsp
Grated nutmeg (optional)	$\frac{1}{4}$ tsp	$\frac{1}{4}$ tsp

Grease a pie dish generously with the butter. Add the rice, pour over the milk, add the salt and sugar and stir well. Sprinkle with the nutmeg if using. Cook in the centre of an oven preheated to cool (150°C/300°F, Gas Mark 2), for about 2 hours. The pudding should be soft and creamy and have a brown skin on top.

4 servings

Apricot Condé

	Metric/UK	US
Short round grain rice (Carolina rice)	100g/4oz	$\frac{2}{3}$ cup
Milk	900ml/ 1½ pints	3¾ cups
Sugar	350g/12oz	1½ cups
Butter	25g/1oz	2 Tbsp
Salt	$\frac{1}{8}$ tsp	$\frac{1}{8}$ tsp
Vanilla essence (extract)	1 tsp	1 tsp
Egg yolks, lightly beaten	6	6
Apricots, peeled, halved and stoned (pitted)	1kg/2lb	2lb
Water	250ml/8floz	1 cup
Kirsch	2 Tbsp	2 Tbsp
Flaked almonds	25g/1oz	$\frac{1}{4}$ cup

Preheat the oven to cool (150°C/300°F, Gas Mark 2). Put the rice, milk, 100g/4oz (½ cup) of the sugar, the butter, salt and vanilla in a flameproof dish. Bring to the boil on top of the stove, stirring continuously, then transfer to the oven. Bake for 1 hour or until all the liquid has been absorbed.

Remove from the oven and stir in the egg yolks. Cook over low heat on top of the stove, stirring, for 3 minutes. Set aside to cool.

Slice 225g/8oz of the apricots. Set aside. Spoon one third of the rice mixture into a greased 20cm/8in soufflé dish. Cover with half of the sliced apricots. Continue making layers, ending with rice. Chill for 2 hours or until firm.

To make the sauce, dissolve the remaining sugar in the water. Add the remaining apricots and simmer for 10 minutes or until tender but firm. Remove 12 apricot halves and set aside. Purée the remainder, return to the pan and boil for 3 minutes. Stir in the kirsch and almonds and set aside to cool.

Unmould the pudding. Arrange the reserved apricot halves over it and pour over the sauce.

6 servings

PASTA

Pasta is made from durum wheat flour and water. Eggs are added, and sometimes spinach to give green noodles. Pasta is dried before being sold. It comes in literally hundreds of shapes and sizes, from thin ribbon noodles to wide sheets of lasagne and the well-known macaroni, spaghetti and vermicelli shapes. There are also novelty pasta shapes, twisted spirals, shells, bows and letters of the alphabet. These smaller varieties are ideal for adding to soups, casseroles and salads. The larger kinds are served with butter, with a sauce such as Bolognese, or stuffed with a savoury meat, cheese or fish mixture. Grated Parmesan cheese is often scattered on top just before serving.

Basic cooking method

Pasta is prepared by cooking in fast boiling water with salt and a little oil added to prevent sticking. Allow 75g/3oz ($\frac{3}{4}$ cup) of pasta per person; for every 50g/2oz ($\frac{1}{2}$ cup) pasta, use 600ml/1 pint ($2\frac{1}{2}$ cups) water. Bring the water to the boil and add the pasta. Do not break long strands, but lower them slowly into the boiling water; when the ends go soft, the rest will fit in. Keep the water boiling steadily, uncovered, until the pasta is just cooked through but not soft and mushy. The time varies with the thickness of the pasta from 12–20 minutes. Drain and rinse in cold water to prevent sticking. Add a knob of butter to the pan and warm through gently before serving or cooking further.

It is not too difficult to make your own pasta and the flavour and tender, melting texture make the effort well worthwhile. The dough should be used the day it is made, as it does not keep well. The same applies to the fresh pasta sold by Italian delicatessens. Dried pasta keeps well in an airtight jar, but it is better to buy it regularly and not store it for too long.

Homemade Pasta

Durum flour, or hard plain (all-purpose) flour	Metric/UK	US
	225g/8oz	2 cups
Salt	$\frac{1}{4}$ tsp	$\frac{1}{4}$ tsp
Eggs	3	3

Eating Spaghetti

To eat spaghetti, hold a spoon in one hand and a fork in the other. Pick up some spaghetti with the fork. (1) Hold the fork against the spoon and turn so that the spaghetti is wrapped around. (2) Lift the fork to your mouth and eat the bundle of spaghetti in one mouthful.

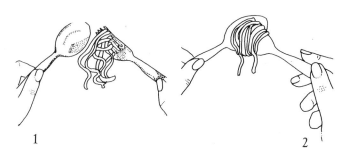

1   2   3

Boiling Spaghetti

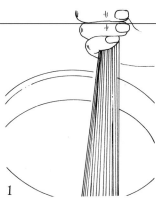

1

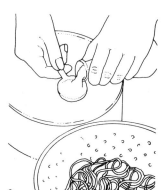

2   3

To cook spaghetti, add a little oil to a pan of boiling water. Grasp the spaghetti at the top and put the ends into the water. (1) As it softens, bend the ends into the pan so that they will all fit into it. (2) Stir, then cook for 10–12 minutes. Drain in a colander and toss with butter before serving. (3).

Sift the flour and salt into a medium-sized mixing bowl. Add the eggs and mix and knead with your hands until the mixture comes away from the sides of the bowl. Form into a ball and knead for 10 minutes on a floured board or slab until smooth and elastic. Cover with a damp cloth and set aside for 30 minutes.

Roll out into thin sheets. The pasta can now be cut into postcard-sized pieces for Lasagne al Forno, made into Ravioli, or cut into thin or thick noodles. Italian-made pasta machines can be bought which knead the dough and extrude it through pre-set holes for any size of noodle.

Makes 225g/8oz (2 cups) quantity

Ravioli Piedmontese.

Ravioli Piedmontese (Pockets of Pasta with Beef and Tomato Stuffing)

RAVIOLI	Metric/UK	US
Homemade pasta in 2 thin square sheets	225g/8oz quantity	2 cup quantity
FILLING		
Butter	50g/2oz	¼ cup
Vegetable oil	1 Tbsp	1 Tbsp
Large onion, finely chopped	1	1
Garlic clove, crushed	1	1
Lean beef, finely minced (ground)	350g/12oz	¾ lb
Beef stock	250ml/8 floz	1 cup
Salt	¼ tsp	¼ tsp
Black pepper	½ tsp	½ tsp
Canned tomatoes, coarsely chopped	225g/8oz	½ lb
Dried rosemary	1 tsp	1 tsp
Dried basil	½ tsp	½ tsp
Parmesan cheese, grated	100g/4oz	1 cup
Eggs, well beaten	2	2

Make the filling first. In a large frying-pan melt the butter with the oil over a moderate heat. Add the onion and garlic and fry until they are golden. Add the beef and fry until it loses its pinkness. Add the stock, salt, pepper, tomatoes and juice, rosemary and basil. Simmer for 10 minutes. Remove from the heat and strain the meat mixture, reserving the cooking liquid. Add the cheese and eggs to the meat mixture and stir well.

To make the ravioli, place one sheet of dough on a flat surface and place a teaspoon of meat filling every 5cm/2in across and down the sheet of pasta. Use a pastry brush with water to draw vertical and horizontal lines between the rows of filling. Place the second sheet of dough exactly on top of the first. Press firmly along the dampened lines to seal each piece of filling in its own pocket. Use a small pastry wheel or sharp knife to cut the dough into separate squares along the dampened lines.

Cook as in the Basic Cooking Method for 8-10 minutes. The ravioli should be tender but not soft and mushy. Drain well on a dampened cloth and serve either with the reserved cooking liquid or a sauce such as Bolognese, or White or Cheese Sauce and grated Parmesan cheese.

6 servings

Spaghetti Bolognese (Spaghetti with Meat Sauce)

	Metric/UK	US
Butter	25g/1oz	2 Tbsp
Olive oil	1 Tbsp	1 Tbsp
Ham, chopped	100g/4oz	⅔ cup
Onion, chopped	1	1
Carrot, chopped	1	1
Celery stalk, chopped	1	1
Beef, minced (ground)	225g/8oz	½lb
Chicken livers, chopped	100g/4oz	¼lb
Canned tomatoes, drained	400g/14oz	14oz
Tomato purée (paste)	2 Tbsp	2 Tbsp
Dry white wine	150ml/5floz	⅔ cup
Chicken stock	300ml/½ pint	1¼ cups
Dried basil	1 tsp	1 tsp
Bayleaf	1	1
Salt and pepper		
Spaghetti	450g/1lb	1lb

In a medium-sized saucepan, melt the butter with the oil over a moderate heat. Add the ham, onion, carrot and celery and cook, stirring occasionally, until the vegetables begin to brown. Add the beef and cook until it loses its pinkness.

Stir in the chicken livers, tomatoes, tomato purée (paste), wine, stock, basil, bayleaf and seasoning. Reduce the heat to low, cover the pan and simmer for 1 hour.

Fifteen minutes before the end of the cooking time, cook the spaghetti according to the basic cooking method. When cooked, transfer it to individual dishes, pour over the sauce and serve at once.

4 servings

Gnocchi alla Romana
[Semolina (Cream of Wheat) Dumplings]

Gnocchi, or Italian dumplings, are not always made from wheat flour—they can also be made from semolina (cream of wheat) or potato flour—but they are treated much like pasta in Italian cooking, often being served with a meat or tomato sauce and Parmesan cheese.

	Metric/UK	US
Milk	600ml/1 pint	2½ cups
Onion, chopped	1	1
Salt	1 tsp	1 tsp
Grated nutmeg	¼ tsp	¼ tsp
Semolina (cream of wheat)	150g/5oz	1¼ cups
Eggs	2	2
Parmesan cheese, grated	100g/4oz	1 cup
Butter, melted	40g/1½oz	3 Tbsp

In a large pan heat the milk, onion, salt and nutmeg over a low heat. Add the semolina (cream of wheat), stirring vigorously. Remove from the heat and beat until thick and smooth. Beat in the eggs and half of the cheese. Pour on to a baking sheet and chill for 30 minutes. Heat the oven to fairly hot (200°C/400°F, Gas Mark 6).

Cut the cold gnocchi mixture into small circles or squares. Arrange in a shallow ovenproof dish. Drizzle over the melted butter and sprinkle with the remaining cheese. Bake for 25 minutes or until golden brown. Serve hot.

2-3 servings

Gnocchi with Flour (Flour Dumplings)

	Metric/UK	US
Egg yolks	4	4
Sugar	2 tsp	2 tsp
Flour	50g/2oz	½ cup
Corn flour (cornstarch)	2 Tbsp	2 Tbsp
Salt	¼ tsp	¼ tsp
Butter, melted	75g/3oz	6 Tbsp
Parmesan cheese, grated	100g/4oz	1 cup
Milk	450ml/¾ pint	2 cups

Place the egg yolks and sugar in a saucepan and beat with a wire whisk until creamy. Sift in the flour, cornflour (cornstarch) and salt. Gradually whisk into the egg yolk mixture until smooth. Stir in 50g/2oz (¼ cup) of the butter and 75g/3oz (¾ cup) of the cheese.

Place the pan over a moderate heat and gradually stir in the milk. Cook for 3-4 minutes or until thick. Remove from the heat. Rinse a baking sheet with water and turn the mixture out on to it, smoothing it into an even layer 1cm/½in thick. Chill for 30 minutes.

Preheat the oven to fairly hot (190°C/375°F, Gas Mark 5). Grease a medium-sized baking sheet. Cut out the gnocchi as in the previous recipe and sprinkle on the remaining melted butter and cheese. Bake for 20 minutes until golden. Serve with Tomato Sauce.

4 servings

One of the great classic dishes of Italy, and one of the most delicious and economical of supper dishes, Lasagne is composed of layers of pasta interspersed with a minced (ground) meat filling, sliced Mozzarella and crumbled ricotta cheese.

Lasagne

	Metric/UK	US
MEAT SAUCE		
Vegetable oil	2 Tbsp	2 Tbsp
Medium-sized onion, thinly sliced	1	1
Garlic clove, crushed	1	1
Medium-sized carrot, chopped	1	1
Celery stalk, chopped	1	1
Streaky (fatty) bacon slices, chopped	3	3
Mushrooms, wiped clean and sliced	100g/4oz	1 cup
Lean beef, finely minced (ground)	700g/1½lb	1½lb
Dried oregano	¼ tsp	¼ tsp
Dried basil	¼ tsp	¼ tsp
Canned tomatoes	400g/14oz	14oz
Tomato purée (paste)	3 Tbsp	3 Tbsp
Single (light) cream	3 Tbsp	3 Tbsp
PASTA		
Lasagne	175g/6oz	6oz
Olive oil	2 Tbsp	2 Tbsp
Béchamel Sauce	450ml/¾ pint	2 cups
Parmesan cheese, grated	100g/4oz	1 cup

To prepare the meat sauce, in a large saucepan, heat the vegetable oil over a moderate heat. Add the onion, garlic, carrot and celery and cook, stirring occasionally until the onion is soft and translucent. Add the bacon and mushrooms and cook for 5 minutes. Add the meat to the pan and cook until it loses its pinkness. Stir in the oregano, basil, salt, pepper, tomatoes and juices and the tomato purée (paste). Reduce the heat to low, cover the pan and simmer the sauce for 1 hour, stirring occasionally.

Stir in the cream and set aside.

To cook the lasagne, half fill a large saucepan with water and add 1 tablespoon of the olive oil.
water to a boil, add half the lasagne to the pan, sheet by sheet, and cook it for 12–15 minutes or until just tender. Remove carefully from the pan and drain on kitchen paper towels.

Preheat the oven to moderate (180°C/350°F, Gas Mark 4). Grease a 1kg/2lb loaf pan or square, oven-proof dish. Place one-third of the meat sauce on the bottom of the dish. Pour over one-third of the Béchamel Sauce, then sprinkle over a quarter of the Parmesan cheese. Cover with a layer of one-third of the lasagne. Repeat these layers until all the ingredients are used up.

Place the pan or dish in the oven and bake for 40 minutes, or until the top is brown and bubbly.

6 servings

VEGETABLES

The success of all vegetable dishes depends greatly on the freshness of the vegetables used. Vegetables are at their peak of freshness and flavour the moment they are picked, and from that moment on their delicacy and nutritive value begin to fade. Really fresh vegetables proclaim their perfection by their very appearance. They look young, firm, crisp and bright in colour and have a fresh smell. Vegetables which look tired dull and limp will taste like that. However carefully you cook them, they will have an unpleasant texture, little flavour and hardly any food value.

Nutrition

We derive a great deal of our vitamin and mineral intake from vegetables, and they are vital to our health and well-being. It is important to eat a wide variety of vegetables, to ensure that you have a good average intake of vitamins and minerals, and this should be remembered when planning meals on a day to day basis. The following chart gives the vitamin content of the more common vegetables.

Vegetables contain considerable amounts of calcium and iron, and there are small amounts of protein in Brussels sprouts, broad (lima) beans, mushrooms, peas, leeks and cauliflower. Root vegetables contain a small amount of carbohydrate, which gives them their filling and sustaining qualities. All in all, the food value of vegetables is not to be dismissed lightly.

Much of this goodness can be lost in cooking, so care must be taken not to over-cook vegetables; in fact, it is a good idea to eat them raw whenever possible.

Buying

If possible, go to a market or store which is busy, clean and thriving. This ensures a rapid turnover of stock, which in turn ensures that you are buying fresh vege-

Vitamins	Vegetable
A	All dark green and orange vegetables; turnip tops, carrots, kale (collards), spinach, broccoli, watercress, cress, cabbage, tomatoes and lettuce.
B	Green vegetables such as broccoli, lettuce and spinach, greens, peas and beans.
C	Kale (collards), Brussels sprouts, turnip tops and broccoli contain a lot; watercress, spinach, cauliflower and cabbage contain a moderate amount; swedes (rutabaga), spring onions (scallions), leeks, radishes, broad (lima) beans, lettuce and tomatoes contain a small amount.

tables. Very small vegetables may be too young to have any flavour, very large ones may be old and coarse. It is vital to choose your vegetables with care. Better still, grow your own, for there is nothing sweeter, fresher or more full of flavour than vegetables picked from your own garden.

Storing

Ideally, vegetables should not be stored for any length of time, but picked or purchased as they are required. However, since this is not always practicable, a few basic rules should be observed. Root vegetables, such as carrots, turnips, swedes (rutabaga), parsnips and potatoes, can be stored in a dry, cool place such as an outhouse or garage for some time. This is ideal for storing surplus garden crops until required. Green and salad vegetables should be stored in the salad drawer in the refrigerator and used as soon as possible. A vegetable rack, standing in a cool position, is useful for the daily turnover of potatoes, roots and other freshly bought vegetables.

Most vegetables freeze well, with the exception of green leaf vegetables such as cabbage and lettuce.

Preparation

All vegetables should be thoroughly cleaned before cooking. A stiff brush is useful for scrubbing root vegetables to remove loose earth and dirt. Do remember that most of the vitamin goodness is stored directly under the skin of roots. New carrots and potatoes are best cooked in their skins, retaining both flavour and goodness; the skins can be rubbed off after cooking. Use a potato peeler to peel other roots and do this as sparingly as possible. Turnips are the exception; you must peel away the green layer beneath the skin, which is bitter. Trim the peeled vegetables with a knife.

Green leaf vegetables should be thoroughly washed to float out small insects, then well drained.

Do not soak vegetables before cooking, as their mineral salts and vitamins dissolve in the water. The exceptions are potatoes, which need to be put in cold water, and Jerusalem artichokes, which should be put in cold water with a squeeze of lemon in it. This stops both turning brown.

Slicing
Roots are usually prepared for cooking by 'blocking' the vegetable into an oblong shape, then neatly slicing downward in two directions, producing even-sized strips. The smaller you cut vegetables, the quicker they will cook.

Dicing
This is taking the slicing process a stage further; the strips are cross-cut into cubes, with a knife.

Shredding
Greens and leaf vegetables have their stalk and coarse ribs cut out with a sharp knife and discarded. The remaining parts are rolled up and cross-cut with a sharp knife to produce thin shreds of vegetable which will cook quickly, retaining the flavour and goodness. French (green) beans should have any stringy fibre down the edges removed. Cabbages can be merely halved and quartered before cooking, or the quarters can be further shredded by cutting into thin slivers.

METHODS OF COOKING

1. Boiling

Put prepared root vegetables into a saucepan, pour boiling water on them so that they are not quite covered, and add 1 teaspoon of salt to each ½kg/1lb of vegetables. Simmer very gently until tender when pierced with a skewer. Drain carefully, then toss in a little melted butter, or sprinkle with chopped parsley, or coat with sauce.

Conservative method This is a delicious way to cook root vegetables, which keeps in all the nutrients and flavour. If the vegetables are mature, slice them thickly. If young and tender, you can leave them whole or cut in quarters. Melt a little butter in a saucepan, then sweat the vegetables in this, with the lid on, for 5–10 minutes. Add boiling water, 150ml/5floz (⅔ cup) to each ½kg/1lb vegetables, plus 1 teaspoon salt. Simmer very gently until tender, approximately 20–30 minutes.

Green vegetables such as leaf vegetables, Brussels sprouts, cauliflower, broccoli, peas and beans should be prepared then plunged into a little boiling, salted water. The cooking time should be kept as short as possible if crispness, flavour and goodness are to be retained; all should be just tender, not soft. They should be carefully drained in a colander before serving, and a knob of butter and black pepper can be added.

Vegetables cook more quickly with a lid on the pan, and less of the flavour escapes as steam.

2. Pressure cooking

Pressure cookers are invaluable for cooking root vegetables quickly without losing flavour, but care must be taken not to overcook or they will turn into soup. Pressure cookers are especially useful for dried vegetables such as peas, beans and lentils, which otherwise take a long time to cook, but on the whole it is not really worth using a pressure cooker for green vegetables.

3. Steaming

Most vegetables can be cooked in a steamer over boiling water. Sprinkle them with salt before steaming—1 teaspoon to ½kg/1lb of prepared vegetables. The steamer must have a tightly fitting lid. Steaming takes slightly longer than boiling but can give very tasty results, especially with delicate new potatoes. Other good vegetables for steaming are leeks, Brussels sprouts and onions; these could all be steamed over a pan of cooking potatoes.

4. Baking

Maincrop potatoes and onions can be baked in their skins in a moderate to hot oven. Choose large potatoes that are all the same size. Onions for baking should be large and firm, with no grit or dirt under the skin. Carrots, parsnips and mushrooms can be put in a dish with butter and seasoning, covered and baked slowly until tender.

5. Grilling (Broiling)

Tomatoes can be grilled (broiled), cut sides up, with a dot of butter and some herbs and seasoning on the cut surface. Stuffed aubergines (eggplants) can be grilled (broiled) to brown the tops.

6. Braising

Plunge the prepared vegetables in boiling water for 2–3 minutes, drain, then fry lightly in butter to coat. Add 150ml/5floz (⅔ cup) to 300ml/½ pint (1¼ cups) of stock to each ½kg/1lb of prepared vegetables. Season, add a knob of butter, cover tightly and cook until tender.

7. Roasting

Root vegetables are often cooked whole around roasting meat in the last hour or so of cooking; potatoes, parsnips, carrots, small turnips, or even onions can be used. There are two methods. One is to put them straight into the hot fat around the meat; the other is to parboil them for 7–8 minutes, drain them and then add them to the hot fat at a later stage— 20–30 minutes before the end of roasting. They should be turned once to cook both sides. If there is no room in the pan, melt some fat in another, add the vegetables and roast separately. The oven should be preheated to hot (220°C/425°F, Gas Mark 7).

8. Frying

Many vegetables can be shallow fried or sautéed over a moderate heat in a little butter; especially suitable are tomatoes, onions, mushrooms, aubergines (eggplants) and courgettes (zucchini). Most other vegetables must be parboiled for 7–8 minutes before frying; drain well, add to butter, oil or fat in a heavy saucepan, and fry over a moderate heat until tender.

Deep frying is used for making potato chips (French fries). Other vegetables, such as onion rings, parsnips

Preparing Artichokes

1

2

3

First cut off the outer leaves. (1) Now scissor the tips from the remaining leaves. (2) And finally remove the hairy choke from the centre of the artichoke. (3).

and cauliflower, can be coated in batter or egg and breadcrumbs and deep fried. Most vegetables must be parboiled and dried first. For potato chips (French fries), see *Potatoes* below, and the recipe for Fish and Chips in Chapter 5. For deep frying, heat fat or oil to 190°C/375°F on a deep fat thermometer, a temperature which will brown a cube of stale bread in 40–50 seconds. Fry until crisp.

Notes on preparation and cooking

Artichoke, globe
Cut off the stalk. Rub cut surfaces with lemon. The choke—the spiky hairs over the heart—can be removed before or after cooking. Spread the top leaves and pull inside leaves out to reveal the choke. With a teaspoon, scrape away the hairs. The rest of the leaves can also be removed before cooking, but half the fun of eating an artichoke is removing the leaves, eating the little bit of flesh in the base of each, and eventually reaching the heart. You can also leave the choke in for each person to remove when he gets to it.

Artichokes are boiled. They take 40–45 minutes to cook with choke, 15–20 minutes without. They can be served hot with melted butter or Hollandaise Sauce, or cold with Vinaigrette or Mayonnaise.

Artichoke, Jerusalem
Peel under running water. Keep in cold water with a little vinegar or lemon juice added until ready to use, or they will discolour. They can be steamed; parboiled for 15 minutes, dried, sliced and deep fried in batter; or made into very good purée soup.

Asparagus
Cut off the woody base of the stems. Tie in a bundle, all heads together and stand in a pan, heads upward. Boil for 10–15 minutes in salted water which comes to just below the heads, covered with a lid or foil. This steams the delicate heads and boils the harder stalks.

Preparing Asparagus

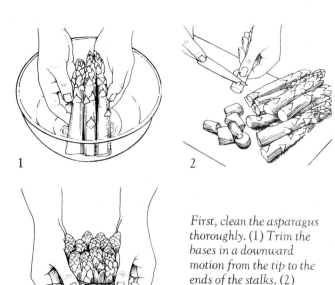

1

2

3

First, clean the asparagus thoroughly. (1) Trim the bases in a downward motion from the tip to the ends of the stalks. (2) Finally, tie the tips together, making sure they are the same size. (3).

Serve with butter, Mayonnaise or Hollandaise, or cold with Vinaigrette.

Aubergine (eggplant)
Before cooking, they should be *dégorged*, that is, have some of their juices removed. Halve, slice or dice them and sprinkle salt on the cut surfaces. Leave to drain in a colander for 15–20 minutes, then rinse in cold water and dry with kitchen paper towels. This operation gives them a less bitter taste and makes them firmer in cooking. If you want to remove the skin, char the aubergine (eggplant) over a gas burner or on an electric burner, turning often; the skin will then come off easily.

Aubergines (eggplant) can be shallow fried in slices, either plain or dipped in flour, or deep fried in batter; grilled (broiled) or baked with butter or oil; or stuffed and baked. They go well with cheese, meat and tomato and are used in Mediterranean dishes such as Moussaka and Ratatouille.

Beans, broad (lima)
Remove from pods unless very young. Top and tail if left in pods. Boil or steam.

Beans, runner (snap or string)
Top and tail, remove stringy edges if necessary. If large, halve or cut into lengths. Boil or steam.

Beetroot (beet)
When preparing raw beetroot (beet) do not remove or pierce the skin, or the beetroot (beet) will 'bleed' and turn white as it cooks. Boil or steam—they take 1–2 hours, depending on size. Beetroot (beets) can often be bought ready cooked. Good in salads, especially marinated in vinegar.

Broccoli
Remove tough stalks and wilted leaves. The stalks need longer cooking than the flowerets; separate them and cook separately.

Brussels sprouts
Cut off dried base and remove yellowed leaves. Cut a deep but small cross in the base of large ones to help them cook quickly. Boil or steam. They can also be used raw in salads.

Cabbage, white
Remove coarse outer leaves, quarter and remove core. Shred finely or cook in quarters. Boil but do not overcook; quarters take 10–15 minutes, shreds 5. Good raw in salads.

Cabbage, red
Quarter and shred. Benefits from long slow cooking, with vinegar to keep it red; otherwise it turns blue. Put it in a casserole in layers with apple slices and sliced onion, vinegar and sugar. Add stock and simmer 1 hour or longer. Fried diced bacon can also be added.

Carrots
Steam or boil; add sugar if old. Good braised in butter, stock and sugar for 10–20 minutes, the liquid should just evaporate. Very good raw in salads.

Cauliflower
Cut off leaves and stalk, separate into flowerets or leave whole. Boil or steam. Do not overcook; it should be still springy, not mushy. Very good raw.

Celery
Remove any old stalks, top, base, and any strings. Cut into lengths, or separate stalks for salads. Blanch 10

minutes before cooking by any method other than boiling. Boil, or fry in butter tightly covered; or braise in white stock. Very good raw. Use leaves and outer stalks for stock.

Chicory (French or Belgian endive)
Leave whole, quarter or separate into leaves. Boil or braise; very good raw. Boiled chicory (endive) is often served with Béchamel or Cheese Sauce.

Collards—See kale.

Corn on the cob
Take off husks and silky threads. Boil ears whole for 5–10 minutes. Do not add salt until after cooking, or they will harden. Serve with butter, salt and pepper.

Courgette (zucchini)
Do not peel. Leave small ones whole, slice larger ones into rounds or sticks. They can be dégorged [see Aubergine (eggplant)] before cooking. Boil, steam or shallow fry. Goes well with onions, tomatoes, aubergines (eggplants) and cheese.

Cucumber
Peeling optional. They can be dégorged [see Aubergine (eggplant)] before cooking or using in salads. Do not boil; shallow frying or baking in butter are better methods. Often used in salads.

Eggplant—See Aubergine.
Endive
A curly member of the lettuce family. See lettuce.
French or Belgian endive—See Chicory.
Kale (collards)
Discard coarse outer leaves. Chop, and boil with just enough water to cover until tender but still slightly crunchy. Drain very well or press out water. Good served with a White or Cheese Sauce.

Leeks
Cut off roots and green tops. Cut down through the white part and wash carefully. You can slice right through or only halfway through. Cook whole, halved, in short sections or in rings. Boil, braise, steam or shallow fry. Boiled or steamed, they are good with Cheese or Hollandaise Sauce.

Lettuce
Do not serve boiled. Blanch for 5 minutes, drain then braise in a little stock with onions, parsley and cloves. Sometimes cooked with fresh peas. More often used raw in salads.

Marrow (summer squash)
Peel, halve lengthwise, scoop out seeds. Dégorge [see Aubergine (eggplant)] if braising or frying. Steam,

braise or shallow fry. Often stuffed or served with Cheese Sauce.

Mushrooms

Cultivated (bought) mushrooms should not be peeled; the peel contains a lot of flavour. Just wash well, dry and trim base of stems. Field mushrooms should be peeled. Halve or slice mushrooms. Fry, steam or bake with butter and herbs.

Onions

Cut off roots and remove papery skin. Whole small onions can be boiled or braised with stock or wine; slices or rings can be shallow-fried, or coated in batter or flour and deep fried.

Parsnip

Trim and peel, cut lengthwise and remove hard core. Steam, boil, deep fry as for potatoes, or roast with meat.

Peas

Remove from pods. Boil, steam or braise with lettuce. 'Mange-tout' or snow peas have edible pods; cook whole or sliced like French (green) beans.

Peppers

Large bell-shaped green or red peppers are mild and sweet. Halve and remove any white pith and seeds. Blanch, stuff and bake or grill (broil); or shallow fry in oil. Often used raw in salads. Red ones ripen and go bad quickly.

Small peppers, also either red or green, are hot—red hotter than green. They are known as chillis (chili peppers). The seeds are far hotter than the pod. Both red and green are used for flavouring, for instance in Chili con Carne and other Latin American dishes.

When dealing with chillis (chili peppers), touch as little as possible with your hands and avoid putting your hands to your face, as the oils cause burning.

Potatoes

Early potatoes are best boiled or steamed; both new and old (or maincrop) can be made into Potato Salad; old are best for chips (French fries) and for roasting, mashing and baking in their jackets. About ½kg/1lb of potatoes will serve 3 people. When buying early potatoes, make sure the earth on them is damp and the skin rubs off easily; this indicates they are fresh.

Do not boil potatoes fiercely. They will absorb water, break up and taste unpleasant. Boiled potatoes can be drained and mashed; add 300ml/½ pint (1¼ cups) boiling milk, seasoning to taste and a knob of butter to 1kg/2lb potatoes and beat until light and fluffy.

To bake potatoes, scrub but do not peel, and arrange, well spaced, in an oven preheated to fairly hot (190°C/375°F, Gas Mark 5). Cook for 1–1½ hours, depending on the size. If the skin is first rubbed with salt, they will be very crisp.

To roast, cut in pieces, and put around meat for the last 60 minutes of cooking, or parboil, dry and add for the last 30 minutes. Turn and baste twice. Or heat fat to very hot in a separate pan, put in the potatoes and roast separately, turning several times.

When making chips (French fries), dry them well before cooking. The fat is hot enough when a chip (French fry) dropped in rises, surrounded by bubbles, to the surface. They take 4–6 minutes to fry to golden. Drain well on kitchen paper towels. If you fry them

again for 1–2 minutes just before serving, they will be extra crisp.

To shallow fry or sauté, add a single layer of potatoes, sliced or diced, to hot butter or oil. Fry, turning frequently, for 10–15 minutes.

Radish
Cut off tops and roots. Usually eaten raw, alone with salt or in salads; they can also be boiled and served with Parsley or Béchamel Sauce.

Rutabaga—See Swede.

Spinach
Wash in several changes of cold water. Do not dry, but put in a saucepan with no extra water. Add a little salt, cover and cook gently for about 10 minutes, shaking occasionally. Drain well.

Summer Squash—See Marrow.

Swede (Rutabaga)
Peel and slice or chop. Boil, or parboil and roast around meat. Boiled swedes (rutabaga) are usually mashed with butter, salt and pepper.

Sweetcorn—See Corn.

Sweet Potatoes and Yams
Hard to peel. For boiling, scrub and halve, and remove skin afterwards. Cook for 30 minutes. For other methods, blanch for 10 minutes, cool, then slip off skin with fingers. Bake, shallow fry or roast as for potatoes. They do not keep well.

Tomatoes
To cook on their own, halve and shallow fry, grill (broil) or bake whole. Brush with oil if grilling (broiling) or baking. They cook very fast. Tomatoes are very good raw, and are used in all kinds of hot dishes and in sauces. To skin tomatoes, plunge them in boiling water for 1 minute, then in cold water. The skins will slip off.

Turnips
Prepare roots like swedes (rutabaga), top like cabbage or kale (collards). Also eaten raw in salads.

Zucchini—See Courgette.

Dried vegetables (peas, beans and lentils)
Wash, cover with boiling water and soak for at least 2 hours, or cover with cold water and soak overnight. If left too long they will ferment; they expand as they soak, so use a big bowl. If they have soaked overnight, drain and cover with fresh water. If not, top up with water to cover. Add 1 teaspoon salt to 225g/8oz (1 cup) dried vegetables, bring to the boil, cover and simmer until tender. If they are soaked overnight they will cook more quickly. Beans take the longest, 1–3 hours, and split peas and lentils the shortest time, 30 minutes–1½ hours. They can be served hot with butter and seasoning, cold with garlic French Dressing or used in soups and stews.

Radis Glacés (Glazed Radishes).

Duchess Potatoes

An elegant potato purée, this can be piped around a meat entrée or piped in small towers and browned in the oven.

	Metric/UK	US
Potatoes, cooked	½kg/1lb	1lb
Butter, softened	25g/1oz	2 Tbsp
Egg yolks	2	2
Salt	1 tsp	1 tsp
White pepper	1 tsp	1 tsp
Grated nutmeg	½ tsp	½ tsp

Preheat the oven to fairly hot (200°C/400°F, Gas Mark 6). Mash or strain the potatoes. Beat in the butter, egg yolks, salt, pepper and nutmeg. Fill a forcing (pastry) bag with the mixture and pipe either a border or round shapes on to a greased baking sheet. Place in the centre of the oven and bake for 10 minutes or until golden.
4 servings

Chicory (Endive) Braised with Butter and Lemon Juice

	Metric/UK	US
Chicory (French or Belgian Endive)	700g/1½lb	1½lb
Water	3 Tbsp	3 Tbsp
Lemon juice	1 tsp	1 tsp
Salt	½ tsp	½ tsp
Butter	25g/1oz	2 Tbsp
Black pepper	¼ tsp	¼ tsp

Preheat the oven to cool (150°C/300°F, Gas Mark 2). Arrange the chicory (endive) heads in one layer in a shallow flameproof casserole. Add the water, lemon juice and ¼ tsp salt. Place over a moderate heat and bring to the boil. Dot the butter on top. Cover with foil and place in the oven. Braise for 1¼ hours, or until tender when pierced with a knife. Season with the remaining salt and the pepper.
4 servings

Stuffed Courgettes (Zucchini)

A sustaining and delicious main course.

	Metric/UK	US
Dried mushrooms	15g/½oz	½oz
Medium-sized courgettes (zucchini)	12	12
Fresh white breadcrumbs soaked in 4 Tbsp milk	50g/2oz	1 cup
Eggs, lightly beaten	2	2
Salt	½ tsp	½ tsp
Black pepper	1 tsp	1 tsp

	Metric/UK	US
Dried oregano	1 tsp	1 tsp
Parmesan cheese, finely grated	175g/6oz	1½ cups
Prosciutto, chopped	50g/2oz	¼ cup
Olive oil	4 Tbsp	4 Tbsp

In a little water soak the dried mushrooms for 45 minutes. Drain and set aside. Boil the courgettes (zucchini) for 7–8 minutes or until just tender. Drain well. Slice lengthways with a sharp knife, then scoop out the flesh carefully and set aside. Preheat the oven to fairly hot (200°C/400°F, Gas Mark 6).

Squeeze any excess moisture from the breadcrumbs and place in a mixing bowl. Add the courgette (zucchini) flesh, eggs, salt, pepper, oregano, half the cheese, the prosciutto and mushrooms. Mix thoroughly.

Spoon a little stuffing into each courgette (zucchini) half and sprinkle the remaining cheese on top. Arrange in an oiled ovenproof dish and drizzle the oil over the top. Bake for 15 minutes or until golden brown. Transfer to a serving dish and serve hot.
6 servings

Radis Glacés (Glazed Radishes)

	Metric/UK	US
Butter	25g/1oz	2 Tbsp
Pink radishes, halved	½kg/1lb	1lb
Sugar	2 tsp	2 tsp
Salt	½ tsp	½ tsp
Water	300ml/ ½ pint	1¼ cups
Chopped parsley	1 Tbsp	1 Tbsp

In a large frying-pan melt the butter over a moderate heat. Add the radishes and sprinkle over the sugar. Cook for 3 minutes, stirring occasionally. Add the salt and water and cook for 10–12 minutes or until tender. Transfer to a warm dish and sprinkle over the parsley.
4 servings

Légumes Nouveaux Flambés (Mixed Fresh Vegetables with Brandy)

	Metric/UK	US
Butter	75g/3oz	⅓ cup
Carrots, chopped	1kg/2lb	2lb
Turnips, chopped	½kg/1lb	1lb
Small white onions	½kg/1lb	1lb
Salt	1 tsp	1 tsp
Black pepper	1 tsp	1 tsp
Brown sugar	2 Tbsp	2 Tbsp
Brandy	75ml/3 floz	⅓ cup
Chopped parsley	2 Tbsp	2 Tbsp

In a large frying-pan melt the butter over a moderate heat. Add the carrots, turnips and onions and shake gently to coat them with the butter. Add the salt, pepper and brown sugar and stir. Reduce the heat to low, cover the pan and cook for 30 minutes, stirring.

Gently heat the brandy in a small saucepan until hot. Remove from the heat and ignite. Carefully pour the brandy into the frying-pan. When the flames die down, cover and cook gently for 5–10 minutes or until the vegetables are tender.
8 servings

Another French favourite, Legumes Nouveaux Flambés which is mixed new (spring) vegetables with Brandy.

SALADS

Almost any vegetable, except some roots, can be used raw
in salads, provided it is fresh, young and crisp. The beauty
of salads is that the valuable vitamin and mineral content
of fresh vegetables is not lost or destroyed by cooking.
Nor is any freshness or the intensity of the flavours lost.
Cooked vegetables, when cold, can also be made into many
delicious salads—Potato Salad is a classic. More
filling salads can be made with cold cooked rice,
pasta or pulses (dried legumes), and salad
enthusiasts use all sorts of other things: nuts, grated
or cream cheese, raisins, or fruit such as orange,
apple and banana. The possibilities are endless; use
your imagination to produce interesting blends of
of flavours and contrasts in texture.

Simple green salads, and cold cooked vegetables such as young French (green) beans or asparagus are usually dressed with French Dressing or Vinaigrette. More substantial salads can be bound together with mayonnaise, sour cream or yogurt (for dressings based on mayonnaise, see page 43); cold rice, pasta and pulses (dried legumes) are also very good with a simple vinaigrette.

Basic French Dressing

Traditionally this is a mixture of olive oil, red or white wine vinegar, salt and pepper. These amounts make about 125ml/4floz ($\frac{1}{2}$ cup). The proportion of oil to vinegar is up to you; use more or less according to personal taste.

	Metric/UK	US
Wine vinegar	2 Tbsp	2 Tbsp
Salt	1 tsp	1 tsp
Black pepper	1 tsp	1 tsp
Olive oil	5 Tbsp	5 Tbsp

In a small bowl or jug, beat the vinegar, salt and pepper with a fork to dissolve the salt. Add the oil and beat well to mix and thicken. If you add crushed garlic, 1 teaspoon French mustard or chopped fresh herbs, and 1 teaspoon sugar if liked, the dressing becomes Vinaigrette.

Preparing vegetables for salad

All raw vegetables for salads should be thoroughly washed, and well dried; lettuce can be dried in a drying basket hanging in an airy place. If the vegetables are wet, the dressing will be diluted and will not coat the salad. Leaf vegetables are shredded or torn into bite-sized pieces. Others can be grated or sliced, or chopped into convenient sections.

Tomatoes
Can be skinned for salads. If you do not mind the skin leave it on; it is the most nutritious part. To make a simple tomato salad, slice or quarter the tomatoes, sprinkle on a little very finely chopped onion, and a little basil, parsley or chervil, then toss lightly in vinaigrette dressing.

Chinese cabbage
An exotic vegetable and usually very cheap, is rather like lettuce but has more flavour. Use like lettuce in green salads. It can also be cooked like cabbage.

Carrots, cauliflower and celery
Are very good eaten raw with a dip of Mayonnaise, cottage or cream cheese with herbs or taramosalata. Unless the carrots are very young, cut them into strips; break the cauliflower into flowerets. Leave the celery in stalks with the leaves on.

Cucumber
Need only be wiped clean, or peeled very thinly. Slice thinly or cut into chunks.

Other salad vegetables, to be mixed as you like, include beetroot (beet), sliced; Brussels sprouts, chopped; cabbage, shredded; celeriac (celery root),

grated; chicory (French or Belgian endive); cress; curly endive (chicory); Florence fennel, sliced, with its delicious taste of aniseed; green peppers, remove the seeds and slice; young leeks; mushrooms; radishes; salsify (oyster-plant) leaves; spring onions (scallions); seakale, use the leaf ends; and watercress, wash very well.

Classic green salad

The perfect side dish for grilled (broiled) meats and fish or roast poultry; also for quick meals of bread and cheese. Choose a deep salad bowl of wood or glass to set off your salad. Look after wood; never submerge it in soapy water and rub it over lightly with a little salad oil from time to time.

Prepare a mixture of any green vegetables; crisp sweet lettuce alone, perfectly prepared and dressed, is very good; contrasting light and dark greens, such as lettuce and watercress, look pretty. Strong tastes, such as green pepper and Florence fennel, may conflict. Put the salad in the bowl and sprinkle over any chopped fresh herbs if you wish. Make a French or Vinaigrette dressing (see above) and pour a little over the salad—just enough to coat it lightly, not so much that it swims in dressing. Use your hands or salad servers to toss and coat the salad evenly until it glistens. Serve immediately. A dressed salad will go limp and soggy in no time at all.

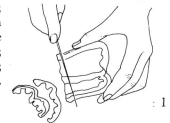

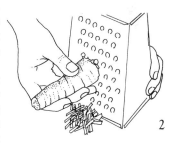

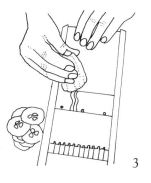

To prepare peppers, remove the white pith and seeds, then chop into rings or slices. (1) Carrot can be grated on an ordinary grater and either scattered over the top of a mixed salad, or served as a salad on its own (perhaps with raisins) and a vinaigrette dressing. (2) Cucumber is best served thinly sliced in salad, and the best way to do this is to invest in a mandolin. Then you just rub the cut edge against it and a perfect product emerges every time. (3)

155

RECIPES

Greek Salad

SALAD	Metric/UK	US
Cos (romaine) lettuce	1	1
Bunch of radishes, peeled and sliced	1	1
Feta cheese, cubed	225g/8oz	2 cups
Dried marjoram	$\frac{1}{4}$ tsp	$\frac{1}{4}$ tsp
Tomatoes, sliced	4	4
Anchovies, chopped	6	6
Black olives, stoned (pitted) and halved	6	6
Chopped parsley	1 Tbsp	1 Tbsp
Black pepper	$\frac{1}{2}$ tsp	$\frac{1}{2}$ tsp
DRESSING		
Olive oil	4 Tbsp	4 Tbsp
White wine vinegar	$1\frac{1}{2}$ Tbsp	$1\frac{1}{2}$ Tbsp
Mixed fresh herbs, chopped	1 Tbsp	1 Tbsp
Spring onions, (scallions), chopped	4	4

Tear the lettuce leaves into pieces and arrange them on a large dish. Scatter the radishes over them. Arrange the feta cheese in the centre and sprinkle it with marjoram. Place the tomatoes in a circle round the cheese and garnish with anchovies and olives. Sprinkle the parsley and pepper on top.

Combine all the dressing ingredients in a small bowl. (Marjoram, chives and lemon thyme could be used as the mixture of fresh herbs.) Pour the dressing over the salad, toss and serve.
4–6 servings

Potato Salad

	Metric/UK	US
Potatoes, cooked	$\frac{1}{2}$kg/1lb	1lb
Mayonnaise	175ml/6floz	$\frac{3}{4}$ cup
Lemon juice	1 Tbsp	1 Tbsp
Olive oil	1 tsp	1 tsp
Salt	$\frac{1}{2}$ tsp	$\frac{1}{2}$ tsp
Black pepper	$\frac{1}{2}$ tsp	$\frac{1}{2}$ tsp
Chopped fresh chives	2 Tbsp	2 Tbsp
Chopped raw leeks	4 Tbsp	4 Tbsp

If made with small potatoes, leave them whole; if with old ones, slice or cube them.

Place three-quarters of the potatoes in a mixing bowl if using sliced potatoes, all if using new. Pour over the mayonnaise and sprinkle with the lemon juice, oil, salt, pepper and 1 tablespoon of the chives. Carefully toss the potatoes with two spoons until they are coated. Spoon into a serving bowl. If using sliced potatoes, arrange the remaining slices over the top. Sprinkle with the remaining chives and scatter the leeks around the edge of the bowl.
4 servings

Salade Niçoise

	Metric/UK	US
Small lettuce	1	1
Cooked potatoes, diced	6	6
French (green) beans, cooked	300g/10oz	10oz
Tomatoes, quartered or cut into wedges	6	6
French Dressing	125ml/4floz	$\frac{1}{2}$ cup
Anchovy fillets, halved	6	6
Black olives, stoned (pitted)	10	10
Capers	2 Tbsp	2 Tbsp

Separate the lettuce into leaves and arrange them on a large serving plate. Combine the potatoes, beans (cut into lengths) and tomatoes in a large mixing bowl with the French dressing. Spoon the vegetables on to the lettuce leaves, garnish with anchovies, olives and capers, and serve at once.
4 servings

Waldorf Salad

	Metric/UK	US
Large red apples, cored and chopped	2	2
Lemon juice	1 Tbsp	1 Tbsp
Celery stalks, chopped	2	2
Walnuts, chopped	100g/4oz	$\frac{2}{3}$ cup
Mayonnaise	175ml/6floz	$\frac{3}{4}$ cup

Put the apples in a salad bowl and sprinkle over the lemon juice. Stir in the celery and walnuts. Combine the remaining ingredients, then pour over the salad. Toss gently until the ingredients are thoroughly coated with the dressing, then serve at once.
4 servings

Nun's Salad

This salad, using black and white ingredients, is a delicious supper dish.

	Metric/UK	US
Cooked chicken, diced	½kg/1lb	2½ cups
Spring onions (scallions), white parts only, chopped	12	12
Potatoes, cooked and diced	½kg/1lb	1lb
Seedless raisins	50g/2oz	⅓ cup
Large black grapes, halved and seeded	225g/8oz	½lb
Large black olives, halved and stoned (pitted)	50g/2oz	½ cup
Salt	½ tsp	½ tsp
Black pepper	¼ tsp	¼ tsp
Large apple, peeled, cored and diced	1	1
Mayonnaise	175ml/6 fl oz	¾ cup

Nun's Salad–a stunning main meal salad.

In a large salad bowl, combine the chicken, spring onions (scallions), potatoes, raisins, half the grapes, the olives, salt, pepper and apple. Pour over the mayonnaise and toss the salad with two large spoons until all the ingredients are well coated. Arrange the remaining grape halves decoratively on top. Chill for 30 minutes before serving.

4 servings

Coleslaw with Caraway

Coleslaw is a crisp, crunchy salad made from shredded white cabbage. It can have any number of additions, from grated onion to grated carrot. This recipe is an interesting variation to serve with cold meat or cold chicken. Or use it as an unusual sandwich filler.

	Metric/UK	US
Large white cabbage, cored and shredded	1	1
Medium-sized onion, finely chopped	1	1
Green pepper, seeded and finely chopped	½	½
Lemon juice	½ tsp	½ tsp
Caraway seeds	1 Tbsp	1 Tbsp

Coleslaw is an American favourite which is rapidly catching on all over the world. Serve as a side salad, or as a sandwich filling—its equally delicious either way.

DRESSING

	Metric/UK	US
Double (heavy) cream	175ml/6floz	¾ cup
Sour cream	90ml/3floz	⅓ cup
French mustard	1 Tbsp	1 Tbsp
Lemon juice	3 Tbsp	3 Tbsp
Sugar	1 Tbsp	1 Tbsp
Salt	½ tsp	½ tsp
White pepper	¼ tsp	¼ tsp

Put the shredded cabbage in a large serving dish and sprinkle with the onion, green pepper and lemon juice. Set aside. Mix together the ingredients for the dressing. Pour the dressing over the cabbage mixture and add the caraway seeds. Using two large forks toss the cabbage mixture until completely coated with dressing. Chill for 1 hour and serve cold.
6 servings

Tomato and Bean Salad

	Metric/UK	US
Tomatoes, thinly sliced and seeded	450g/1lb	1lb
French (green) beans, trimmed and cooked	450g/1lb	1lb
Dried basil or chopped fresh basil	1 tsp	1 tsp
DRESSING		
Wine Vinegar	3 Tbsp	3 Tbsp
Olive Oil	6 Tbsp	6 Tbsp
Prepared mustard	½ tsp	½ tsp
Sugar	½ tsp	½ tsp
Garlic clove, crushed	1	1
Salt and pepper		

Put all the dressing ingredients into a screw-top jar, cover and shake vigorously. Arrange the tomatoes and beans in a serving dish and pour over the dressing. Toss the salad gently until all the vegetables are well coated. Generously sprinkle over the basil. Chill in the refrigerator untill you are ready to serve.
4 servings.

159

FRUIT

With the development of hothouse gardening and air freihgt, most kinds of fruit can be enjoyed all the year round. Temperate climate fruits such as apples, plums, gooseberries and strawberries can be bought at the same time as the exotic Chinese gooseberries (Kiwi fruit) persimmons and limes, or hot-climate fruits like peaches, pineapples, melons, grapefruit and bananas.

This profusion is marvellous; but it is all too easy to neglect fruits. They are low in calories, but provide a convenient package of vitamins, minerals and carbohydrates. They are very good eaten unadorned, or with cream or lemon juice, at the end of a heavy meal, but they can also be cooked and made into many delicious dishes.

Buying

As with vegetables, it is important to buy from a reliable source with a quick turnover of goods, to ensure freshness. Always choose unmarked, unbruised fruit which smells aromatic and fresh. Fruit is best used at its peak of ripeness; the flavour, juiciness and vitamin content are then at their height.

Buy fruit in small quantities, as you require it, though peaches, avocados, melons and bananas can be put in a warm dark place to ripen for a few days. Examine twice a day and refrigerate when ripe (except bananas, which blacken internally when chilled). Avocados and bananas ripen more quickly in a paper-bag. Always wash fruit before use, to get rid of insecticides that may have been sprayed on them during cultivation.

COOKING METHODS

To cook fruit on its own, the main methods are poaching, stewing in syrup and puréeing. Some fruits can also be baked, fried or made into fritters; and prepared raw fruit can be flambéed or given an interesting topping. Suggestions for individual fruits are in the fruit list below.

Many substantial dishes can be made using fruit. For flans and pies see the chapter on pastry; for crumbles, fritters and other hot desserts, also ice-cream, see the chapter on desserts.

To skin fruit, such as peaches, before cooking, pour over boiling water and leave for 1 minute. Then put them in cold water. The skins will slip off quite easily.

1. Poaching

Drop the prepared fruit into just enough boiling water to cover, and reduce the heat to low so that the liquid just simmers. Other liquids such as wine can also be used. Cook slowly, and do not overcook; cooked fruit should be tender but not mushy. When it is cooked, remove it from the liquid, or it will go on cooking. If you are serving it in its cooking liquid, cool the pan quickly by putting the bottom into cold water. Sweeten to taste.

2. Stewing in syrup

For every $\frac{1}{2}$kg/1lb fruit, allow between 50g/2oz ($\frac{1}{4}$ cup) and 100g/4oz ($\frac{1}{2}$ cup) sugar and 150ml/5floz ($\frac{2}{3}$ cup) to 300ml/$\frac{1}{2}$ pint (1$\frac{1}{4}$ cups) water. Allow less sugar for sweet fruit, and less water for soft fruit such as black-currants. Put the water and sugar in a large pan, stir over a moderate heat until the sugar is dissolved, put in the prepared fruit and lower the heat to simmer. Cover with a lid to keep in the steam. Soft fruit takes about 5 minutes, firm fruit 10–20 minutes.

If you put the sugar, water and fruit into the pan at the same time, the fruit is more likely to go mushy.

3. Puréeing

To cook fruit for purées, cut it into small pieces and put in very little water, 1cm/½in to 2.5cm/1in depth in the pan. Cook slowly, stirring occasionally, until tender. Fruit cut in small pieces cooks more quickly. Mash it with the cooking liquid into a purée, sweetening now rather than earlier, as less sugar is needed. To make a fruit fool, cool, stir in whipped cream and chill.

Dried fruit

These are invaluable in winter when fruit can be expensive and scarce. In many hot desserts, dried fruit can be substituted for fresh. Dried fruit must be soaked before cooking. Cover the fruit with cold water and soak for at least 12 hours. Drain in a colander and discard the water.

Preparing, cooking and serving various fruit

Many of these fruits are delicious eaten uncooked on their own or with sugar and cream or lemon juice.

Apples
Wash carefully, peel thinly, cut into quarters and remove core. To use raw, in sweet or savoury salads, rub over with lemon juice to prevent discolouring. Good stewed, puréed, in tarts, crumbles, Apple Pie and Apple Fritters. For cooking, use the larger, sourer apples. Also good baked whole; core, score the skin down the sides, fill with raisins, mincemeat, sugar, honey or a stoned (pitted) date, and cook for at least 1 hour in an oven preheated to moderate (180°C/350°F, Gas Mark 4).

Apricots
Wash, remove stalks, halve with a sharp knife and twist to remove stones (pits). Use in fruit salads, poached, stewed, puréed, in tarts and flans.

Bananas
Cut off stalks, peel, remove strings, use at once, or dip in lemon, orange, lime or grapefruit juice, to prevent discolouring. Use in fruit salads, baked or fried in butter and in Banana Fritters.

Blackberries
Wash and pick over carefully. Use in fruit salad, tarts and flans, Summer Puddings, in pies with apples.

Cherries
Wash well, remove stalks. Stone (pit) with a cherry stoner (pitter) or skewer. Use Morello (Bing) cherries in fruit salads, tarts, flans and pies.

Currants (red and black)
Pick over, remove any stalks. Wash in a colander and drain on kitchen paper towels. Use in cheesecakes, pies, tarts and flans, and ice cream.

Figs, fresh
Always eaten fresh, when very ripe. Eat only the soft red flesh unless you particularly like skin.

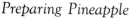
Preparing Pineapple

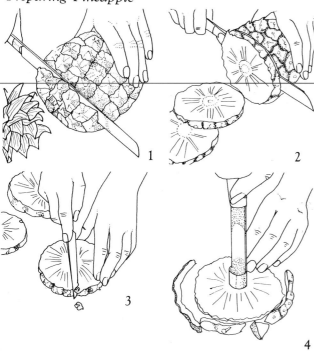

Cut away the leafy foliage and take a small slice from the bottom. 1
Cut the pineapple into thin slices, using a sharp, serrated knife. 2

Using the point of the knife, remove the woody eyes from the flesh. 3
Cut away the skin, keeping as close to the flesh as possible. 4

Grapes
Can be halved and seeded or left whole, seeded or unseeded; eat on their own or use in fruit salad.

Grapefruit
As an appetizer or breakfast, cut in half crossways, allowing half per person. The flesh can be separated from the skin with a sharp curved saw edged knife or 'grapefruit tool'. Serve with or without sugar. Or prepare as oranges and use in fruit salad. Empty half grapefruits make pretty containers for fruit salad.

Gooseberries
Wash, top and tail with a sharp knife. Eat dessert varieties uncooked, use acid ones in fools, crumbles, tarts, pies and flans, or in a savoury sauce for mackerel.

Greengages
Serve on their own, or halve and stone (pit) and use in pies.

Kumquats
Serve whole, eat with the skin. Used fresh as a garnish for duck.

Lemons
Though not eaten on their own, lemons are essential for cooking and garnishing, and their sharp taste can turn many a dull dish into a successful one. Three parts of the lemon are used; zest, rind and juice. The zest or oil is produced by rubbing a sugar cube over the outer skin and using the crushed cube to flavour. The rind is grated, taking care to leave out the bitter white pith. The juice is squeezed out and strained carefully.

Limes
Use like lemons. Use juice in fruit salads or squeezed over melon.

Lychees
Pinch the outer skin to crack it and peel off. Serve on their own or add to fruit salad.

Mangoes
Do not cut until just before serving, or the aroma is lost. Serve whole with only the skin cut; to eat, peel the skin back with a knife and scoop out the pulp with a spoon. Or cut in slices above and below the stone (pit).

Melons
Slice large ones into crescents, halve the small ones. Remove seeds. Scoop out the flesh with a teaspoon or melon baller for fruit salads. On their own as an appetizer, serve with ground ginger, lemon or lime juice or port wine sprinkled over.

Nectarines
Need no peeling. Eat fresh as a dessert.

Oranges
Remove the rind and white pith with a saw knife. With a sharp knife remove each section from the membrane, or slice the whole orange across into thin rounds. Save the juice and serve them in it or add it to fruit salad. They can also be used for flavouring in the same way as lemons.

Passion fruit
Use to flavour fruit drinks and pies; or serve as a

dessert fruit with a little sugar.

Pawpaws
Prepare like melon. Serve with sugar as a dessert or breakfast; or dice and mix into fruit salad.

Peaches
Stone (pit) as apricots for a dessert. Slice for fruit salad. Use in flans and pies; purée for ice-cream.

Pears
Prepare as apples. Use in fruit salads, or poached or stewed.

Persimmons
Wash and lightly chill, to serve fresh with a pointed spoon. To eat, dig the flesh out of the skin. Use the pulp in ice-cream.

Pineapple
Cut off the leaves. The peel can be cut off in a spiral before slicing; or slice the fruit into rounds and cut the peel from each slice. Remove the hard core and 'eyes' beneath the skin. Leave in rings or cut into chunks. Use in fruit salad. Rings can be made into fritters.

Plums and damsons
Wash well, remove stalks. Halve with a sharp knife and remove stones (pits). Use in tarts, flans, crumbles or pies, or poached or stewed.

Pomegranates
Serve fresh as a dessert, with the top sliced off. To eat, take out the seeds with a spoon and suck the flesh from the seeds.

Raspberries
Pick over, wash in a colander if they look dirty or dusty; avoid over dampening. Best of all with sugar and cream; also use in tarts, shortcake, cheesecake, mousses and ice-cream. To make a purée, simply blend or mash without cooking.

Rhubarb
Cut off leaves and thick ends. Wipe with a damp cloth and cut into short lengths. Use stewed, or in pies, crumbles, tarts, flans and fools; goes well with the tastes of orange rind or juice, cinnamon and ginger. Or, for an expensive treat, add a little gin.

Strawberries
Hull, pick over for dust. Wipe with damp kitchen paper towels if necessary. Use soon. Best of all with sugar and cream; also use in tarts, shortcake, cheesecake, mousses and ice-cream. To make purée, simply blend or mash without cooking. Or serve simply with iced white wine or champagne.

Ugli fruits
Prepare like grapefruit. They need no sugar but are better chilled before eating.

Summer Pudding: line a mould with bread, spoon in raspberries dredged with sugar and top with more bread. Chill with a weight on top.

RECIPES

Fraises Romanoff (Strawberries Romanoff)

To add sparkle to a bowl of strawberries, turn them into this gloriously refreshing dessert.

	Metric/UK	US
Fresh strawberries, hulled	1kg/2lb	2lb
Orange-flavoured liqueur	125ml/4floz	½ cup
Fresh orange juice (strained)	50ml/2floz	¼ cup
Crème Chantilly	300ml/ ½ pint	1¼ cups

Place the strawberries in a deep bowl and pour over the liqueur and orange juice. Cover the bowl and chill for 2 hours, basting the berries occasionally with the liquid in the bowl.

Transfer the strawberries and the liquid to a serving dish. Fill a forcing (pastry) bag with the cream and pipe it around and over the dessert in decorative whirls.
4-6 servings

Apricot Salad

This unusual salad is a good accompaniment for hot or cold ham.

	Metric/UK	US
Ripe apricots, peeled and halved	1kg/2lb	2lb
DRESSING		
Sour cream	4 Tbsp	4 Tbsp
Tarragon vinegar	3 Tbsp	3 Tbsp
Sugar	1 Tbsp	1 Tbsp
Salt	½ tsp	½ tsp
Black pepper	½ tsp	½ tsp
Tarragon leaves, chopped	2 or 3	2 or 3

Remove the apricot stones (pits). Arrange the fruit in a glass serving bowl. Crack the stones (pits) with a hammer and remove the kernels. Chop them and set aside.

Put the sour cream into a bowl and stir in the vinegar, sugar, salt, and pepper. Taste and adjust the seasoning if necessary. Pour the dressing over the apricots. Sprinkle with the tarragon leaves and chopped kernels.
4 servings

Fraises Romanoff is the French version of strawberries and cream—the different 'French' touch is the addition of orange-flavoured liqueur to the whipped cream.

Fresh Fruit Salad

	Metric/UK	US
Sugar	50g/2oz	¼ cup
Water	175ml/6floz	¾ cup
Lemon juice	1½ Tbsp	1½ Tbsp
Apple	1	1
Pear	1	1
Orange	1	1
Peach	1	1
Banana	1	1
Small honeydew melon	½	½

Dissolve the sugar in the water and lemon juice over a low heat, stirring continuously. Increase the heat and boil the syrup for 2–3 minutes. Remove the pan from the heat and allow the syrup to cool.

Peel, core and chop the apple and pear, peel the orange and peach and chop them, peel and slice the banana crossways, and remove the seeds from the melon before chopping the flesh. Put the cooled syrup into a serving bowl and, while you chop the fruit, add it to the syrup.

Place the bowl in the refrigerator to chill for 30 minutes before serving.
4 servings

Pears in Red Wine

	Metric/UK	US
Large firm pears	6	6
Sugar	175g/6oz	¾ cup
Water	125ml/4floz	½ cup
Cinnamon stick	5cm/2in	2in
Rind of 1 lemon		
Red wine	125ml/4floz	½ cup

Peel the pears carefully, then place them with the sugar, water, cinnamon stick and lemon rind in a large saucepan. Cover and cook for 10 minutes over a moderate heat. Add the wine, reduce the heat to very low and simmer, turning occasionally, for a further 20–25 minutes, or until the pears are tender but firm.

Using a slotted spoon, transfer the pears to a serving dish and set aside. Increase the heat to high and boil the cooking liquid for about 8 minutes, or until it has thickened slightly. Remove the pan from the heat and strain the liquid over the pears. Allow the dish to cool, then place it in the refrigerator to chill for at least 1 hour before serving.
6 servings

Melon with Ham

Try this classic appetizer with its interesting combination of tastes.

	Metric/UK	US
Large honeydew melon, quartered and seeded	1	1
Smoked fillet (tenderloin) of pork or smoked Parma ham, very thinly sliced	175g/6oz	6oz
Lemon juice	1 Tbsp	1 Tbsp
Finely grated fresh root (green) ginger	1 tsp	1 tsp

Using a sharp knife, remove the skin from the melon quarters. Cut the flesh into 1cm/½in slices. Return the melon slices to the skin, alternating with slivers of smoked pork or ham. Pour over the lemon juice and chill for 30 minutes.

Transfer the melon to serving dishes and sprinkle over the ginger. Serve immediately.
4 servings

Glazed Oranges

	Metric/UK	US
Oranges	4	4
Water	300ml/½ pint	1¼ cups
Sugar	225g/8oz	1 cup
Orange-flavoured liqueur or brandy	1 Tbsp	1 Tbsp

Peel two of the oranges with a sharp knife and discard the peel and white pith. Set aside. Thinly pare the rind from the other two oranges and cut it into long, thin strips. Place the rind in a small saucepan. Remove the white pith from the oranges. Slice a strip off the bottom of each orange so that they will stand up, and put them on a shallow glass serving dish. Set aside.

Pour the water over the rind and bring it to the boil over a moderately high heat. Boil for 5–6 minutes or until the strips are just tender and beginning to curl. Remove the pan from the heat and lift out the strips with a slotted spoon. Wash them under cold water and leave to drain on kitchen paper towels. Reserve 175ml/6floz (¾ cup) of the cooking liquid.

Combine the reserved cooking liquid and the sugar in a small saucepan over a low heat. Cook, stirring continuously until the sugar has dissolved. Then boil the syrup, without stirring, until the temperature registers 120°C/240°F on a sugar thermometer or until a teaspoon of the mixture dropped into cold water forms a soft ball. Add the orange rind and continue boiling until the syrup turns a rich golden brown. Remove from the heat and stir in the liqueur.

Pour the syrup over the oranges and place the dish in the refrigerator. Chill for 2 hours before serving.
4 servings

Compote of Dried Fruit

This makes a delightful dessert or it can be used to accompany cold meat or poultry.

	Metric/UK	US
Mixed dried fruit (apples, apricots, sultanas or raisins, prunes, figs, etc)	700g/1½lb	4 cups
Water	450ml/¾ pint	2 cups
Dry red wine	150ml/5floz	⅔ cup
Sugar	225g/8oz	1 cup
Cinnamon stick	5cm/2in	2in
Rind of 1 lemon, cut in thin strips		

Cover the fruit with cold water and soak for at least 12 hours. Drain the fruit well in a colander.

In a large saucepan, bring the water, red wine, sugar, cinnamon and lemon rind to a boil, stirring until the sugar has dissolved. Add the drained fruit, reduce to low and simmer for 10–15 minutes or until tender. Using a slotted spoon, transfer the fruit to a serving dish. Cover with foil and keep warm.

Remove and discard the cinnamon stick. Return the pan to a high heat and boil the liquid for 30 minutes or until it has reduced and thickened. Pour over the fruit and serve warm, or chill for 1 hour to serve cold.
6–8 servings

Banana Flambé

	Metric/UK	US
Bananas	6	6
Butter	40g/1½oz	3 Tbsp
Lemon juice	1 Tbsp	1 Tbsp
Brandy or rum	2 Tbsp	2 Tbsp
Light brown sugar	1 Tbsp	1 Tbsp

Peel the bananas and halve them lengthwise. In a large frying-pan, melt the butter over a moderate heat. Add the bananas and fry them gently on each side for 3–4 minutes, or until they are just browned. Add the lemon juice to the pan and cook for a further 1 minute.

Warm the brandy or rum, set light to it and pour it, flaming, over the bananas. Sprinkle with the sugar and serve at once, spooning the liquid from the pan over each serving.
4 servings

Grapefruit and Orange Salad

This is good with glazed ham or roast lamb.

	Metric/UK	US
Medium-sized grapefruit	2	2
Large orange	1	1
Small cucumber	½	½

Fresh mint leaves

DRESSING

Corn oil	3 Tbsp	3 Tbsp
Lemon juice	½ tsp	½ tsp
Sugar	1 tsp	1 tsp
Black pepper	½ tsp	½ tsp
Salt	½ tsp	½ tsp

With a sharp knife, segment the grapefruit and orange, removing the membrane, and place in a shallow salad bowl. Cut the cucumber in half lengthways, then into 5mm/¼in slices crossways. Arrange decoratively around the grapefruit mixture.

In a small bowl, combine the dressing ingredients until they are well blended. Pour over the salad and decorate with mint leaves. Chill for 30 minutes before serving.

4 servings

Refreshing Grapefruit and Orange Salad can be served with meat, or as an unusual appetizer.

DESSERTS

*Desserts are both the fitting end to a meal and the climax
to it. They can be hot or cold, complicated or simple,
cheap or almost more expensive than the savoury
course. It can be a pudding, such as tapioca or sago,
a pie such as apple pie, or a gelatine (gelatin) based
mousse; often it is a special cake (for some possible
dessert cakes see the next chapter).
The addition of a dessert at the end of the meal can make
the meal more flexible—a hearty soup followed by a
pie with cream, say, makes a perfect weekday supper,
and a dessert based on fruit can not only make a pleasant
end to the meal but also a nutrious one.*

1. HOT DESSERTS

There is nothing so mouthwatering as the aroma of a hot dessert on a cold winter's evening. Hot desserts are often based on pastry, crumble or sponge recipes with delicious fruity fillings. Serve them with your own Egg Custard Sauce or whipped cream to make a really satisfying end to a meal. Custard can make a dessert on its own, such as Crème Caramel. Other good hot desserts are made with batters, such as crêpes or fritters; and for a spectacular end to the meal, there are sweet hot soufflés and sweet omelettes, or the luxurious Italian Zabaglione.

For fruit pies, flans and suet puddings, see the chapter on Pastry.

Crumbles

These are delicious toppings for fruit desserts, and very simple to prepare. The fat is simply rubbed into the flour, and the sugar and flavourings are stirred in. The crumbly mixture is sprinkled on top of the fruit and baked in the oven until golden brown. The fruit can be cold cooked fruit, but quickly-cooked raw fruit such as gooseberries, red and white currants, blackcurrants, bilberries (blueberries), apples, plums, rhubarb and apricots can all be used in a crumble; they bake gently at the same time as the crumble topping. A crumble should not be cooked at a high heat, or the fruit will boil over and spoil the top.

BASIC CRUMBLE TOPPING

	Metric/UK	US
Flour	100g/4oz	1 cup
Butter, cut into small pieces	75g/3oz	6 Tbsp
Sugar	50g/2oz	¼ cup

Preheat the oven to moderate (180°C/350°F, Gas Mark 4). Sift the flour into a bowl and rub in the butter until the mixture resembles fine breadcrumbs. Stir in the sugar and any spice being used. This is enough topping for 700g/1½lb prepared fruit, which is put in a lightly greased baking dish with 100g/4oz (½ cup) sugar and about 2 tablespoons of water. Use less water for very soft berry fruit, more for firmer fruits such as plums. Spread the crumble mixture on top and bake in the oven until golden brown—about 45 minutes.

Sponge puddings

These are made from creamed sponge mixtures, often with a little liquid in the form of milk or cream added. They are cooked by steaming in a basin (mold) set in a large saucepan of boiling water for about 2 hours. This produces a moist, fragrant sponge to complement the flavourings used. The method of making creamed sponge is the same as in the chapter on Cakes.

Custard

Although the prepacked powdered variety is very popular —and useful—you can make your own stirred custard sauce quite easily, using egg yolks to thicken it. This creamy sauce makes a superb accompaniment to hot desserts.

BASIC CUSTARD SAUCE

	Metric/UK	US
Egg yolks	4	4
Sugar	2 Tbsp	2 Tbsp
Milk	600ml/ 1 pint	2½ cups
Vanilla essence (extract)	a few drops	a few drops

Beat the egg yolks with the sugar and a little of the milk. Heat the remaining milk until hot but not boiling (or the eggs will curdle). Stir the milk into the egg mixture, strain and return to the rinsed-out pan. Place a cold, clean bowl nearby. Continue to cook the custard, stirring continuously, over a moderate heat until it thickens enough to coat the back of the wooden spoon. As soon as it thickens, pour the custard into the waiting bowl to stop the cooking process. Serve at once.

Baked Custard (Crème Caramel)

Custard can also be baked to make a hot or cold dessert and a delicious version of baked custard is Crème Caramel. It can be served plain, or baked in a ring mould (tube pan) then filled with fruit when cold.

	Metric/UK	US
CARAMEL		
Sugar	100g/4oz	½ cup
Water	50ml/2floz	¼ cup
CUSTARD		
Milk	600ml/ 1 pint	2½ cups
Sugar	90g/3½oz	7 Tbsp
Vanilla essence (extract)	1 tsp	1 tsp
Whole eggs	2	2
Egg yolks	2	2

To make the caramel, dissolve the sugar in the water, stirring, over a low heat. When dissolved, increase the heat to high and boil, without stirring, for 3–4 minutes or until nut brown. Remove from the heat and pour into a baking dish or individual ramekin dishes.

Make the custard as in the Basic Custard Recipe, stopping when the eggs have been added to the milk. Pour the mixture into a jug.

Preheat the oven to warm (170°C/325°F, Gas Mark 3). Strain the custard mixture into the prepared dish. Place in a deep baking pan and add enough boiling water to come halfway up the dishes. Bake in the lower part of the oven for 40 minutes or until firm and set, but do not allow the custard to simmer or it will curdle.

Remove from the oven and cool, then chill thoroughly. Loosen the edges with a knife, then turn out on to a serving dish.
6 servings

Custard can be made to a slightly thicker consistency and used as an integral part of other desserts. It must be able to support the weight of fruit or whipped cream, so use your own judgement when adding egg yolks.

BATTERS

These can be of two types. The first is a coating or fritter batter, into which small pieces of food such as apple rings or pieces of banana are dipped before frying in hot oil. The second type of batter is a pancake or crêpe batter, which can be filled and flavoured in many different ways.

1. Fritter batter

This is a basic fritter batter. A richer batter can be used, such as the one given in the Apple Fritters recipe below.

	Metric/UK	US
Flour, sifted	100g/4oz	1 cup
Pinch of salt		
Tepid water	6 Tbsp	6 Tbsp
Cooking oil	4 tsp	4 tsp
Egg whites	2	2

Mix the flour, salt, water and oil to a smooth batter, drawing the flour gradually into the liquid. Beat the egg whites until stiff, then fold into the batter mixture with a metal spoon. Fritters can be shallow fried (see Apple Fritters below) or deep fried (see Banana Fritters).

2. Crêpe batter

	Metric/UK	US
Flour	150g/5oz	1¼ cups
Castor (superfine) sugar	1 Tbsp	1 Tbsp
Egg yolks	3	3
Butter, melted	65g/2½oz	5 Tbsp
Milk	125ml/4floz	½ cup
Cold water	125ml/4floz	½ cup
Cherry-flavoured liqueur (optional)	3 Tbsp	3 Tbsp
Vegetable oil	2 Tbsp	2 Tbsp

Crêpe Batter

Sift the flour and sugar into a mixing bowl. Stir in the egg yolks and melted butter with a wooden spoon. Gradually add the milk and water and beat until smooth. Stir in the liqueur. Cover and leave for about 1½–2 hours.

With a brush, lightly grease a medium-sized heavy frying-pan. Heat until it is very hot. Pour about 4 tablespoons (use your judgement) of batter into the pan and quickly tilt it to spread out the batter thinly. Pour out any excess. (You now know the quantity to add to the pan). Cook for 1 minute or until golden underneath. Flip the crêpe over with a palette knife or spatula and cook the other side for about 30 seconds. Slide on to an ovenproof plate and keep warm while making the rest of the crêpes.

Crêpes can be filled with fruit purée, jam or jelly or even ice-cream.
4–6 servings

Hot soufflés

Hot soufflés depend upon stiffly beaten egg whites to make them rise. These soufflés collapes quickly, so they must be eaten immediately. Most are quite simple to make and mouthwatering. All hot sweet soufflés are made in a similar way.

Sweet omelettes

These have a little icing (confectioner's) sugar added to the egg mixture.

Strawberry Omelette

This is delectable served with whipped cream. Other fruit such as raspberries or blackberries may be substituted.

Add 175g/6oz hulled, crushed strawberries to 2 tablespoons double (heavy) cream. Set aside. Add 40g/1½oz icing sugar (⅓ cup confectioner's sugar) to the basic egg mixture. Proceed as before. Use the strawberry and cream mixture to fill the omelette. Dust with icing (confectioner's) sugar and serve.

To make crêpe batter, put the flour in a bowl, then add egg yolks and melted butter.

Now using a wooden spoon, slowly fold the egg yolks and butter into the flour.

Finally, add the milk and water to the bowl and beat well until all the ingredients make a smooth batter.

RECIPES

Coffee Souffle

	Metric/UK	US
Sponge finger biscuits (lady fingers), broken into small pieces	6	6
Coffee-flavoured liqueur	75ml/3 floz	$\frac{1}{3}$ cup
Icing (confectioner's) sugar	25g/1oz	4 Tbsp
Butter	40g/1$\frac{1}{2}$oz	3 Tbsp
Flour	25g/1oz	$\frac{1}{4}$ cup
Hot milk	175ml/6 floz	$\frac{3}{4}$ cup
Strong black coffee	50ml/2 floz	$\frac{1}{4}$ cup
Sugar	1 Tbsp	1 Tbsp
Egg yolks	5	5
Egg whites	6	6
Walnuts, chopped	100g/4oz	1 cup

Place the sponge (lady) fingers in a shallow dish and sprinkle over 50ml/2floz of the liqueur. Leave for 30 minutes, then mash with a fork to a smooth paste.

Preheat the oven to moderate (180°C/350°F, Gas Mark 4). Grease a straight-sided soufflé dish of 1.5L/ 2$\frac{1}{2}$ pint (2 quart) capacity. Sprinkle all over with the icing (confectioner's) sugar and shake out any excess. Make a roux with the butter and flour, then stir in the hot milk gradually to make a thick sauce. Cook for 2 minutes. Stir in the remaining liqueur, black coffee and sponge (lady) fingers mixture. Set aside to cool a little. Beat the sugar with the egg yolks and add gradually to the cooled sauce.

Beat the egg whites until stiff and fold into the sauce. Spoon into the prepared dish and sprinkle with the walnuts. Bake in the centre of the oven for 35–45 minutes or until the soufflé is well risen and lightly browned. Serve immediately.
6 servings

Railway Pudding

	Metric/UK	US
Butter	100g/4oz	$\frac{1}{2}$ cup
Sugar	100g/4oz	$\frac{1}{2}$ cup
Eggs	2	2
Double (heavy) cream	2 Tbsp	2 Tbsp
Grated rind of 1 small lemon		

Hot soufflés are very special–this Coffee Soufflé is not difficult to make, and its taste more than repays any effort involved.

	Metric/UK	US
Vanilla essence (extract)	$\frac{1}{2}$ tsp	$\frac{1}{2}$ tsp
Baking powder	1 tsp	1 tsp
Flour	175g/6oz	1$\frac{1}{2}$ cups
Sweet red cherries, halved and stoned (pitted)	225g/8oz	1$\frac{1}{2}$ cups

Grease a 1.2L/2 pint pudding basin (2$\frac{1}{2}$ pint steaming mold). Set aside. Make the sponge mixture using the creaming method (see page 216), stirring in the cream, lemon rind and vanilla after beating in the eggs. Stir in the cherries after the flour and baking powder have been folded in. Spoon the mixture into the pudding basin (mold) and cover the top with greaseproof or waxed paper, then foil. Make a deep pleat across the top to allow for expansion. Tie the paper tightly around the rim of the basin (mold). Place the bowl in a pan of boiling water to reach halfway up the basin (mold), and steam for about 2 hours, adding boiling water as necessary.

Remove the paper, then turn the pudding out on to a warmed serving dish. Serve immediately.
6 servings

Apple Fritters

	Metric/UK	US
Flour	100g/4oz	1 cup
Salt	pinch	pinch
Whole egg	1	1
Egg yolk	1	1
Cooking oil	1 Tbsp	1 Tbsp
Milk	150ml/5 floz	$\frac{2}{3}$ cup
Cooking apples, peeled and cored	$\frac{1}{2}$kg/1lb	1lb
Juice of 1 lemon		
Castor (superfine) sugar		
Butter or cooking fat	100g/4oz	$\frac{1}{2}$ cup

Sift the flour and salt into a medium-sized mixing bowl. Make a well in the centre of the flour and put in the egg, egg yolk and the oil. With a wooden spoon, mix the eggs and oil, slowly incorporating the flour and gradually adding the milk. Mix to a smooth batter and beat well. Cover and set aside for 30 minutes.

Slice the apples into rings 5mm/$\frac{1}{4}$in thick. Sprinkle with lemon juice and sugar.

In a large frying-pan melt the butter or fat over a high heat. Use a skewer to dip the apple slices into the batter and drop them one by one into the hot fat. Cook on both sides until they are golden brown. Arrange on a plate and dredge with more sugar.
4 servings

Coriander Fruit Crumble

	Metric/UK	US
Cooking apples, peeled, cored and thinly sliced	700g/1½lb	1½lb
Fresh blackberries, washed and stalks removed	225g/8oz	½lb
Brown sugar	2 Tbsp	2 Tbsp
Ground cinnamon	1 tsp	1 tsp
CRUMBLE TOPPING		
Flour	100g/4oz	1 cup
Butter	75g/3oz	6 Tbsp
Sugar	50g/2oz	¼ cup
Ground coriander	2 tsp	2 tsp

Preheat the oven to moderate (180°C/350°F, Gas Mark 4). Grease a 1.8L/3 pint (2 quart) baking dish. Put in the fruit and sprinkle generously with the brown sugar and cinnamon.

Make the crumble as in Basic Crumble Topping, above, adding the coriander with the sugar. Sprinkle the crumble on top of the fruit and bake for about 45 minutes or until golden brown.
4–6 servings

Coriander Fruit Crumble makes an economical and homely dessert. Serve with whipped cream.

Banana Fritters

This recipe can be made with Basic Fritter Batter (see page 174).

	Metric/UK	US
Large bananas	6	6
Castor (superfine) sugar	225g/8oz	1 cup
Fritter Batter freshly prepared	100g/4oz	1 cup
Vegetable oil for deep frying		
Fresh orange juice	250ml/8floz	1 cup
Orange-flavoured liqueur	2 Tbsp	2 Tbsp

Cut the bananas in half lengthways then cut in half crossways. Roll in 50g/2oz (¼ cup) of the sugar.

Place the fritter batter in a small, deep bowl. Heat the oil to 180°C/350°F on a deep-fat thermometer. Coat a few pieces of banana with batter and drop carefully into the hot oil. Fry for 3–4 minutes or until golden and crisp. Remove from the oil with a slotted spoon and drain on kitchen paper towels. Transfer to a hot serving dish and keep warm. Fry the remainder in the same way.

Place the remaining sugar, orange juice and liqueur in a small saucepan. Heat slowly until the sugar dissolves, then boil without stirring for 3 minutes or until thickened slightly. Serve with the fritters.
4 servings

Crêpes Suzette

Crêpes Suzette–an all–time classic.

Crêpe Batter	Metric/UK	US
Crêpe Batter	150g/5oz	1¼ cups
Sugar lumps	4	4
Medium-sized oranges	2	2
Castor (superfine) sugar	4 Tbsp	4 Tbsp
Unsalted butter, softened	175g/6oz	¾ cup
Orange juice	75ml/3floz	⅓ cup
Orange-flavoured liqueur	5 Tbsp	5 Tbsp
Brandy	3 Tbsp	3 Tbsp

Make the crêpes according to the basic recipe and keep hot.

Rub the sugar lumps over the oranges to absorb the zest (oil). Crush the lumps in a small bowl with a wooden spoon. Peel the oranges carefully, removing the white pith. Chop the rind finely and add to the sugar lumps. Add half of the sugar and the butter. Cream with a wooden spoon until light and fluffy. Stir in the orange juice and 3 tablespoons of the liqueur.

In a small frying-pan, melt the orange butter over a low heat. Dip each crêpe in the hot mixture until well soaked. Fold each crêpe into quarters and arrange in a warm serving dish. Sprinkle over the remaining sugar and any remaining melted orange butter.

In a small saucepan, warm the remaining liqueur and brandy. Do not boil. Pour the liquid over the crêpes. Ignite with a match and shake gently. When the flames die down, serve.

4–6 servings

Zabaglione

	Metric/UK	US
Egg yolks	4	4
Castor (superfine) sugar	4 Tbsp	4 Tbsp
Marsala	4 Tbsp	4 Tbsp
Grated lemon rind	2 tsp	2 tsp

In a heatproof bowl beat the egg yolks and sugar together until the mixture is thick and yellow. Set over a saucepan of hot water and stir in the Marsala and lemon rind. Continue beating over low heat until the mixture becomes very thick and frothy. Pour into individual glasses and serve immediately.

4–6 servings

2. COLD DESSERTS

Many cold desserts are based on the setting qualities of custard—trifle, for instance, in which sponge, fruit, custard and cream are arranged in attractive layers, or those of gelatine (gelatin). Some combine custard and gelatine (gelatin), as in a Bavarois or Bavarian Cream. Cold Fruit Charlottes combine custard, gelatine (gelatin) and whipped cream with cold fruit purée; they are made in a mould, then turned out to show the case of sponge (lady) fingers. Charlotte Russe is presented in the same way but is made from custard, whipped cream and lemon jelly (gelatin). Another spectacular dessert using gelatine (gelatin) is cold soufflé, which is easy to make and freezes extremely well.

No chapter on cold desserts can leave out ice-cream and it is well worth making your own. Home-made ice-cream is very good on its own, but if you have a bombe mould you can make your own decorative frozen desserts made from several layers of differently flavoured ice-cream.

Eggs, the basis of so many cooking transformations, provide yet another in meringues—stiffly beaten egg whites mixed with sugar and baked to snowy crispness.

Gelatine (gelatin)

Gelatine (gelatin) is a solid made from boiling bones, cartilage and tendons. It can also be made from fish and from seaweed. It is tasteless and odourless. When dissolved in a liquid it will set on cooling, and melt when warmed. It is simple to use, provided you observe a few basic rules.

1. Measure the gelatine (gelatin) accurately and use the exact amount stated in the recipe. It is available in both powdered and sheet form. An envelope of powdered gelatine (gelatin) usually contains 15g/½oz (¼oz in US), which is approximately the same as 2 level tablespoons (1 tablespoon in US); 20g/¾oz sheet gelatine gives equivalent setting power.

2. Normally this quantity will set 600ml/1 pint (2½ cups) of clear liquid, but in hot weather or for acidic juices such as lemon, use half as much again. Beware of using too much, as this gives a rubbery texture.

3. Always dissolve gelatine (gelatin) in warm water or lemon juice, without boiling. Boiling spoils it and gives a poor set. Sheet gelatine (gelatin) must be soaked for 2–3 hours in a little cold water before dissolving over low heat.

4. When adding gelatine (gelatin) to other ingredients, try to have them all at the same room temperature, neither hot nor cold.

5. Do not dissolve gelatine (gelatin) in milk or the milk will curdle. To make milk jelly (gelatin), dissolve the gelatine (gelatin) in water and when it is cool and beginning to set, add it slowly to cool but not cold milk.

6. If anything solid—fruit, nuts—is to be added to the

jelly (gelatin), stir them in when it is on the point of setting or they will sink to the bottom. When making fruit jelly (gelatin), the best fruits to use are those with bright colours and a strong flavour, such as blackcurrants, oranges, lemons and pineapple. Lemon jelly (gelatin) should always be strained to give a sparkling result. Pineapple juice contains an enzyme which destroys the setting properties of gelatine (gelatin), so it must be boiled first for 2–3 minutes to kill the enzyme.

Lemon Jelly (*Gelatin*)

	Metric/UK	US
Lemons	2 large or 3 small	2 large or 3 small
Water	to make up to 600ml/ 1 pint	to make up to 2½ cups
Sugar	50–75g/ 2–3oz	¼–⅓ cup
Gelatine (gelatin)	15–20g/ ½–¾oz	2 envelopes

Pare the rind thinly from the lemons. Put them in a saucepan with about 300ml/½ pint (1¼ cups) water. Simmer for 10 minutes. Strain and stir in the sugar. Measure the liquid. Squeeze the juice from the lemons and measure. Dissolve the gelatine (gelatin) in a little cold water. The water for dissolving the gelatine (gelatin), the lemon juice and the simmered liquid from the rind should add up to 600ml/1 pint (2½ cups). Heat the lemon juice and sugar mixture together, and strain over the dissolved gelatine (gelatin). Pour into a dampened mould or use as required.

This method can also be used for oranges.

4–6 servings

ICE-CREAM

If you are thinking of making a lot of ice-cream, then it is worth buying an electric ice-cream maker, which is equipped with paddles to churn the ice-cream continually while freezing. This breaks up the ice crystals, and aerates the mixture.

There are two basic mixtures for making ice-cream. One is based on a thick custard and is best suited for coffee, chocolate and ginger flavours; the other is based on a mousse, and is used in fruit ice-creams such as raspberry, strawberry, blackcurrant, peach, apricot or lemon. These would curdle if made with a custard base.

Meringue Base

To make a meringue circle, first draw a large circle on non-stick silicone (parchment) paper–use a plate or board as a guide.

When the meringue mixture is stiff, spread about one-third over the circle to make a base of about 6mm/¼in thick.

Pipe the remaining mixture around the edge of the circle. Cook until crisp then, when it has cooled completely, transfer to a serving plate.

1. Custard base

	Metric/UK	US
Milk	300ml/ ½ pint	1¼ cups
Vanilla essence (extract)	½ tsp	½ tsp
Egg yolks	4	4
Castor (superfine) sugar	50g/2oz	¼ cup
Double (heavy) cream	300ml/ ½ pint	1¼ cups

Make a custard as in Basic Custard Sauce, using the milk, vanilla, egg yolks and sugar. Remove from the heat when thickened and strain into a bowl. Whip the cream until it begins to thicken. Fold into the cooled custard. When it is cold, put into an ice-cream container and freeze in the freezer or in the freezing cabinet of a refrigerator. When the mixture is beginning to freeze firmly around the edges, after about 30 minutes, take it out and beat it to a smooth consistency. Replace in the freezer and freeze again until almost solid. Take it out and beat it thoroughly again. Freeze until firm, then serve.

Chocolate Ice-cream Add 50g/2oz melted plain chocolate (2 squares semi-sweet chocolate) to the custard.
Coffee Ice-cream Add 2 teaspoons coffee essence (extract) to the custard.
Ginger Ice-cream Add 50g/2oz (⅓ cup) finely-chopped preserved (crystalized) ginger and 1 tablespoon ginger syrup to the custard.

2. Mousse base

	Metric/UK	US
Vanilla essence (extract)	1 tsp	1 tsp
Double (heavy) cream	450ml/¾ pint	2 cups
Egg yolks	3	3

Sugar	50g/2oz	¼ cup
Water	75ml/3floz	⅓ cup
Fruit purée	250ml/8floz	1 cup
Egg whites, stiffly beaten	3	3

Mix the vanilla with the cream. Beat the egg yolks until they are well blended. Set aside.

Dissolve the sugar in the water over a low heat. Bring to the boil and boil, without stirring, until the temperature reaches 110°C/220°F on a sugar thermometer, or a little cooled syrup taken between thumb and forefinger will form a short thread when drawn out. Pour the syrup over the egg yolks in a steady stream, beating constantly. Continue beating until the mixture is thick and fluffy. Add the fruit purée. Mix in the cream and fold in the egg whites with a metal spoon. Spoon into a container and freeze as before.

Ice-cream can be used to fill crêpes, to accompany fresh fruit or hot desserts, to fill Swiss (jelly) rolls or it can be transformed into a dramatic dinner party dessert.

Meringue

Meringue makes a sweet crisp base for many desserts. It can be piped into baskets, large or small, then filled with whipped cream and fruit of your choice. Alternatively, it can be dried in large discs of the same size and sandwiched with nut- or chocolate-flavoured creams. The possibilities are endless and can give you plenty of scope for your inventiveness.

BASIC MERINGUE

	Metric/UK	US
Egg whites	4	4
Castor (superfine) sugar	225g/8oz	1 cup

Beat the egg whites until you can hold the bowl upside down without their falling out. Beat in 4

tablespoons of the sugar. Continue beating for 1 minute or until glossy. Carefully fold in the remainder of the sugar with a metal spoon. Use and shape the mixture as required.

To make a simple meringue topping for fruit pies and desserts, halve these quantities and proceed in the same way. Pipe the mixture over the filling, taking it right to the edges. Bake in the centre of an oven preheated to moderate (180°C/350°F, Gas Mark 4), for 20–25 minutes. The top should be crisp and lightly golden, the inside of the meringue soft and marshmallow like. Serve at once.

Note When making meringues, meringue discs or baskets, it is best to use non-stick silicone baking paper to line the baking sheets. The meringues slip off easily when ready, with no danger of broken crumbled shells that have stuck to the baking sheet.

To make meringue discs and baskets

Draw a circle or circles on the silicone paper, using a plate as a guide, to the size stated in the recipe. This is usually 23cm/9in for large discs or baskets, and about 6–7.5cm/2½–3in for small individual discs or baskets. Lay the paper carefully on a greased baking sheet. Preheat the oven to very cool (140°C/275°F, Gas Mark

One excellent way to serve a meringue basket is to fill it with whipped fresh cream and a combination of chopped fresh fruit— then you have the classic Australian Pavlova.

1), or as stated in the recipe. (It should be no hotter than moderate.)

Spread some of the meringue mixture 5mm/¼in thick evenly over the circle(s) drawn on the paper. Alternatively, you can pipe the circle using a pastry bag fitted with a 2.5cm/1in nozzle, working in decreasing circles from the drawn guideline. This will give you flat discs suitable for building up in layers with cream fillings.

To make baskets, carefully pipe around the edge of the circle to form the raised edge. Bake for at least 1 hour, then turn off the heat and leave in the oven for at least 30 minutes until crisp on the outside, but still slightly soft and melting inside. Remove from the oven and leave to cool. Carefully peel off the silicone paper, place on a flat serving dish and fill with your chosen fruit or cream mixture when cold.

RECIPES

Bombe Coppelia

	Metric/UK	US
Coffee-flavoured ice-cream, slightly softened	1.8L/ 3 pints	3¾ pints
Egg yolks	8	8
Sugar	100g/4oz	½ cup
Dark rum	3 Tbsp	3 Tbsp
Water	1 Tbsp	1 Tbsp
Double (heavy) cream	300ml/ ½ pint	1¼ cups
PRALINE		
Castor (superfine) sugar	75g/3oz	⅓ cup
Blanched almonds	75g/3oz	¾ cup

Make the praline as described on p 234 for Nougatine Cakes. Carefully line a chilled 1.8L/3 pint (4 pint) metal bombe mould with an even, thick layer of the coffee ice-cream, retaining a little. Press firmly into place with a smooth glass bowl. Leave the bowl in the mould and freeze for 1 hour or until firm.

Use the remaining ingredients and the praline to make a mousse-based ice-cream, adding the rum to the sugar and water, and the praline before adding the cream. Pour this ice-cream into the centre of the bombe until it is filled, and freeze until firm. Spread the remainder of the coffee ice-cream smoothly over the praline ice-cream. Cover with the lid or foil and freeze overnight. Unmould on to a serving dish by dipping the bombe quickly in hot water first.
10–12 servings

Meringue Basket with Strawberries

	Metric/UK	US
1 × 23cm/9in Meringue Basket, cooked and cooled		
Double (heavy) cream, whipped and sweetened to taste	450ml/ ¾ pint	2 cups
Fresh strawberries, hulled and washed	225g/8oz	½lb

Place the meringue basket on a flat serving plate. Spoon in the cream and pile on the strawberries attractively.
4–6 servings

A stunning mixture of ice cream, cream and praline is Bombe Coppelia— and it tastes good.

Charlotte Russe

	Metric/UK	US
Lemon-flavoured jelly (gelatin), cooled but liquid	125ml/4floz	½ cup
Sponge finger biscuits (lady fingers)	28–30	28–30
Milk	300ml/ ½ pint	1¼ cups
Egg yolks	3	3
Vanilla essence (extract)	½ tsp	½ tsp
Sugar	2 Tbsp	2 Tbsp
Gelatine (gelatin)	1 Tbsp	1 Tbsp
Hot water	75ml/3floz	⅓ cup
Double (heavy) cream	250ml/8floz	1 cup

Use the lemon jelly (gelatin) to coat the bottom of a metal Charlotte mould. When it has almost set, place the sponge (lady) fingers around the sides with the ends in the jelly (gelatin).

As in Basic Custard Sauce, make a custard from the milk, egg yolks, vanilla and sugar. While it cools, dissolve the gelatine (gelatin) in the hot water. When the custard is cool, add the dissolved gelatine (gelatin) and mix well. Whip the cream and fold it in when the custard is on the point of setting. Spoon into the lined mould and place in the refrigerator to set. Just before serving, trim the edges of the sponge (lady) fingers to a level with the cream filling.

Unmould as for Wine Jelly. A ribbon can be tied around to keep the sponge (lady) fingers in place.
4–6 servings

Cold Lemon Soufflé

	Metric/UK	US
Gelatine (gelatin)	15g/½oz	2 envelopes
Hot water	4 Tbsp	4 Tbsp
Eggs, separated	5	5
Castor (superfine) sugar	100g/4oz	½ cup
Finely grated rind and juice of 3 lemons		
Double (heavy) cream	300ml/ ½ pint	1¼ cups

Wrap a high collar of double greaseproof (waxed) paper tightly around the outside of a straight-sided 15cm/6in soufflé dish and secure firmly. It should extend considerably above the top of the dish. The aim is to give the effect of a risen hot soufflé—though

*Small meringue baskets
filled with unsweetened
chestnut purée is the
French classic Chamonix.*

in fact cold soufflés do not rise, as they are not cooked.
If you prefer, use a larger dish and dispense with the
paper collar.

Dissolve the gelatine (gelatin) in the hot water. Put
the egg yolks, sugar and lemon rind in a heatproof bowl
over a pan of hot water and beat until pale and fluffy.
Alternatively, use an electric mixer without heat. Beat
until the mixture is thick enough to leave a ribbon
trail on itself when the beater is lifted. Remove from
the heat. Add the lemon juice and continue beating
until the mixture has cooled. Stir in the gelatine
(gelatin) mixture very thoroughly, and continue stirring
until you begin to feel a slight 'drag' on the spoon.
Whip the cream until thick but not stiff, and fold it
into the lemon mixture.

Beat the egg whites until stiff, and carefully fold them
into the lemon mixture. Spoon into the soufflé dish—
it will come above the top of the dish, but be held by

the paper collar. Chill until set.

Carefully peel off the collar, using a table knife to
ease it away from the soufflé. To decorate, press flaked
(shredded) almonds or chocolate curls on to the sides
above the dish and pipe whirls of whipped cream on
the top. Serve cold.
6 servings

Chamonix

	Metric/UK	US
Small meringue baskets, cooked and cooled	6	6
FILLING		
Double (heavy) cream	250ml/8floz	1 cup
Castor (superfine) sugar	4 Tbsp	4 Tbsp
Vanilla essence (extract)	$\frac{1}{2}$ tsp	$\frac{1}{2}$ tsp
Brandy	2 Tbsp	2 Tbsp
Canned, unsweetened chestnut purée	225g/8oz	$\frac{1}{2}$lb

Beat the cream with half of the sugar and the vanilla until thick. Beat the remaining sugar and brandy into the chestnut purée. Pipe the chestnut mixture around the inside of the baskets, leaving a hollow in the centre of each one. Spoon some whipped cream into the centre of each basket.

6 servings

Orange Caramel Trifle

	Metric/UK	US
Trifle sponge squares, each sliced into 2 layers (pound cake slices)	6	2
Orange-flavoured liqueur	2 Tbsp	2 Tbsp
Fresh orange juice	2 Tbsp	2 Tbsp
Sugar	275g/10oz	1¼ cups
Custard Sauce	300ml/ ½ pint	1¼ cups
Large oranges, peeled and thinly sliced	4	4
Double (heavy) cream, stiffly whipped	150ml/5floz	⅔ cup

An elegant version of a traditional British favourite–that's Orange Caramel Trifle.

Place the sponge squares (pound cake slices) in a flat-bottomed dish. Sprinkle with the liqueur and orange juice and set aside for 30 minutes. Melt the sugar in a heavy pan and cook until it turns golden brown. Remove from the heat and keep the caramel warm over a pan of hot water.

Arrange one-third of the soaked cake slices in a glass serving bowl. Spoon over one-third of the custard. Lay on one-third of the orange slices and trickle over one-third of the caramel in a thin stream.

Continue with the layers, ending with a layer of caramel-coated orange slices. Chill for at least 2 hours. Pipe whirls of whipped cream over the top of the trifle before serving.

4–6 servings

Chocolate Bavarois.

Chocolate Bavarois

	Metric/UK	US
Milk	750ml/ 1¼ pints	3 cups
Plain (semi-sweet) chocolate, grated	100g/4oz	4 squares
Egg yolks	4	4
Castor (superfine) sugar	75g/3oz	⅓ cup
Gelatine (gelatin)	15g/½oz	2 envelopes
Hot black coffee	125ml/4floz	½ cup
Vanilla essence (extract)	1 tsp	1 tsp
Double (heavy) cream	150ml/5floz	⅔ cup
Rum	2 Tbsp	2 Tbsp

Grease a 1.2L/2 pint (2½ pint) mould with a little oil. Invert over kitchen paper towels to drain off any excess. Heat the milk with the chocolate, stirring to melt the chocolate. Make a custard sauce with the chocolate, milk, egg yolks and sugar as in Basic Custard Sauce, putting all the ingredients in a large heatproof bowl over a pan of hot water to thicken, and taking care not to curdle the custard. Dissolve the gelatine (gelatin) in the coffee. Add the vanilla and stir into the custard. Strain the mixture into a bowl. Place over a bowl of crushed ice and stir until the custard becomes thick and begins to set.

Whip the cream until thick but not stiff and fold it into the custard with the rum. Pour the mixture into the mould. Cover with foil and chill until completely set. Unmould as for Wine Jelly.

4–6 servings

Pavlova

	Metric/UK	US
MERINGUE BASKET		
Egg whites	5	5
Castor (superfine) sugar	275g/10oz	1¼ cups
Cornflour (cornstarch)	2 tsp	2 tsp
Vanilla essence (extract)	½ tsp	½ tsp
Malt vinegar	1 tsp	1 tsp
FILLING		
Double (heavy) cream	300ml/ ½ pint	1¼ cups
Orange-flavoured liqueur	1–2 Tbsp	1–2 Tbsp
Fresh exotic fruit (e.g. passion fruit, pineapple, white peaches, Chinese gooseberries or kiwi fruit)	½kg/1lb	1lb

Preheat the oven to warm (150°C/300°F, Gas Mark 2). Make the meringue from the egg whites and sugar in the usual way, folding in the cornflour (cornstarch), vanilla and vinegar with the remainder of the sugar. Form into a basket and bake for 1 hour. Turn off the heat and leave in the oven for 30 minutes to crisp on the outside. The meringue should still be very soft and melting inside. Take the basket out of the oven and cool.

Beat the cream and liqueur together until thick. Fill the meringue basket with the cream and pile the fruit on top.

6 servings

Wine Jelly (Gelatin) with Fruit

	Metric/UK	US
Lukewarm water	250ml/8floz	1 cup
Dry white wine	450ml/ ¾ pint	2 cups
Lemon juice	2 Tbsp	2 Tbsp
Sugar	100g/4oz	½ cup
Gelatine (gelatin) (dissolved in 4 Tbsp hot water)	20g/¾oz	3 envelopes
Strawberries, hulled and halved	12	12
Peach, peeled, stoned (pitted) and sliced	1	1
Bananas, thinly sliced	2	2
Redcurrants, trimmed	100g/4oz	1 cup

Place the water, wine, lemon juice and sugar in a large bowl and stir until the sugar has dissolved. Stir in the dissolved gelatine (gelatin). Pour one quarter of the mixture into a 1.2L/2 pint ring mould (2½ pint tube pan) and chill until set. Keep the remainder at room temperature.

Dry the fruit carefully on kitchen paper towels. Remove the mould (pan) from the refrigerator. Make a neat layer of strawberries on the gelatine (gelatin) mixture, cover with a layer of peaches, a layer of bananas and finally a layer of redcurrants. Pour over the remaining gelatine (gelatin) mixture. Chill until completely set.

To unmould, run a knife around the edges of the mould (pan). Invert over a serving dish and place a hot, wet cloth over it for a minute. Give the mould (pan) a sharp shake. The jelly (gelatin) will slide out easily.

4 servings

Jelly (gelatin) with fruit has long been a family favourite, and it's given a lift here by the addition of dry white wine. Top with cream.

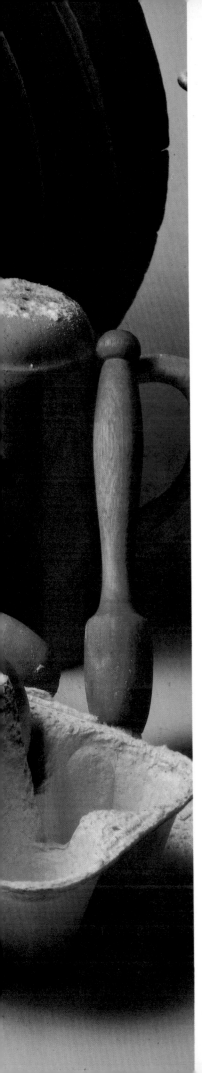

PASTRY

Pastry is an unleavened dough made from shortening (fat), flour and liquid. It is used either to provide a lining for a filling or to encase or envelope a filling completely. Such fillings can be sweet or savoury. There are several different types of pastry, ranging from the simple everyday shortcrust used in flans and quiches, to the more exotic choux pastry (paste), which provides the basis for some of the most glorious cakes of classic French haute cuisine.

Quantity

It is useful to note that when a recipe calls for, for instance, 225g/8oz (2 cups) pastry, it means pastry made from that quantity of flour.

Ingredients

Flour
Usually plain (all-purpose) white wheat flour. Self-raising (self-rising) flour is only used when a heavy ingredient such as suet is included.

Salt
Most dough has salt added—between $\frac{1}{8}$ teaspoon and 1 teaspoon.

Sugar
Sugar is added to sweet pastry doughs.

Shortening
The more shortening in relation to flour, the richer the dough. Butter is usually used, but margarine, suet, lard, vegetable fat (shortening) or oil, or goose or duck fat can be used. If using margarine, make sure it is hard, not soft 'whipped' margarine.

Liquid
A small amount of liquid is added to the flour and shortening mixture to bind it. Water is usually used, but eggs, milk, cream, sour cream and buttermilk may be used.

Flavourings
Cheese, herbs, spices and essences (extracts) may be added.

Yeast
Yeast is added to some pastry doughs such as that used for Danish pastries.

Making pastry: basic points

There are many different kinds of pastry, but several techniques apply to all pastry-making. The basic points to remember are:

1. Unless the dough is made with yeast or already cooked, keep the ingredients and implements cool. Your hands should be freshly washed in cold water. For some pastries, such as puff, the ingredients should be chilled.

2. Again, with the exception of yeast and cooked doughs, handle as little as possible. If you can, use a table knife or electric mixer to rub the fat into the flour. When doing this with your fingers, use the fingertips and

Sift flour and salt together then add fat. Use a sharp knife to cut the fat into the flour until the pieces are small and well coated.

Rub the fat into the flour until the mixture resembles fine breadcrumbs. To do this rub the ingredients between your fingers.

Sprinkle about 2 tsp of cold water over the surface of the mixture and carefully stir this into the ingredients with the knife.

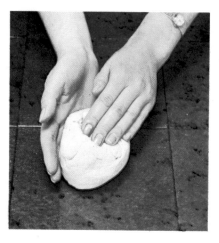

Add more water, in small quantities, until the mixture clings together in small lumps. Continue cutting with a knife until it makes large lumps.

Add the remaining water and stir in. Use your fingers to test if the mixture is moist enough to stick together, it should leave the sides of the bowl clean.

Draw the lumps together to make a dough and place on an unfloured surface. Knead lightly until it is smooth. Chill before using.

work quickly. The more you handle the dough, the stickier and less manageable it becomes. If using a mixer, switch off the minute the ingredients are like breadcrumbs.

3. When rolling out dough, place it on a lightly floured working surface and use a lightly floured rolling pin. Roll the dough lightly, away from you. Do not turn it over, or it will absorb too much flour from the working surface. If it is sticky or contains a lot of shortening or needs a lot of rolling, chill it, first folding it like puff pastry, to make rolling easier.

4. Usually pastry should be baked, or at least start its baking time, at a high oven temperature. Long, slow baking produces hard, tasteless pastry.

If you have a freezer, it is well worth making a large quantity of pastry at one time, as it freezes perfectly. Divide it into easy to use portions before freezing. Remove from the freezer at least 30 minutes before cook-

ing. Pie and flan cases can also be frozen—it is best to freeze them uncooked.

Types of pastry

The basic pastry types are shortcrust, rich shortcrust, puff, rough puff, flaky, suetcrust, hot water crust, choux and strudel. The difference between them is mainly determined by the method used to incorporate the shortening into the flour. In puff, rough puff and flaky pastry, the shortening—generally butter—is added either in one large or several smaller pieces and rolled and folded into the flour and liquid. The result is light and flaky. In closer textured pastries such as shortcrust, the shortening is cut into small pieces and rubbed into the flour until the mixture resembles fine or coarse breadcrumbs. For even closer-textured pastry, such as choux or hot water crust, the shortening is

melted with the liquid and stirred or beaten into the flour. The eggs in choux pastry open out the texture; strudel pastry also contains eggs but they are added in a different way. It requires a lot of kneading and has to be rolled out very thinly.

All types of pastry doughs are suitable for covering pies and enveloping sweet or savoury fillings. Close textured pastry, such as shortcrust and rich shortcrust, are more suitable for lining flans and pie dishes and baking blind.

1. Shortcrust Pastry

Basic shortcrust pastry can be used for making sweet or savoury pies or tarts.

	Metric/UK	US
Flour	175g/6oz	1½ cups
Salt	¼ tsp	¼ tsp
Butter	40g/1½oz	3 Tbsp
Vegetable fat (shortening)	40g/1½oz	3 Tbsp
Iced water	2–3 Tbsp	2–3 Tbsp

Sift the flour into a medium-sized mixing bowl. Add the butter and vegetable fat (shortening) and cut them into small pieces with a table knife. With the finger tips, rub the fat into the flour until the mixture resembles fine breadcrumbs. Add 1 tablespoon of the iced water and mix it into the flour using the knife. With your hands, mix and knead the dough until it is

smooth. Add a little more iced water if necessary. The dough should be smooth, soft, pliable and silky, leaving the sides of the bowl clean. Chill for 30 minutes. The pastry is now ready to be used.

2. Rich Shortcrust Pastry

Use for rich or sweet fillings. Rich desserts taste delicious in it.

	Metric/UK	US
Flour	175g/6oz	1½ cups
Salt	⅛ tsp	⅛ tsp
Butter, chilled	75g/3oz	6 Tbsp
Sugar	1 Tbsp	1 Tbsp
Small egg, lightly beaten	1	1
Iced water	1–2 Tbsp	1–2 Tbsp

Proceed as for the Basic Shortcrust method until the mixture resembles fine breadcrumbs. Stir in the sugar. Mix the egg with 1 tablespoon of iced water and use this to make the dough, adding more water if necessary. Chill for 30 minutes before use.

Cheese Pastry is based on rich shortcrust pastry, with the addition of grated cheese in the proportion, 4 tablespoons of grated cheese per 100g/4oz (1 cup) of flour. Cheese pastry can be substituted in savoury flans and tartlets, where a cheese flavour is complementary to the filling. It can also be made into cheese straws or biscuits (crackers).

Sift the flour and salt into a bowl, then chill. Put about half the water into a bowl with ice.

Make a well in the flour and add half the chilled water. Beat with your fingers until it is creamy.

Add the rest of the water and flour and form into a ball. Knead lightly and chill for 30 minutes.

  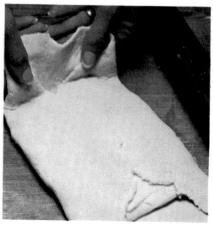

Work the fat until it is spreadable. Spread out carefully on greaseproof or waxed paper to make a large rectangle.

Unwrap the chilled dough and roll out on a floured surface to a large circle. Peel off paper from the fat and put in the centre of the dough circle.

Lift the short edges over and press the same way. You will now have a rectangle of dough. Push it into shape with a knife, if necessary.

Turn the rectangle so that the long sides face you. Rolling in one direction, lightly roll out until the dough is twice its size. Rest.

Fold again, then rest for 15 minutes. Unwrap the dough—the fold should be on your left, the longest sealed edge on the right. Roll, fold and rest.

Repeat this operation until the dough has been rolled and rested six times. Wrap and chill for about 2 hours before using.

3. Puff Pastry

This is considered to be the queen of all pastries. It is the best in flavour and texture and generally only the finest ingredients should be used. Use best quality flour and unsalted butter. Add a squeeze of lemon juice to the iced water, to help counteract the greasiness of the butter. Uncooked pastry dough can be stored in the refrigerator for 3 days or deep frozen for up to 3 months. The object is to produce thin layers of dough interspersed with thin layers of butter. Puff pastry is used for sweet or savoury bouchées (mouthfuls), vol-au-vents (pastry cases shaped into an oval, square or round and filled with a savoury mixture in a creamy sauce), and little savouries such as Portuguese Shrimp Rissoles which are deep fried.

	Metric/UK	US
Flour	450g/1lb	4 cups
Salt	½ tsp	½ tsp
Butter	450g/1lb	2 cups
Iced water with lemon juice added	250ml/8floz	1 cup

Sift the flour and salt into a large mixing bowl. With a table knife cut 100g/4oz (½ cup) of the butter into the flour. Quickly rub it into the flour with your fingertips and add enough of the iced water to make a firm dough. Form the dough into a ball and chill for 15 minutes. Form the remaining butter into a flat oblong slab about 2cm/¾in thick. The easiest way is to put it between two sheets of greaseproof or waxed paper and beat it with the back of a wooden spoon or a wooden mallet. The consistency of the butter and the dough should be as nearly the same as possible—that is, they should be pliable but not sticky.

Roll out the dough into a rectangle about 5mm/¼in thick. Place the slab of butter in the centre and fold the dough over to make a neat parcel. Keep the corners pulled out and squared. Chill for 10 minutes. Place the dough, folds down, on a floured board and roll out gently into a rectangle. Pull the corners square and fold into three. Chill again. Roll out and fold. Chill for 15 minutes. Repeat this twice more. Chill for a final 15 minutes.

The dough is now ready for use.

A classic example of a raised pie is Melton Mowbray Pie. The dough is hot water crust, one of the easier pastries to make.

4. Rough Puff Pastry

This rich pastry is easy to make, but does not rise so well as puff pastry. It is mainly used for pie crusts and turnovers. It is particularly good for meat pies.

	Metric/UK	US
Flour	225g/8oz	2 cups
Salt	$\frac{1}{2}$ tsp	$\frac{1}{2}$ tsp
Butter or half butter/half other fat	175g/6oz	$\frac{3}{4}$ cup
Iced water	4–6 Tbsp	4–6 Tbsp

Sift the flour and salt into a medium-sized mixing bowl. Add the butter, cut into walnut-sized pieces. Pour in 4 tablespoons of the iced water and quickly mix to a dough with a knife. It will be lumpy at this point. Add a little more water if the dough looks too dry.

Shape into a ball and place on a lightly floured board. Roll out into an oblong. Pull the corners square. Fold the dough in three, turning it so that the open end faces you.

Roll out again to an oblong shape, pull the corners and fold again in three. Repeat this once more, then chill for 30 minutes. If the dough looks streaky, repeat the rolling and folding once more. The dough is now ready to use.

5. Flaky Pastry

A light, butter pastry used for mincemeat or fruit pies.

	Metric/UK	US
Flour	175g/6oz	$1\frac{1}{2}$ cups
Salt	$\frac{1}{4}$ tsp	$\frac{1}{4}$ tsp
Butter	50g/2oz	$\frac{1}{4}$ cup
Cold water	3–4 Tbsp	3–4 Tbsp
Lard	50g/2oz	$\frac{1}{4}$ cup

Sift the flour and salt into a mixing bowl. Divide the butter into two equal pieces and add one piece to the flour. Rub it into the flour until it resembles fine

Step-by-Step to Hot Water Crust Pie

To make the case for a raised pie, warm hot water crust pastry is moulded around the outside of a greased storage jar until 1cm/½in thick.

Now support the dough case with greaseproof or waxed paper and place on a baking sheet. The filling should be added now.

Finally, dampen the edges of the case, put the dough lid on top and very carefully crimp the edges to seal in the filling.

breadcrumbs. With a spatula, mix in the water to form a firm dough.

Put the dough on a floured board and shape it into a square. Roll it out into an oblong and dot two thirds of it with small pieces of half the lard. Fold over one third of the dough, then the other third, to make a neat parcel. Press the edges gently with a rolling pin to seal them.

Turn the dough round so the sealed ends face you, and roll out again into an oblong. Dot with pieces of the remaining lard, fold in three, seal the edges, turn the dough and roll out as before.

Repeat this process with the remaining butter. Chill for 10 minutes before using.

6. Suetcrust Pastry

This is simple to make and can be used for sweet or savoury dishes, baked or steamed. It can also be made into balls and cooked in stock to make dumplings.

Suet is the fat found around the kidneys of sheep and bullocks. If you buy fresh suet, discard the membranes and fibres, then chop or mince (grind) very finely. Commercially prepared suet, which is ready shredded, can be easily bought.

	Metric/UK	US
Flour	225g/8oz	2 cups
Salt	½ tsp	½ tsp
Shredded suet	100g/4oz	½ cup
Cold water	150ml/5floz	⅔ cup

Sift the flour and salt into a mixing bowl. Use a table knife to stir in the suet and water, mixing to form a firm dough. Chill for 10 minutes. The dough is now ready to use.

7. Hot Water Crust Pastry

This is the traditional pastry used for raised pies such as pork, veal, ham, and game.

	Metric/UK	US
Flour	350g/12oz	3 cups
Salt	1 tsp	1 tsp
Water	150ml/5floz	⅔ cup
Vegetable fat (shortening) or lard	100g/4oz	½ cup
Egg yolk, lightly beaten	1	1

Sift the flour and salt into a large mixing bowl. Bring the water and fat to the boil over a high heat, stirring until the fat has melted. Remove the pan from the heat. The pastry must be made quickly before the fat can solidify. Pour in the egg yolk and the water and fat mixture. Gradually draw the flour into the liquids with a wooden spoon to form a dough. Knead well on a lightly floured board until smooth and shiny. Roll to shape and use at once.

8. Choux Pastry

This is a delicious light pastry which is used in cream puffs, éclairs, profiteroles and savoury cheese recipes. It can also be used for more elaborate dishes such as Gâteau St. Honoré. It is named 'choux'—the French for cabbage—because it puffs up during baking into a cabbage shape.

	Metric/UK	US
Water	300ml/ ½ pint	1¼ cups
Butter, cut into small pieces	75g/3oz	6 Tbsp
Salt	1 tsp	1 tsp
Flour	275g/10oz	2½ cups
Large eggs	5	5

In a large heavy saucepan, bring the water to the boil. Add the butter and salt. Sift the flour on to a sheet of greaseproof or waxed paper or foil. When the butter has melted, remove the pan from the heat and shoot in the flour at once. Beat until the paste is smooth and pulls away from the sides of the pan. Add the eggs, one by one, beating after each addition until the mixture is thick and glossy. Do not overbeat. Use while still warm.

Choux Puffs (see the recipe on page 212) is easy to make once you have mastered the techniques of making choux pastry. Serve as a dessert or snack.

9. Strudel Pastry

This dough requires careful handling and should be rolled and pulled until it is transparently thin. The dough does not keep well, so make it up just before you use it. Strudel pastry can be filled with sweet fillings such as mincemeat, apple, dried fruit or chocolate, or with savoury fillings such as minced (ground) beef or liver pâté. You can make one large strudel to cut up into small pieces, pull it into horseshoe shape or make up small individual shapes for snacks or desserts.

	Metric/UK	US
Flour	275g/10oz	2½ cups
Salt	½ tsp	½ tsp
Egg, lightly beaten	1	1
Tepid water	200ml/7floz	Scant 1 cup
Unsalted butter, melted	25g/1oz	2 Tbsp

Sift the flour and salt into a large mixing bowl. Mix the egg, water and butter in a small mixing bowl. With a wooden spoon, stir the egg mixture into the flour and mix well. Knead well until a firm dough is formed and continue kneading for about 10 minutes, or until smooth and elastic. Place in a large, warm mixing bowl. Cover the bowl and set aside to rest for about 30 minutes.

Spread out a large clean cloth on a table or work surface. Sprinkle with a little flour. Place the dough on the cloth and roll out as thinly as possible. With the back of your hands, lift and stretch the dough, trying not to tear it. Trim the outer edges with scissors to neaten them. Fill as required.

French Pastry (Pâte)

The French use similar ingredients in their pastry but it is mixed by a different method. The flour is sifted on to a flat floured surface and the butter (in rough cubes), egg yolks and sugar, if used, are placed in a well in the centre. The sugar can be icing (confectioner's), which gives a very soft dough, or castor (superfine). Use the fingertips of one hand to mix the egg, butter and sugar. Gradually incorporate the flour. As soon as the flour has all been worked in, clean your fingers, then knead the dough lightly with the heel of your hand. Do not overmix or the dough will become sticky. Form the mixture into a ball and chill in the refrigerator for about 1 hour before rolling out and using.

Step-by-Step to Strudel Pastry

To make Apfelstrudel, roll out strudel dough as thinly as possible on a cloth sprinkled with flour.

Using the backs of your hands, pull the dough until it stretches over the table and is wafer thin.

Brush the stretched dough with melted butter and cover generously with dry breadcrumbs.

Place the sliced apples on the edge nearest to you, about 7.5cm/3in from the edge.

Lift the cloth and use it to roll the dough over the filling. Continue rolling until all dough is rolled.

Brush the top of the roll with melted butter and sprinkle with breadcrumbs before cutting and cooking.

The best known pâtes are:

1. Pâte sucrée

A rich, sweet pastry. Use in place of Shortcrust Pastry with sweet fillings, for a melting pastry dessert.

	Metric/UK	US
Flour	175g/6oz	1½ cups
Butter, at room temperature	75g/3oz	6 Tbsp
Icing (confectioner's) sugar, sifted	75g/3oz	¾ cup
Egg yolks	3	3

Mix as for Basic Pâte.

2. Pâte brisée

Similar to shortcrust pastry. The proportions of fat to flour are the same, but the method of mixing, with the addition of an egg, is as for Basic Pâte.

3. Pâte à pâté

An excellent rich crust for Pâté en Croûte, such as veal and pork in pastry.

	Metric/UK	US
Flour	350g/12oz	3 cups
Salt	½ tsp	½ tsp
Egg yolks, lightly beaten	2	2
Water	4–5 Tbsp	4–5 Tbsp

Mix as for Basic Pâte.

Preparing a Flan Dish

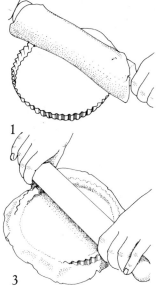
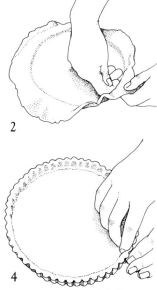

Roll out the dough 4cm/ 1½in larger than the ring. Put the ring on a baking sheet. (1) Lift the dough and centre over the ring. Unroll into the ring and ease into place. (2) Press gently into shape, making sure it fits round the bottom edge. (3) Bend surplus over rim and remove with the rolling pin. (4)

Biscuit (Crumb) Crust

A popular and delicious alternative to a shortcrust pastry case is one made from biscuit (cookie or graham cracker) crumbs. This is used for sweet dishes only, such as cheesecake and chiffon desserts, and it provides an interesting flavour and crunchy contrast to creamy fillings. Use digestive (graham crackers) or shortbread biscuits (cookies) which have a coarse crumbly texture. Crush them between two sheets of greaseproof or waxed paper or in a polythene (plastic) bag, using a rolling pin.

	Metric/UK	US
Digestive biscuits (cookies or graham crackers), crushed	175g/6oz	2¼ cups
Sugar	2 Tbsp	2 Tbsp
Butter, melted	75g/3oz	6 Tbsp

Preheat the oven to moderate (180°C/350°F, Gas Mark 4). Sift the crushed biscuits (cookies or crackers) through a coarse strainer into a mixing bowl. Add the sugar and melted butter and stir until well mixed. Scatter over the bottom of a greased 23cm/9in flan tin or cake pan with a removable bottom and press down with the back of a spoon. Coat the sides with crumbs and press flat and smooth. Bake for 10 minutes, then allow to cool. Remove from the tin or pan and place on a flat serving dish. Fill.

TECHNIQUES OF USING PASTRY

Lining a pie plate for an open pie

Roll out the dough to 5mm/¼in thick, and 10cm/4in wider than the plate (pan). Lift the dough on the rolling pin and cover the bottom and sides of the plate (pan). Trim with a knife to 1cm/½in from the plate (pan) edge and fold the dough under the rim. Decorate the edge by pressing down along the rim with your thumb.

Covering a (deep) pie dish

Roll out the dough evenly to about 5mm/¼in thick, and 10cm/4in wider than the dish. Cut a 2.5cm/1in wide strip from the outer edge of the dough, place it on the moistened rim of the dish and seal the ends together with a little water. Fill the pie dish to just below the rim, place a funnel in the centre, and lift the dough over the dish with the rolling pin, taking care not to stretch it. Press the lid to the rim and cut off any excess dough.

Preparing a double crust pie

Divide the dough into two portions, one slightly larger than the other. Roll out the larger portion to a little less than 5mm/¼in thick, and about 2.5cm/1in wider than the top of the pie dish (pan). Lift the dough over the pie dish (pan) with the rolling pin and press it into the dish (pan) without stretching the dough. Trim off excess with a knife. Put the prepared filling into the dish (pan), making a slight mound in the centre.

Roll out the smaller portion of dough to about 1cm/½in larger than the top of the pie dish (pan). Brush the rim of the lining with water, place the dough lid over the filling, trim the edges and knock up (flute). Another method is to trim the top crust to within 5mm/¼in of the dish (pan) and tuck the overhang under the edge of the bottom crust. Make a slit in the centre of the dough to allow steam to escape during cooking.

Knocking up (Fluting)

This prevents the edges of the double crust pies from coming apart during cooking. Make a series of shallow parallel cuts, at right angles to the edge, with the back of a knife in the dough edges or press with the prongs of a fork; or crimp the pastry with the thumb and forefinger. You can also decorate the edges of a pastry cover for an unlined pie, with cuts, indentations or crimping.

Making a raised pie

A hinged pie mould can be used, but you can manage without. To make a raised pie to contain pork, veal, ham or game, mould the freshly-made dough over the outside of a lightly greased glass storage jar turned upside down. This makes the pie case. Turn over, tie a band of greaseproof or waxed paper or foil round the dough to support it, remove the jar, and put the case on a baking sheet. Spoon in the prepared filling, dampen the edges of the case, fit a round dough lid on top to cover completely, and crimp to seal the edges.

Baking blind

Cooking dough before it is filled is known as baking blind. Flan cases and tartlets are often cooked in this way.

Preheat the oven to fairly hot (200°C/400°F, Gas Mark 6). Roll out the dough to a circle about 5mm/¼in thick. Carefully lift the dough on the rolling pin and lay over a 23cm/9in flan ring or flan tin on a baking sheet or a pie pan. Ease the dough down and press against the edges of the tin, ring or pan. Trim any overhanging edges with a knife. Prick the pastry base with a fork. Line with foil or greaseproof or waxed paper and weigh this down with dried beans or rice. Place in the oven and bake for 10 minutes. Remove the foil or paper and beans and continue baking for 5 minutes until the pastry is golden brown. Remove from the oven and allow to cool. It can now be filled.

Glazing

A glaze is brushed on dough before baking to give it a good finish. Beaten egg yolk, lightly beaten egg white, egg white and sugar, whole beaten egg, milk, milk and sugar, or cream can be used. Egg yolk gives the shiniest glaze. Sweet pastry can be brushed with water and then sprinkled with sugar for a pretty sparkling finish.

Asparagus Quiche (see recipe on page 207) is made from shortcrust pastry. It can be served either hot or cold.

RECIPES

Beef Steak and Kidney Pudding

	Metric/UK	US
Suetcrust Pastry Dough (double the basic recipe quantities)	450g/1lb	4 cups
FILLING		
Braising (chuck) steak, cut into small cubes	700g/1½lb	1½lb
Ox (beef) kidney, cut into small pieces	225g/8oz	½lb
Flour	2 Tbsp	2 Tbsp
Salt	¼ tsp	¼ tsp
Black pepper	⅛ tsp	⅛ tsp
Chopped fresh mixed herbs	2 tsp	2 tsp

Roll out the dough to a large round, 1cm/½in thick. Cut a large wedge-shaped piece out of the round and reserve it. Line a 1.5L/2½–3 pint pudding basin (3½–4 pint steaming mold) with the large piece of dough. Dampen the cut edges and bring them together. Press the dough to the shape of the basin (mold). Trim the top edge.

Fill a large saucepan with water and bring to a boil. Meanwhile, toss the steak and kidney pieces in flour, salt, pepper and mixed herbs. Put the meat in the lined basin (mold) and fill up to two-thirds full with cold water. Knead the reserved piece of dough and the trimmings together and roll out into a round to fit the top of the basin (mold). Dampen the edges of the dough and place on top of the meat. Press together to seal. Cover with greased foil or a cloth, loosely, to allow for expansion. Tie a piece of string under the rim of the basin (mold) leaving a loop to make it easier to remove.

Put into the boiling water, making sure that the water does not reach the top of the basin (mold), and cover. Steam for 3 hours, adding more water if necessary. Remove the foil or cloth before serving. Serve steaming hot.

6 servings

Veal and Ham Pie

	Metric/UK	US
Hot Water Crust Pastry dough	350g/12oz	3 cups
Egg, lightly beaten	1	1

Economical and filling– Beef Steak and Kidney Pudding is made from suet crust pastry and a beef and kidney filling.

FILLING

	Metric/UK	US
Fillet (tenderloin) of veal, cut into 1cm/½in cubes	1kg/2lb	2lb
Lean cooked ham, cut into cubes	225g/8oz	1⅓ cups
Salt	½ tsp	½ tsp
Black pepper	½ tsp	½ tsp
Dry mustard	¼ tsp	¼ tsp
Hard-boiled (hard-cooked) eggs	2	2
Gelatine (gelatin)	7g/¼oz	½ envelope
Veal or chicken stock	175ml/6floz	¾ cup

Grease a 23cm/9in oval hinged mould (or use a glass storage jar, see page 199). Dust with flour, shaking off the excess. Cut off one third of the dough and keep warm. Roll out the remainder into a large oval to fit the bottom and sides of the mould. Line the mould and chill for 30 minutes on a baking sheet. Preheat the oven to fairly hot (200°C/400°F, Gas Mark 6).

In a large bowl, combine the veal, ham, salt, pepper and mustard with a fork. Spoon half the meat filling into the dough case. Put in the eggs and cover with the remainder of the meat mixture. Roll out the remaining dough to make a lid. Place on top of the pie. Trim to fit, dampen the edges and seal by crimping with your fingers.

Brush beaten egg over the top of the pie. Cut a slit in the centre of the lid. Bake for 30 minutes. Reduce the heat to moderate (180°C/350°F, Gas Mark 4).

Heat the gelatine (gelatin) and stock in a small saucepan until the gelatine (gelatin) has dissolved. Remove the pie from the oven. Pour the stock mixture through the slit into the pie filling. Return to the oven and bake for a further 1½ hours or until the meat is tender. Leave to cool for at least 4 hours. Serve at room temperature.

4–6 servings

Cheese Straws

	Metric/UK	US
Flour	100g/4oz	1 cup
Salt	¼ tsp	¼ tsp
Cayenne pepper	⅛ tsp	⅛ tsp
Unsalted butter, cut into small pieces	75g/3oz	6 Tbsp
Cheddar cheese, grated	25g/1oz	¼ cup
Egg yolk, lightly beaten	1	1
Iced water	1 Tbsp	1 Tbsp

Sift the flour, salt and cayenne into a mixing bowl. Rub in the fat. Stir in the grated cheese. Mix to a smooth dough with the beaten egg and water. Chill for 1 hour.

Preheat the oven to fairly hot (200°C/400°F, Gas Mark 6). Roll out the dough to a rectangle about 5mm/¼in thick. Cut into strips 5cm x 5mm/2 x ¼in. Arrange on an ungreased baking sheet and bake in the centre of the oven for about 15 minutes or until golden brown. Cool.

About 30 straws

Portuguese Shrimp Rissoles

	Metric/UK	US
Puff pastry dough (half original quantity), chilled	225g/8oz	2 cups
FILLING		
Shrimps, shelled and chopped	½kg/1lb	1lb
Hard-boiled (hard-cooked) egg, finely chopped	1	1
Béchamel Sauce	175ml/6floz	¾ cup

Vol-au-vent d'Eté is a puff pastry case filled with eggs, walnuts and cream, bound with béchamel.

	Metric/UK	US
Cayenne pepper	⅛ tsp	⅛ tsp
Paprika	1 Tbsp	1 Tbsp
Salt	¼ tsp	¼ tsp
Chopped parsley	1 Tbsp	1 Tbsp
Oil for deep frying		

Roll out the dough to an oblong about 5mm/¼in thick. Using a sharp knife cut it into 7.5cm/3in squares. Combine the filling ingredients thoroughly in a large bowl. Place a teaspoon of the filling on each square. Moisten the edges with a little water and fold over to make a triangle. Press the edges firmly together to seal.

Heat the oil to 180°C/350°F on a deep fat thermometer. With a slotted spoon, lower 4 or 5 rissoles into the hot oil. Fry for 2 minutes or until puffed up and golden brown. Remove with a slotted spoon. Drain on kitchen paper towels. Serve hot.

About 30 rissoles

Vol-au-vent d'Ete (Puff Pastry Case with Lettuce and Egg)

This basic vol-au-vent case can be used for many other varieties of filling.

	Metric/UK	US
Puff Pastry dough, chilled	450g/1lb	4 cups

	Metric/UK	US
Egg, beaten	1	1
Butter	25g/1oz	2 Tbsp
Lettuces, shredded	2	2
Salt	$\frac{1}{2}$ tsp	$\frac{1}{2}$ tsp
Black pepper	$\frac{1}{2}$ tsp	$\frac{1}{2}$ tsp
Sugar	1 tsp	1 tsp
Fresh white breadcrumbs	3 Tbsp	3 Tbsp
Béchamel Sauce	250ml/8floz	1 cup
Hard-boiled (hard-cooked) eggs, sliced	6	6
Walnuts, coarsely chopped	175g/6oz	$1\frac{1}{2}$ cups
Double (heavy) cream	125ml/4floz	$\frac{1}{2}$ cup
Grated nutmeg	$\frac{1}{2}$ tsp	$\frac{1}{2}$ tsp

To make the vol-au-vent case: divide the dough in half and roll out two equal-sized ovals. Place one on a baking sheet. Cut a smaller oval from the second oval, this forms the lid. Dampen the bottom of the oval ring with water. Place it on top of the large base oval on the baking sheet to form the case. Press together. Flake up the sides of the case with a knife to help the pastry rise. With a sharp knife, make a criss-cross pattern across the tops of both the case and the lid. Place them in the refrigerator to chill for 30 minutes.

Preheat the oven to very hot (240°C/475°F, Gas Mark 9). Paint the tops of the case and lid with lightly beaten egg, avoiding sealing the cut sides, as they will not rise.

Bake both case and lid for 20 minutes. Remove the lid from the oven and transfer to a wire rack to cool.

Reduce the oven to moderate (180°C/350°F, Gas Mark 4). Discard any soft dough from the centre of the case. Return to the oven and continue baking for about 30 minutes or until crisp and golden brown. Allow to cool on a wire rack.

In a medium-sized saucepan, melt the butter over a moderate heat. Add the lettuces, cover and simmer for 10 minutes. Add the salt, pepper and sugar. Remove from the heat and strain. Discard the liquid. Return the lettuce to the pan. Add the breadcrumbs and stir well. Add the Béchamel Sauce, eggs, walnuts, cream and nutmeg. Stir gently. Pile into the vol-au-vent shell. Bake in the preheated moderate oven for 5-7 minutes or until heated through. Serve hot.

4-6 servings

Asparagus Quiche

	Metric/UK	US
1 x 23cm/9in uncooked flan case (pastry shell) made with Shortcrust Pastry		
FILLING		
Lean cooked ham, chopped	175g/6oz	1 cup
Single (light) cream	125ml/4floz	$\frac{1}{2}$ cup
Milk	75ml/3floz	$\frac{1}{3}$ cup
Eggs	3	3
Cheddar cheese, grated	25g/1oz	$\frac{1}{4}$ cup
Salt	$\frac{1}{4}$ tsp	$\frac{1}{4}$ tsp
White pepper	$\frac{1}{2}$ tsp	$\frac{1}{2}$ tsp
Asparagus tips, cooked and drained	12	12

Preheat the oven to fairly hot (200°C/400°F, Gas Mark 6). Cover the bottom of the flan case (pastry shell) with ham. Set aside. In a mixing bowl, combine the cream, milk, eggs, grated cheese, salt and pepper. Beat well. Pour the mixture over the ham. Arrange the asparagus tips on top like the spokes of a wheel, tips to the centre. Bake in the centre of the oven for 35-40 minutes or until set and golden brown. Serve hot or cold.

4-6 servings

Rhubarb Flan

	Metric/UK	US
Sugar	100g/4oz	$\frac{1}{2}$ cup
Water	250ml/8floz	1 cup
Fresh rhubarb, cut into 5cm/2in lengths	$\frac{1}{2}$kg/1lb	1lb
Ground cinnamon	$\frac{1}{2}$ tsp	$\frac{1}{2}$ tsp
Rich Shortcrust Pastry dough	225g/8oz	2 cups
Egg, lightly beaten, to glaze	1	1

In a medium-sized saucepan, dissolve the sugar in the water over a low heat. Bring to a boil. Add the rhubarb and cinnamon and bring back to the boil. Reduce the heat to moderate and simmer for 20-25 minutes until the rhubarb is tender. Remove from the heat and allow to cool. Preheat the oven to moderate (180°C/350°F, Gas Mark 4).

Roll out two-thirds of the dough into a round 5mm/$\frac{1}{4}$in thick. Ease it into a 23cm/9in flan ring or pie pan and trim with a sharp knife. Fill the case with the rhubarb mixture and smooth flat with a spatula. Roll out the remaining dough into a rectangle 5mm/$\frac{1}{4}$in thick. Cut it into 8 strips 1cm/$\frac{1}{2}$in wide. Lay over the filling to form a lattice. Glaze the dough with the beaten egg. Bake for 40 minutes or until golden brown.

6 servings

Spotted Dick

	Metric/UK	US
Flour	225g/8oz	2 cups
Salt	1 tsp	1 tsp
Sugar	2 Tbsp	2 Tbsp
Baking powder	2 tsp	2 tsp
Ground cloves	$\frac{1}{8}$ tsp	$\frac{1}{8}$ tsp
Shredded suet	75g/3oz	$\frac{1}{3}$ cup
Currants	100g/4oz	$\frac{2}{3}$ cup

	Metric/UK	US
Sultanas or raisins	50g/2oz	⅓ cup
Water	6 Tbsp	6 Tbsp
Strawberry jam	6 Tbsp	6 Tbsp
Milk	3 Tbsp	3 Tbsp

Sift the flour, salt, sugar, baking powder and cloves into a large mixing bowl. Stir in the suet, currants, sultanas or raisins, and water, mixing to a smooth, pliable dough. Add more water if the dough is too stiff.

Roll out the dough to a rectangle 5mm/¼in thick. Spread the jam over the surface, leaving a margin around the edge. Brush the edges with the milk. Roll up the dough, Swiss (jelly)-roll style, pressing the edges together to seal. Wrap the roll loosely in foil or cheesecloth, making a pleat to allow for expansion.

Half fill a large saucepan or steamer with water. Place over a high heat and bring to the boil. Put the pudding on a trivet or the top of the steamer, cover and

Below: A Cheesecake, with cream cheese filling.
Right: Normandy Pear Tart.

place over the water. Reduce the heat to moderate. Steam for 2½ hours, adding more water if necessary.

Unwrap the pudding and transfer to a warmed serving dish. Serve hot.

6–8 servings

Cheesecake

	Metric/UK	US
1 basic quantity of Biscuit (Crumb) Crust		
FILLING		
Full fat cream cheese	700g/1½lb	3 cups
Castor (superfine) sugar	75g/3oz plus 2 tsp	⅓ cup plus 2 tsp
Eggs, separated	3	3
Cornflour (cornstarch)	1 Tbsp	1 Tbsp
Lemon juice	2 Tbsp	2 Tbsp
Grated lemon rind	1 tsp	1 tsp
Currants	50g/2oz	⅓ cup
Glacé (candied) cherries, chopped	40g/1½oz	¼ cup

Sour cream	150ml/5floz	$\frac{2}{3}$ cup
Vanilla essence (extract)	$\frac{1}{2}$ tsp	$\frac{1}{2}$ tsp

Preheat the oven to moderate (180°C/350°F, Gas Mark 4). Press the crumb mixture into the bottom only of a 23cm/9in loose-bottomed cake pan. Set aside.

In a large mixing bowl, combine the cream cheese and the 75g/3oz ($\frac{1}{3}$ cup) of sugar with a wooden spoon. Add the egg yolks and beat until smooth. Mix together the cornflour (cornstarch) and lemon juice. Stir the lemon rind, currants, glacé (candied) cherries and cornflour (cornstarch) mixture into the cream cheese mixture.

In another bowl, beat the egg whites until stiff. With a metal spoon, fold the egg whites into the cheese mixture. Spoon into the prepared pan and bake for 30 minutes or until the centre is firm when pressed.

Combine the sour cream, remaining sugar and the vanilla and beat well. Remove the pan from the oven and spread the sour cream mixture over the top. Return to the oven and bake for 5 minutes. Cool, then remove from the pan and chill before serving.

6 servings

Normandy Pear Tart

	Metric/UK	US
Rich Shortcrust Pastry dough	225g/8oz	2 cups
Walnuts, finely chopped	40g/1$\frac{1}{2}$oz	$\frac{1}{3}$ cup
FILLING		
Sugar	50g/2oz	$\frac{1}{4}$ cup
Water	150ml/5floz	$\frac{2}{3}$ cup
Large pears, peeled, halved and cored	4	4
GLAZE		
Egg white, beaten	1	1
Sugar	2 Tbsp	2 Tbsp
TO DECORATE		
Double (heavy) cream, stiffly whipped	150ml/5floz	$\frac{2}{3}$ cup
Chopped walnuts	2 Tbsp	2 Tbsp

Prepare the dough, adding the walnuts with the dry ingredients, and chill. In a medium-sized saucepan dissolve the sugar in the water. Add the pears and cook for 15 minutes or until tender. Set aside to cool. Preheat the oven to fairly hot (190°C/375°F, Gas Mark 5).

Roll out two thirds of the dough into a round and use to line a 23cm/9in flan ring or loose-bottomed pie pan. Remove the pears from the syrup with a slotted spoon and arrange them, pointed ends to the centre and cut sides down, in the pastry case. Dampen the edges of the

209

dough. Roll out the remainder of the dough to a round large enough to make a lid for the tart. Use a pastry cutter 7.5cm/3in in diameter to cut out a hole in the centre. Lay the lid on top of the pears and gently press the edges together. Trim off any excess. Brush the top with the egg white and dust with the sugar. Bake for 30–35 minutes or until golden and firm. Remove from the flan ring or pan. Spoon the whipped cream into the centre of the tart and sprinkle over the chopped walnuts. Serve at once.

6 servings

American Apple Pie, with a shortcrust pastry with cream added. Serve hot and crisp with vanilla ice–cream for a truly superb dessert.

American Apple Pie

	Metric/UK	US
PASTRY		
Flour	275g/10oz	$2\frac{1}{2}$ cups
Salt	$\frac{1}{4}$ tsp	$\frac{1}{4}$ tsp
Vegetable fat (shortening) or lard	100g/4oz	$\frac{1}{2}$ cup
Margarine or butter	50g/2oz	$\frac{1}{4}$ cup
Iced water	6 Tbsp	6 Tbsp
Single (light) cream, to glaze	1 Tbsp	1 Tbsp
FILLING		
Sugar	175g/6oz	$\frac{3}{4}$ cup
Ground cinnamon	1 tsp	1 tsp
Ground allspice	$\frac{1}{4}$ tsp	$\frac{1}{4}$ tsp
Grated nutmeg	$\frac{1}{4}$ tsp	$\frac{1}{4}$ tsp
Cornflour (cornstarch)	1 Tbsp	1 Tbsp
Cooking apples, peeled, cored and thickly sliced	1kg/2lb	2lb
Lemon juice	1 Tbsp	1 Tbsp
Butter, cut into small pieces	25g/1oz	2 Tbsp

This is a shortcrust pastry with a greater proportion of fat. The method of preparation is the same as for Basic Shortcrust Pastry. Prepare the dough and chill for 30 minutes.

Grease the bottom and sides of a deep 23cm/9in pie dish (pan). Divide the dough into two portions, one slightly larger than the other. Roll out the larger portion of dough into a round big enough to line the pie dish (pan). Lift it carefully into position and trim off the excess dough with a knife. Preheat the oven to fairly hot (190°C/375°F, Gas Mark 5).

Mix together the sugar, spices and cornflour (cornstarch) in a large bowl. Add the apple slices and lemon juice and toss thoroughly until well coated. Fill the pie with the apple mixture, doming it in the centre. Dot with the butter. Roll out the remaining dough to about 30cm/12in in diameter and lift it on top of the pie. Trim the edges and knock up (flute). Brush with the cream. Make two small cuts in the centre to allow steam to escape, then bake in the oven for 40 minutes or until golden brown. Dust with sugar, and serve hot.

6 servings

Apfelstrudel

	Metric/UK	US
Strudel Pastry dough	275g/10oz	2½ cups
FILLING		
Cooking apples, peeled, cored and thinly sliced	1.35kg/3lb	3lb
Sugar	100g/4oz	½ cup
Ground cinnamon	1 tsp	1 tsp
Raisins	75g/3oz	½ cup
Almonds or walnuts, chopped	75g/3oz	¾ cup
Grated rind of 1 lemon		
Butter, melted	100g/4oz	½ cup
Dry white breadcrumbs	50g/2oz	½ cup

In a large mixing bowl, combine the apples, sugar, cinnamon, raisins, nuts and lemon rind. Preheat the oven to hot (230°C/450°F, Gas Mark 8).

Roll out the dough very thinly on a cloth. Brush the dough with half of the melted butter. Sprinkle with nearly all the breadcrumbs, and spoon the apple mixture in a long strip, 7.5cm/3in away from the nearest edge. Using the cloth, lift the dough over the filling and roll it up like a Swiss (jelly) roll, tucking in the ends. Brush with the remaining melted butter and sprinkle on the remaining breadcrumbs. Cut the roll into slices. Divide the strudel between two greased baking sheets, keeping the seams underneath. Bake for 10 minutes, then reduce the heat to fairly hot (200°C/400°F, Gas Mark 6). Continue baking for 20 minutes or until golden brown.
About 10 strudels

Quince and Apple Turnovers

	Metric/UK	US
Rough Puff Pastry dough, chilled	225g/8oz	2 cups
FILLING		
Cooking apples, peeled, cored and sliced	350g/12oz	¾lb
Small quince, peeled, cored and thinly sliced	1	1
Butter	1 Tbsp	1 Tbsp
Apricot jam	1 Tbsp	1 Tbsp
Currants	1 Tbsp	1 Tbsp
Ground cloves	¼ tsp	¼ tsp
Soft brown sugar	50g/2oz	⅓ cup
GLAZE		
Egg	1	1
Sugar	1 tsp	1 tsp

Place the apples and quince in a medium-sized sauce-

Delicate Quince and Apple Turnovers are made with a covering of springy, melting rough puff pastry.

pan. Cover with water and bring to the boil. Add the butter, jam, currants, cloves and sugar, and stir until the sugar has dissolved. Reduce the heat to low and simmer for 20–30 minutes or until the fruit has become a pulp. Set aside to cool.

Preheat the oven to hot (220°C/425°F, Gas Mark 7). Roll out the dough into a square about 5mm/¼in thick. With a table knife, cut the dough into 10 squares. Place 2 teaspoons of the filling on each dough square. Fold each one over to form a triangle and press the edges together to seal them.

Place the triangles on the baking sheet. Make a small hole in the centre of each one to let out the steam, and brush with the egg beaten with the sugar to glaze. Place in the oven and bake for 20–30 minutes or until the pastry is puffed up and golden brown. Place on a wire rack to cool.
10 turnovers

Choux Puffs

	Metric/UK	US
Choux Pastry (paste) dough	275g/10oz	2½ cups
Egg	1	1
Water	½ tsp	½ tsp

Preheat the oven to hot (220°C/425°F, Gas Mark 7). Fit a forcing (pastry) bag with a 5mm/¼in nozzle for small puffs and a 1cm/½in nozzle for large puffs and fill with the pastry dough. Pipe out into round mounds of equal size, leaving a good space around each one to

allow for expansion, on a greased baking sheet. Beat the egg lightly with the water. Brush with beaten egg.

Bake in the centre of the oven for 10 minutes, then reduce the heat to fairly hot (190°C/375°F, Gas Mark 5) and continue baking for 20–30 minutes or until golden brown and crisp. Remove from the oven and make a small, sharp slit in the side of each puff to allow steam to escape. Return to the turned-off oven for 5 minutes to dry, then cool on a wire rack.

To make sweet Choux Puffs, pipe in whipped cream through the slit when cold, then dust with sugar or top with melted sweet chocolate.
8 large or 16 small puffs

Savoury Choux Puffs

	Metric/UK	US
Choux Pastry (paste) dough	275g/10oz	2½ cups
FILLING		
Cream cheese	225g/8oz	1 cup
Single (light) cream	2 Tbsp	2 Tbsp
Salt	⅛ tsp	⅛ tsp
Black pepper	½ tsp	½ tsp
Lemon juice	1 tsp	1 tsp
Caviare or roe	2 Tbsp	2 Tbsp

Prepare one batch of small Choux Puffs (see previous recipe). Beat all the filling ingredients together thoroughly, then pipe into the slit in the side of each puff.
16 small puffs

Pineapple Flan

	Metric/UK	US
1 x 23cm/9in flan case (pastry shell) made with Rich Shortcrust Pastry, baked blind and cooled		
FILLING		
Canned pineapple syrup	250ml/8floz	1 cup
Fresh pineapple, finely chopped	350g/12oz	2½ cups
Flour	1 tsp	1 tsp
Lemon juice	2 Tbsp	2 Tbsp
Kirsch	2 Tbsp	2 Tbsp
Eggs, lightly beaten	3	3

Preheat the oven to moderate (180°C/350°F, Gas Mark 4). Boil the syrup over a moderate heat for 5 minutes. Add the pineapple, bring to the boil again and cook for 5 minutes. Remove from the heat. Mix the flour and lemon juice to a smooth paste. Beat in the kirsch and eggs, a little at a time. Slowly beat in the hot pineapple mixture. Pour into the flan case (pastry shell). Place in the oven and bake for 20–30 minutes or until set and slightly brown. Serve hot or cold.
4–6 servings

Plum Flan

	Metric/UK	US
1 x 23cm/9in uncooked flan case (pastry shell), made with Rich Shortcrust Pastry		
FILLING		
Plums, halved and stoned (pitted)	1kg/2lb	2lb
Castor (superfine) sugar	175g/6oz	¾ cup
Ground cinnamon	1 tsp	1 tsp
Ground allspice	½ tsp	½ tsp
Slivered (shredded) almonds, toasted	50g/2oz	½ cup

Preheat the oven to fairly hot (200°C/400°F, Gas Mark 6). Arrange the plum halves decoratively, cut sides down, in the flan case (pastry shell) and set aside. In a small bowl, combine the sugar, cinnamon and allspice. Sprinkle evenly over the plums. Place in the oven and bake for 35–40 minutes, or until the pastry is crisp and golden and the plums are tender. Remove from the oven and sprinkle over the almonds. Serve hot.
6 servings

CAKES

*Cake-making is one of the traditional cooking arts
still lovingly practised today. It is an art which can
give endless satisfaction—both to those who make the cakes
and those who eat them! Cakes also freeze well, so
the old 'bake-in' makes sense in a modern context
too, when you can bake one for the pot, and two or
three for the freezer at the same time. Cakes are
versatile, too, ranging from simple plain sponge cakes to
exotic gâteaux, from small individual cakes and
pastries to elaborately iced and filled offerings.*

PARIS
GÂTEAUX.

CAKES

Ingredients

It is important to have all the ingredients at room temperature, so remove fat and eggs from the refrigerator at least 1 hour before starting the preparation. Use soft fine flour, and use self-raising (self-rising) and plain (all-purpose) flours as specified in the recipe. Do not interchange them. If self-raising (self-rising) flour is called for and you only have plain (all-purpose) add baking powder in the proportion of 4 level teaspoons baking powder to 450g/1lb plain flour (4 cups all-purpose flour). Margarine is perfectly satisfactory for cake making, but if you use butter the flavour will be even more delicious. Measure all the ingredients accurately, as this is one area of cooking where exact proportions are extremely important. Flour is sifted before use to remove lumps and aerate it.

Raising (leavening) agents

Cake mixtures are made to rise by incorporating air or gas in the mixture, which expands when heated and raises the cake to the required lightness. When you beat in eggs, you are incorporating air; by using bicarbonate of soda (baking soda) plus an acid such as cream of tartar, or a ready-made combination of the two such as baking powder, or self-raising (self-rising) flour, you produce carbon dioxide. Most mixtures depend partly on air and partly on another raising (leavening) agent to make them light. The batter should not be beaten after the flour is added, or a heavy cake will result.

Folding

This useful technique is a way of combining an aerated mixture with another ingredient without driving the air out by too vigorous mixing. Put the substances to be mixed together in a bowl. The folding motion consists of two steps; first cut across the centre of the mixture with a large metal spoon, then run the spoon around the edge of the bowl, ending with a folding motion towards the centre. Make sure the spoon goes right to the bottom of the bowl. Give the bowl a quarter turn and repeat. Eight or ten folds should be enough. The last bits of the aerated mixture can be broken up and incorporated as you pour the batter into the cake mix.

Preparation of pans

Use the correct size of tin or pan, as specified in the recipe. Never fill it more than two thirds full, or the batter will rise over the sides and make an open-textured cake.

For most cakes it is sufficient to grease the tin or pan carefully with butter or melted lard on the bottom and sides. The easiest way is to melt the fat and grease the tin or pan with a brush. If you miss even a small bit, the cake may stick and break when turned out. Then dust flour all over the inside and tap out the excess. A

Lining a Deep Tin

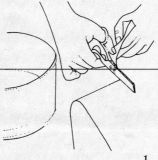
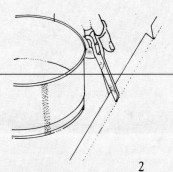
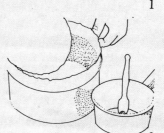

Cut out paper for base, then sides, about 6cm/2½in deeper than the tin. (1) Make a fold along a longer edge and crease. Cut the fold diagonally at 1cm/½in intervals. (2) Grease and arrange the strip on the tin. Add paper and grease again. (3)

rich cake which requires long cooking, or a sponge cake with little fat in it, should be baked in a tin or pan lined with greaseproof or waxed paper or foil, to prevent burning. Cut a disc the exact size of the bottom. To line the sides, cut a strip 1cm/½in wider than the depth of the tin or pan and long enough to go round it. Bend down 1cm/½in along one side and snip regularly. Put the snipped side at the bottom so that the bent edge lies flat on the bottom, and lay the disc over the cut edges.

Baking

Preheat the oven to the required temperature. Place large cakes in the centre of the oven and small cakes nearer the top. Do not open the oven for the first 15 minutes of cooking or the centre of the cake will fall in. Check 5 minutes before the end of cooking time with a skewer inserted into the centre of the cake. If it does not come out clean, then bake for a further 5 minutes, and check again. Alternatively, press the sponge lightly in the centre with the fingertips.

When the cake is ready, remove it from the oven and let it stand for a few minutes to cool. Run a table knife carefully around the edges to loosen it, then turn it out on to a wire cooling rack. Leave the cake to become cold before cutting, filling or icing.

Storing

Cakes are generally at their best when newly baked. However, fruit cakes mature and improve in flavour if left in an airtight container for several weeks. Store sponge cakes or rich cakes in an airtight container for not more than a day or two. Cakes and gâteaux which are filled and decorated with fresh cream should be stored, covered, in the refrigerator.

METHODS OF CAKE-MAKING

1. Rubbing-in method

This method is used for some plainer cakes, scones and biscuits (cookies). The proportion of fat is usually only about quarter to half the quantity of flour. The fat is rubbed into the flour lightly with the fingertips, as in preparing pastry. Add fruit or flavouring then eggs or milk as required.

2. Creaming method

Use a wooden spoon or electric food mixer for this method. Beat the sugar with the margarine or fat until the mixture is light in colour and fluffy in texture. This dissolves the sugar crystals and incorporates air into the mixture. The eggs are lightly beaten in, one by one, then the sifted flour is folded in with a metal spoon. Continue folding until all the flour has been mixed in, but do not overmix or all the air which you have beaten in during the initial stages will be knocked out, giving a heavy, flat cake.

Basic sponge cakes are made by this method. Equal weights of self-raising (self-rising) flour, eggs, castor (superfine) sugar and fat are used. The batter is divided into two sandwich (layer cake pans) tins and the baked cakes are sandwiched together, most simply, with jam.

Endless varieties of this type of cake are possible, using chocolate, coffee, lemon, orange or any chosen flavouring. Sandwich the cakes together with a complementary flavour of buttercream and dust with sifted icing (confectioner's) sugar or cover with glacé icing. The Chocolate Peppermint Cake on page 236 is a good example.

Rich fruit cakes are also made by this method; the

The Creaming Method

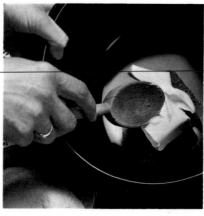

Preheat the oven to moderate (180°C/ 350°F, gas mark 4). Sift icing (confectioners') sugar over two sandwich tins (tart pans).

Sift 175g/6oz (1½ cups) of self-raising flour into a bowl. Cream 175g/6oz (¾ cup) of softened butter in a second bowl until light.

Add 175g/6oz (¾ cup) of castor (superfine) sugar to the fat in the bowl and beat vigorously until the mixture is light and fluffy.

Whisk 3 eggs lightly, then beat them into the mixture, a little at a time with a wooden spoon, beating after each addition.

Using a rubber spatula scrape the mixture down the sides of the bowl and off the spoon. Beat again, then fold in the flour.

Add milk to make a dropping consistency if necessary and divide between the prepared pans (tins). Bake for 25–30 minutes or until cooked.

fruit is added before the flour is folded in. They require long, slow cooking to produce a well risen, firm cake. Cakes made by the creaming method have a firm consistency, so they are ideal for cutting and shaping, as for instance in Battenburg Cake.

3. Melting method

This method makes moist cakes which keep well. Plain (all-purpose) flour is usually used with the addition of bicarbonate of soda (baking soda) or baking powder as the raising (leavening) agent. When bicarbonate of soda (baking soda) is used, often treacle (molasses) or syrup is included in the recipe as it acts as the acid which produces carbon dioxide to raise the cake. Moist brown sugar is preferable to white sugar as it increases the keeping quality and makes the colour richer. Sift the dry ingredients into a large mixing bowl and make a well in the centre. Gently melt the fat with the sugar, syrup and other liquid ingredients. Then stir the liquid into the dry ingredients to make a soft dough.

4. Whisking method

This is the true sponge cake method, depending for lightness on the air beaten in with the eggs, rather than on a raising (leavening) agent. Cakes made by this method need not contain fat. Eggs and castor (superfine) sugar are whisked together, entrapping air in the mixture until they are light, thick and mousse-like. Use a wire whisk or electric mixer to do this. The flour is then lightly folded in with a metal spoon, to prevent the air escaping from the mixture. These cakes have a drier texture and do not keep at all well. However, fat in the form of melted butter or oil can be folded in after preparation to produce a moister, richer sponge known as Genoese Sponge Cake. This is often used as a basis for rich gâteaux.

Basic sponge mixture can be placed in spoonsful on a baking sheet to bake, making delicious little sponge drops to accompany fruit and ice-cream desserts.

Swiss (jelly) rolls are made with a whisked sponge mixture. The baked sponge is spread with filling, then rolled up tightly.

Small cakes

Small cakes can be made in paper cases using the creaming method sponge. They should be neatly and carefully iced and decorated. Genoese Sponge can be made into small rich cakes for icing, by making the sponge in a square or rectangular baking tin or pan and cutting into squares once it has cooled.

Scones (biscuits)

These are a type of small, plain cake made by the rubbing-in method, using flour, a raising (leavening) agent, a very small proportion of fat, and liquid to bind the mixture. They do not keep well, except in a freezer,

and are best eaten freshly baked and still warm.

Drop-scones (griddle scones or pancakes) are made from batter, cooked in small rounds on a hot greased griddle or heavy frying-pan, and eaten hot with butter and maple syrup or jam.

Biscuits (cookies)

Biscuits (cookies) are simple to make, very economical and absolutely delicious. If made from a soft dough, they can be shaped by dropping the mixture in spoonsful on to a baking sheet; these are Dropped Biscuits (Cookies). A stiffer dough can be chilled in the refrigerator and cut into shapes before baking—these are Shaped Biscuits (Cookies). A simple example is Shortbread, which can be cut into fingers with a sharp knife or pressed into a traditional wooden shortbread mould. The dough can also be cut out with a pastry (cookie) cutter into round or any fancy shapes. Piped Biscuits (Cookies) are shaped by squeezing the dough through a large forcing (pastry) bag fitted with a star nozzle. Refrigerator Biscuits (Cookies) are made from a special stiff dough which is shaped into rolls and

The Whisking Method

Preheat the oven and prepare the tins (pans). Sift the flour, baking powder and dry flavourings. Beat eggs.

Add sugar to the eggs and set over a saucepan of hot water. The bowl must not touch the water.

Whisk the eggs and sugar together with a rotary beater or whisk until it leaves a trail.

Remove from the heat and continue whisking briskly until the mixture cools slightly.

Carefully and quickly fold in the flour, about a quarter at a time until it has been incorporated.

Pour the mixture into the prepared tins (pans) and bake until the cakes are cooked.

219

stored in the refrigerator for up to 3 weeks; slice off thin wafers of dough as required and bake until crisp.

FILLINGS AND TOPPINGS

Many cakes and biscuits (cookies) benefit from a creamy filling or icing to enhance their appearance and to make them richer and less dry to eat. Use a broad, flat bladed palette knife or spatula to spread the creams and icings, giving a smooth finish. Invest in a nylon forcing (pastry) bag with several nozzles to vary your decoration. Your skills will soon improve with a little practice.

Buttercream and Crème au Beurre Mousseline freeze extremely well. Make a large batch at one time in a basic flavour, then use with the addition of chosen flavours as required. You can freeze cakes which have been filled, iced and decorated, although you do lose a little of the shine on the icing when defrosted. Crème Pâtissière, having a custard base, does not freeze, but Fondant Icing will store in a cupboard for weeks. Cakes filled or decorated with whipped cream freeze extremely well also.

FILLINGS

Buttercream

A quick and easy filling for sponge sandwich (layer) cakes and sweet biscuits (cookies).

	Metric/UK	US
Unsalted butter	100g/4oz	½ cup
Icing (confectioner's) sugar, sifted	225g/8oz	2 cups
Flavouring		

Beat the butter until soft, white and shiny. Gradually beat in the sugar until smooth and creamy. Add a few drops of milk if the mixture is too stiff to spread easily. Flavour and colour to complement the cake: for orange or lemon, beat in a little finely grated rind and add a few drops of the juice to give a smooth, creamy texture; for coffee, beat in a little coffee essence (extract) to taste; for chocolate, dissolve 4 level teaspoons of cocoa powder in a little boiling water, and beat in gradually.
To fill one 23cm/9in cake

Crème au Beurre

There are three types of Crème au Beurre, which are used for filling and decorating cakes and pastries. These are a little more complicated to prepare than Buttercream, but absolutely delicious.

1. SIMPLE CREME AU BEURRE

	Metric/UK	US
Milk	150ml/5floz	⅔ cup
Castor (superfine) sugar	50g/2oz	¼ cup
Egg yolks	2	2
Unsalted butter	175g/6oz	¾ cup

Make the milk, sugar and egg yolks into custard as in Basic Custard Sauce. Pour the custard through a strainer into a bowl and allow it to cool. Cream the butter until white and smooth. Gradually beat in the cooled custard and continue beating until smooth and creamy. Flavour as required.
To fill one 20cm/8in cake

2. CREME AU BEURRE MOUSSELINE

	Metric/UK	US
Sugar	75g/3oz	6 Tbsp
Water	5 Tbsp	5 Tbsp
Egg yolks	2	2
Unsalted butter	100g/4oz	½ cup

Dissolve the sugar in the water over a low heat. Cover and bring to a boil. Boil rapidly, without stirring, until it reaches 105°C/215°F or makes a short thread when a little of the cooled syrup is stretched gently between the thumb and forefinger. Remove from the heat immediately. Lightly beat the egg yolks in a small bowl and add the sugar syrup in a steady stream, beating until thick and mousse-like. Cream the butter until soft and white. Gradually beat in the egg mousse until smooth. Flavour as required. If the mixture begins to curdle, simply place over a pan of hot water and beat until smooth.
To fill one 20cm/8in cake

3. CREME AU BEURRE MERINGUEE

This is light and useful for sandwiching meringue layers together. A cooked meringue is added to the butter and can be flavoured as required.

	Metric/UK	US
Icing (confectioner's) sugar	100g/4oz	1 cup
Egg whites	2	2
Unsalted butter	100g/4oz	½ cup

Sift the sugar into a heatproof bowl and add the egg whites. Place the bowl over a pan of simmering water and beat until the meringue is very thick and will hold its shape. Remove from the heat and continue beating for a few minutes. Cream the butter as before and gradually beat in the meringue. Curdling can be remedied as in Crème au Beurre Mousseline.
To fill one 20cm/8in cake

Crème Pâtissière

This is also known as pastry custard or confectioner's custard. It has a wide variety of uses from filling choux puffs and éclairs to spreading on cakes and in pastry cases to be topped with fresh fruit. It does not keep for more than a few days in the refrigerator.

	Metric/UK	US
Egg yolks	2	2
Sugar	50g/2oz	¼ cup

Decorating with Icing Sugar

To decorate a cake with icing (confectioners') sugar, place a doily on top and sift over the sugar.

Gently lift the doily from the top of the cake with your fingertips, so that the pattern remains.

	Metric/UK	US
Cornflour (cornstarch)	1 Tbsp	1 Tbsp
Flour	1 Tbsp	1 Tbsp
Vanilla essence (extract)	$\frac{1}{2}$ tsp	$\frac{1}{2}$ tsp
Milk	300ml/ $\frac{1}{2}$ pint	$1\frac{1}{4}$ cups
Egg white (optional)	1	1

Beat the egg yolks and sugar until creamy. Sift in the cornflour (cornstarch) and flour and add the vanilla. Gradually mix in about one quarter of the milk. Heat the remainder of the milk without boiling and then add it to the egg mixture, beating well. Pour into the saucepan and heat gently, stirring, until the mixture just reaches the boil. Remove from the heat and beat until smooth. Allow to cool.

If you want to lighten the custard cream, beat the egg white until stiff. Fold the egg white into a quarter of the cream mixture, then fold that into the remaining cream. Cook over a low heat for 1–2 minutes, stirring occasionally. Allow to cool before using.
About 350ml/12floz (1½ cups)

Crème Chantilly

This is simply a flavoured, sweetened whipped cream.

	Metric/UK	US
Double (heavy) cream, chilled	300ml/ $\frac{1}{2}$ pint	$1\frac{1}{4}$ cups
Vanilla essence (extract)	1 tsp	1 tsp
Castor (superfine) sugar	1 tsp	1 tsp

In a mixing bowl, beat the cream until it begins to thicken. Add the vanilla and sugar and continue beating until the mixture is stiff and forms soft peaks.
About 350ml/12floz (1½ cups)

TOPPINGS

Glacé Icing

This is a simple water icing which can be coloured and flavoured and used to ice the tops of cakes.

	Metric/UK	US
Icing (confectioner's) sugar, sifted	225g/8oz	2 cups
Warm water or strained fruit juice	$1\frac{1}{2}$ Tbsp	$1\frac{1}{2}$ Tbsp
Flavouring or colouring		

Mix the sugar with most of the warm water or juice. Beat hard until it is smooth, shiny and will coat the

Glacé Icing

Beat warm water or juice into sifted icing (confectioners') sugar until the ingredients are mixed.

Beat the mixture vigorously for about 3 minutes, or until it is shiny, thick and smooth.

Pour the icing on to the cake and spread it evenly over the top and sides with a palette knife.

back of the spoon thickly. Thin a little if required. It is easy to make it too soft. Flavour and colour as required, keeping the colouring very discreet. Pour over the cake at once, spread smoothly to the edges and add any decoration while the icing is still soft. Allow to set.

To ice one 20cm/8in cake

Marbling

This is an effective but simple decoration for cakes covered with white glacé icing. Add a few drops of food colouring to 1 tablespoon of prepared glacé icing. The colour should be sufficiently bold to contrast with the white icing. Use a small forcing (pastry) bag, or make a small greaseproof or waxed paper forcing (pastry) bag. Draw parallel lines over the surface of the cake with the coloured icing, about 1cm/½in apart. Use a skewer to draw aside the icing in lines at right angles to the coloured lines. First draw the skewer from left to right, then from right to left. Leave to set.

Cooked Frostings

Frostings are a type of soft icing which can fill or ice a cake. Chopped nuts are often added with the flavouring.

BASIC FROSTING

	Metric/UK	US
Sugar	225g/8oz	1 cup
Water	5 Tbsp	5 Tbsp
Egg white	1	1
Cream of tartar	⅛ tsp	⅛ tsp
Vanilla essence (extract)	½ tsp	½ tsp

Dissolve the sugar in the water over a low heat. Bring to the boil and boil rapidly until the temperature reaches 115°C/240°F on a sugar thermometer. In a medium-sized mixing bowl, beat the egg white with the cream of tartar until it forms stiff peaks. Pour the sugar syrup in a steady stream on to the beaten egg white, beating continuously until the frosting is thick enough to spread. Stir in the vanilla.

To ice one 20cm/8in cake

Marbling

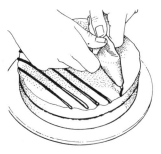 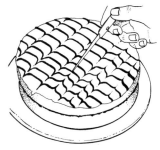

Pipe a contrasting colour of icing in lines over the white icing.

Make a leafy pattern by altering the lines with a knife, as shown.

Fondant Icing

This is a sweet, smooth icing used for cakes and gâteaux. It can be stored in an airtight jar in the refrigerator for 2–3 weeks.

	Metric/UK	US
Sugar	450g/1lb	2 cups
Water	200ml/7floz	1 cup less 2 Tbsp
Cream of tartar	$\frac{1}{8}$ tsp	$\frac{1}{8}$ tsp

Use a spotlessly clean, heavy-based saucepan. Dissolve the sugar in the water slowly, then bring to the boil. Add the cream of tartar (dissolved in a few drops of water) and boil rapidly until the syrup reaches 115°C/240°F on a sugar thermometer. Remove from the heat and pour on to a flat surface to cool. Do not stir or scrape the pan or the mixture will become gritty and uneven. When it is cool enough to handle, work the fondant with a palette knife or spatula until it turns opaque and white. Knead hard with your hands until smooth and pliable. Roll into balls and place in polythene (plastic) bags to mature for several hours before using.

Use Fondant Icing in its finished state to mould and shape sweets (candies). To use the icing as a frosting or coating, combine it with 3 or 4 tablespoons of sugar syrup until it is thick and creamy but pours and spreads easily.

To make the sugar syrup, take 250ml/8floz (1 cup) water and proceed as before, but remove from the heat when the temperature reaches 110°C/220°F and the mixture looks syrupy. Allow to cool completely before using.

To ice a cake, gently warm the prepared fondant in a heatproof bowl over hot water. Gradually add enough of the sugar syrup and flavouring to make a smooth, thick pouring consistency. Place the cake on a wire rack over a tray to catch drips. Carefully pour the warm fondant over the top of the cake so that it eventually covers the top and sides completely. Avoid spreading and moving with a knife — it should spread fairly evenly by itself. Leave to cool before cutting the cake. It gives a shiny, beautiful finish to a special cake and is worth the effort.

About 450g/1lb (4 cups)

Seven Minute Frosting

	Metric/UK	US
Sugar	350g/12oz	$1\frac{1}{2}$ cups
Water	4 Tbsp	4 Tbsp
Cream of tartar	$\frac{1}{4}$ tsp	$\frac{1}{4}$ tsp
Salt	$\frac{1}{8}$ tsp	$\frac{1}{8}$ tsp
Egg whites	2	2

Put all the ingredients into a medium-sized heatproof bowl. Beat for 1 minute. Place the bowl over a saucepan of simmering water and continue beating for 7 minutes. Remove from the heat and continue beating until the frosting is thick enough to spread.

To ice one 23cm/9in cake

Rough Icing

Put a blob of icing on the centre of your cake board and set the cake on top.

Put all the icing on the cake. Work back and forth to remove bubbles, then spread over the sides.

Using the blade of a knife or the handle of a teaspoon, rough the icing up in peaks.

Almond Paste

 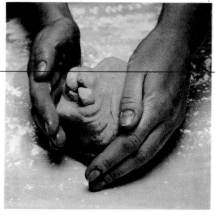 

To make marzipan (almond paste), sift the icing (confectioners') and castor (superfine) sugars into a bowl with the ground almonds.

Add the lemon juice, almond essence (extract) and some of the egg and beat well. Add more egg if you need more liquid.

Mix to a smooth paste. Turn out on to a board sprinkled with icing (confectioners') sugar. Knead for 3 minutes until smooth and oily.

Royal Icing

This is a pure white icing which is traditionally used for icing Christmas, wedding and rich fruit cakes. It produces a smooth, hard finish which can be decorated as elaborately as you wish.

	Metric/UK	US
Icing (confectioner's) sugar sifted	450g/1lb	4 cups
Egg whites, lightly beaten	2	2

Place the sugar in a large mixing bowl. Add the egg whites and stir gently with a wooden spoon until smooth. Beat gently for 2 minutes, then vigorously for 10 minutes until the icing is fairly thick and holds stiff peaks.
To ice two 23cm/9in cakes

To Ice a Rich Fruit Cake

Place the fruit cake on a board and brush all over lightly with Apricot Glaze. Roll out Almond Paste to about 1cm/½in and cut in a strip as wide as the side of the cake. Press the strip gently against the sides of the cake and trim neatly to fit. Roll out the remainder of the almond paste to a round slightly larger than the top of the cake. Gently place on top of the cake. Press into position and trim any excess to make a neat, smooth finish all over.

Spread the prepared Royal Icing over the top and sides of the cake, smoothing it carefully with the blade of a knife over the top and sides. Leave to harden for 4–5 days before decorating.

To give a 'snow effect', gently pull the icing upwards in soft peaks with a rounded palette knife or spatula and leave to harden for 1–2 days.

Apricot Glaze

Useful for glazing fruit flans (pies) and tartlets, brushing over cakes before icing, holding almond paste on to cakes and glazing Danish pastries. These quantities are for making in bulk.

	Metric/UK	US
Sugar syrup	150ml/5floz	⅔ cup
Apricot jam	450g/1lb	1lb (1⅓ cups)
Juice of ½ lemon		

Make the sugar syrup as in Fondant Icing. Put the jam, syrup and lemon juice into a pan and heat almost to boiling. Rub through a wire strainer into a clean pan. Boil gently for a few minutes until the glaze hangs in drops from a wooden spoon. Store in a covered bowl in the refrigerator.

Almond Paste

	Metric/UK	US
Icing (confectioner's) sugar	100g/4oz	1 cup
Castor (superfine) sugar	100g/4oz	½ cup
Ground almonds	225g/8oz	2 cups
Lemon juice	1 tsp	1 tsp
Almond essence (extract)	3 drops	3 drops
Egg, lightly beaten	1	1

Work the ingredients into a smooth ball. Do not over-knead.
About 225g/8oz (2 cups)

PIPING

This is the most effective method of decorating cakes with Royal Icing or Buttercream. Use a small grease-proof or waxed paper bag for small quanitities and a large forcing (pastry) bag for large quantities. The consistency is very important; it must be smooth to be

Decorating with Almond Paste

To colour almond paste, work edible food colouring into it. Deep colours, such as the green used here, look better than light tones.

For holly leaves, draw a leaf shape on to a card. Use the card as a template to cut shapes. Mark the veins with a knife.

Another way to do it is to cut out small rounds using a plain cutter. Then simply cut away the edges of the circle with a smaller cutter.

piped evenly and easily, but stiff enough to hold the piped shape. There are many different shaped nozzles available which can produce many interesting swirls and flowers.

Buttercream piping

Cover the cake with prepared buttercream and coat the sides with chopped nuts or other decorations. Use a large, plain nozzle fitted in a piping (pastry) bag and pipe lines across the cake. Pipe a border with an up and down movement or a border of 'rosettes' with a star nozzle. The patterns are essentially bolder with this type of soft icing.

Piping with Royal Icing

Attractive borders can be made using small shaped nozzles, in shells, spirals or zig-zag patterns. Thin lines. can be drawn and messages piped with thin, plain nozzles. Make flowers in advance, piped on a piece of greaseproof or waxed paper and set aside to dry. Place them in position on the iced cake with a small dot of icing.

The icing pattern can be as simple or as elaborate as you choose. The golden rule is always to practice first on greaseproof or waxed paper if you are a little unsure of yourself, before proceeding with the finished cake.

Making a Piping Bag

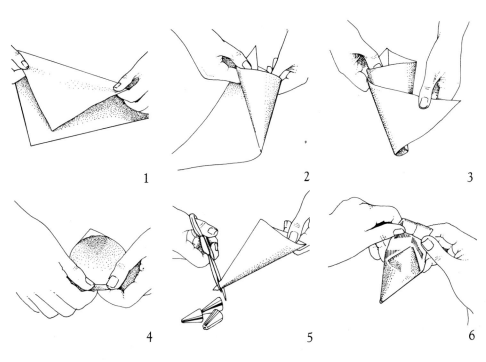

1   2   3

4   5   6

Cut a 25cm/10in square from greaseproof or waxed paper. Fold diagonally to make two triangles. (1) With the base facing away, bring up the lefthand corner of the base to meet the top of the triangle. (2) Holding the two points together, bring up the righthand corner and wrap around the back. (3) Fold the three corners towards the inside of the cone. (4) Cut off the point of the bag to fit the chosen nozzle. Slip on the nozzle. (5). Fill the bag at an angle, no more than half full. Fold down to secure. (6)

RECIPES

Dundee Cake

	Metric/UK	US
Butter	225g/8oz	1 cup
Castor (superfine) sugar	225g/8oz	1 cup
Flour	275g/10oz	2½ cups
Baking powder	½ tsp	½ tsp
Eggs	5	5
Raisins	100g/4oz	⅔ cup
Currants	100g/4oz	⅔ cup
Sultanas (seedless raisins)	100g/4oz	⅔ cup
Mixed candied fruit	50g/2oz	⅓ cup
Glacé (candied) cherries	50g/2oz	⅓ cup
Grated rind of 1 orange		
Grated rind of 1 lemon		
Mixed spice (apple pie spice)	½ tsp	½ tsp
Ground cinnamon	½ tsp	½ tsp
Blanched almonds, halved (to decorate)	50g/2oz	½ cup

Line a 20cm/8in diameter, deep cake tin (pan) with greaseproof or waxed paper or foil then grease. Preheat the oven to warm (170°C/325°F, Gas Mark 3).

Prepare the batter by the creaming method. Add the spices at the same time as the flour. Turn the mixture into the tin (pan) and smooth it flat. Arrange the halved almonds on top of the cake. Bake in the lower part of the oven for about 2 hours. Test with a skewer. Turn off the heat and leave the cake in the oven for about 10 minutes. Remove and allow to cool in the tin (pan) until you can turn it out on to a rack to become completely cold. Peel off the paper or foil.

Orange Cake Fingers

	Metric/UK	US
Castor (superfine) sugar	75g/3oz	⅓ cup
Eggs	2	2
Flour	75g/3oz	¾ cup
Ground almonds	2 Tbsp	2 Tbsp
Grated rind of 2 oranges		
Orange-flavoured liqueur	1 tsp	1 tsp

Preheat the oven to moderate (180°C/350°F, Gas Mark

Dundee Cake, a rich fruit cake made by the creaming method.

4). Grease and flour an 18×23cm/7×9in Swiss (jelly) roll tin.

Place the sugar and eggs in a heatproof bowl over a pan of hot water. Beat until the mixture is thick and pale and will make a trail on itself when the whisk is lifted. (If using an electric beater, no heat is needed). Remove from the heat. Use a metal spoon to fold in the flour and almonds. Fold in the orange rind and liqueur. Pour into the tin and bake for 30 minutes or until the cake springs back when lightly pressed. Cool for 5 minutes, then turn out on to a wire rack. Cool. Cut into fingers before serving.
About 20 fingers

Almond Cake

This cake uses ground almonds instead of flour.

	Metric/UK	US
Egg yolks	6	6
Castor (superfine) sugar	100g/4oz	½ cup
Ground almonds	175g/6oz	1½ cups
Milk	2 Tbsp	2 Tbsp
Egg whites	6	6
ICING		
Icing (confectioner's) sugar	450g/1lb	4 cups
Hot water	2 Tbsp	2 Tbsp
Egg white	1	1
Almond essence (extract)	¼ tsp	¼ tsp
Slivered (shredded) almonds (to decorate)	50g/2oz	½ cup

Preheat the oven to moderate (180°C/350°F, Gas Mark 4). Line a Swiss (jelly) roll tin with greaseproof or waxed paper or foil. Grease and set aside.

Beat together the egg yolks and sugar. Fold in the ground almonds and milk. Beat the egg whites until they are stiff and gently fold into the batter. Place in the tin and bake for 15–20 minutes or until golden and cooked through. Cool for 5 minutes, then turn out on to a clean sheet of greaseproof or waxed paper or foil dusted with cornflour (cornstarch). Discard the lining. Leave to cool. For the icing, put the sugar, water and egg white in a heatproof bowl over a pan of hot water. Beat until the icing is glossy and will coat the back of the spoon. Stir in the almond essence (extract). Set aside to cool.

Use a sharp knife to cut the cake into 4 rectangles the same size. Place one rectangle on a serving dish. Spread with a little of the icing and continue to make layers with the cake and icing. Spread the remaining icing evenly over the top and sides of the cake. Sprinkle the top with the slivered (shredded) almonds.

Classic Madeira Cake, made with self-raising flour.

Chocolate Roulade

	Metric/UK	US
Eggs, separated	5	5
Castor (superfine) sugar	175g/6oz	¾ cup
Dark (semi-sweet) cooking chocolate	175g/6oz	6 squares
Cold water	3 Tbsp	3 Tbsp
TO FILL		
Double (heavy) cream	250ml/8floz	1 cup
Vanilla essence (extract)	½ tsp	½ tsp

Preheat the oven to hot (220°C/425°F, Gas Mark 7). Grease a Swiss (jelly) roll tin. Line with greaseproof or waxed paper or foil and grease. Set aside.

Beat the egg yolks and sugar together until the mixture is pale, thick and fluffy. Melt the chocolate and water in a small pan over a low heat, stirring continuously. Remove from the heat. When cool, beat into the egg yolk mixture. Beat the egg whites until they are stiff. Fold into the chocolate mixture carefully with a metal spoon. Spoon into the tin and bake for 10 minutes.

Reduce the heat to warm (170°C/325°F, Gas Mark 3). Bake for a further 10 minutes or until a skewer inserted into the cake comes out clean. Remove from the tin

and cover with a damp cloth. Leave for 15 minutes.

Turn the cake out on to a fresh piece of sugared greaseproof or waxed paper or foil. Chill for 30 minutes. With a sharp knife, make a shallow cut across the cake at one end to make rolling easier. Using the paper or foil to lift, roll the cake carefully, rolling the paper or foil inside so it can be unrolled again. Keep it rolled until it is completely cold. Then, unroll the cake carefully and remove the paper or foil. Whip the cream with the vanilla until thick and spread over the cake. Roll up the cake again, and sprinkle with icing (confectioner's) sugar before serving.

Madeira Cake

	Metric/UK	US
Butter	225g/8oz	1 cup
Castor (superfine) sugar	225g/8oz	1 cup
Self-raising (self-rising) flour	225g/8oz	2 cups
Eggs	5	5
Grated rind of 1 lemon		
Juice of ½ lemon		
Candied citron peel	3 strips	3 strips

Preheat the oven to moderate (180°C/350°F, Gas Mark 4.) Grease and flour a 15cm/6in round, deep tin (pan). Make the cake batter by the creaming method, adding a tablespoonful of the flour with each egg to avoid curdling. Stir in the lemon rind and juice. Spoon into the prepared tin (pan) and sprinkle with 1 tablespoon

of sugar. Bake for 30 minutes. Place the candied citron peel on top, return to the oven and continue baking for 45–50 minutes or until cooked through. Turn on to a wire rack to cool.

Viennese Fingers

	Metric/UK	US
Butter, softened	225g/8oz	1 cup
Icing (confectioner's) sugar	50g/2oz	½ cup
Flour	225g/8oz	2 cups
Grated orange rind	2 tsp	2 tsp
Orange juice	1 Tbsp	1 Tbsp
Dark plain chocolate (to decorate)	175g/6oz	6 squares
BUTTERCREAM		
Unsalted butter, softened	50g/2oz	¼ cup
Icing (confectioner's) sugar sifted	100g/4oz	1 cup
Vanilla essence (extract)	⅛ tsp	⅛ tsp

Grease two baking sheets. Preheat the oven to moderate (180°C/350°F, Gas Mark 4). Prepare the dough using the creaming method. Fill a large forcing (pastry) bag, fitted with a star-shaped nozzle, with the mixture and pipe out 24 fingers, each about 7.5cm/3in long on to the baking sheets. Bake for 10–15 minutes or until golden and firm. Leave the biscuits (cookies) to cool for 5 minutes, then transfer to a wire rack to cool

completely. Make the Buttercream as in the basic recipe and use to sandwich together pairs of biscuits (cookies).

Melt the chocolate in a small heatproof bowl over a pan of hot water. Dip each end of each biscuit (cookie) into the melted chocolate and place on greaseproof or waxed paper to harden and dry.

This type of biscuit (cookie) dough can be shaped to an S-shape, a star shape or whatever shape you choose, using a forcing (pastry) bag and a large star nozzle.
About 24 fingers

Chocolate Refrigerator Biscuits (Cookies)

	Metric/UK	US
Flour	175g/6oz	1½ cups
Baking powder	1 tsp	1 tsp
Salt	¼ tsp	¼ tsp
Butter	100g/4oz	½ cup
Sugar	100g/4oz	½ cup
Vanilla essence (extract)	½ tsp	½ tsp
Egg, beaten	1	1
Plain (semi-sweet) chocolate, melted	40g/1½oz	1½ squares

Make the basic dough using the creaming method. Divide the dough in half. Add the melted chocolate to one half. Chill well.

229

Roll out each portion of dough into a long thin strip and place in a tin (pan) in alternate layers of chocolate and plain dough. Chill until required. Cut off in thin slices with a sharp knife. Bake on greased baking sheets in an oven preheated to fairly hot (200°C/ 400°F, Gas Mark 6) for about 7–8 minutes or until crisp.

About 30 biscuits (cookies)

Flour, rice flour, sugar and butter are the only ingredients in this traditional Scottish Shortbread. It can be made either in a special mould (as here), or a baking sheet.

Shortbread

	Metric/UK	US
Flour	225g/8oz	2 cups
Rice flour	100g/4oz	1 cup
Castor (superfine) sugar	100g/4oz	½ cup
Butter	225g/8oz	1 cup

Grease a large baking sheet and set aside. Sift the flours and sugar into a mixing bowl. Rub the butter into the dry ingredients with your fingertips until the mixture is like coarse breadcrumbs. Knead gently until it forms a stiff dough. Divide the dough in half and shape each half into a neat flat circle, or press into a mould. Crimp the edges with your fingertips. Chill for 20 minutes.

Mark the circles with a knife like the spokes of a wheel. Preheat the oven to moderate (180°C/350°F, Gas Mark 4). Bake the shortbread for 10 minutes, then reduce the oven to warm (150°C/300°F, Gas Mark 2). Continue baking for 30–40 minutes or until crisp and lightly golden.

Allow to cool a little, then sprinkle the tops with a little castor (superfine) sugar. Transfer to a wire rack to cool. Cut through the marks completely to make triangles of shortbread when cold.

About 12 biscuits (cookies)

Ginger and Cream Wafers

	Metric/UK	US
Butter	100g/4oz	½ cup
Castor (superfine) sugar	50g/2oz	¼ cup
Light brown sugar	50g/2oz	⅓ cup
Black treacle (molasses)	2 Tbsp	2 Tbsp
Clear honey	1 Tbsp	1 Tbsp
Egg	1	1
Flour	350g/12oz	3 cups
Ground ginger	1½ tsp	1½ tsp
FILLING		
Double (heavy) cream	300ml/ ½ pint	1¼ cups
Grated lemon rind	1 tsp	1 tsp
Castor (superfine) sugar	1 Tbsp	1 Tbsp

Preheat the oven to moderate (180°C/350°F, Gas Mark 4). Grease two large baking sheets and set aside. Use the creaming method to mix the butter and sugars.

Stir in the treacle (molasses) and honey. Beat in the egg and fold in the sifted flour and ginger. Mix and knead the dough until smooth. Chill for 30 minutes.

Roll out the dough on a floured surface to 1–2mm/ 1/16 in thick. Cut into rounds using a 6cm/2½in round pastry (cookie) cutter. Bake half of them on the baking sheets for 10–12 minutes. Transfer to a wire rack to cool. Bake the remainder.

When cold, beat the cream until stiff with the lemon rind and sugar, and use to sandwich pairs of biscuits (cookies) together.

About 36 biscuits (cookies)

Cherry-filled Cakes

	Metric/UK	US
Butter, melted	75g/3oz	6 Tbsp
Eggs	3	3
Castor (superfine) sugar	100g/4oz	½ cup
Self-raising (self-rising) flour	100g/4oz	1 cup

Vanilla essence (extract)	½ tsp	½ tsp
Basic quantity of Glacé Icing, coloured with 1 drop of red food colouring		
Candied angelica		
FILLING		
Canned stoned (pitted) red cherries, drained	150g/5oz	1 cup
Icing (confectioner's) sugar	2 Tbsp	2 Tbsp
Ground almonds	2 Tbsp	2 Tbsp

Preheat the oven to moderate (180°C/350°F, Gas Mark 4). Grease a 25×18cm/10×7in cake tin (pan) and set aside. Make the batter by the whisking method and pour into the tin (pan). Bake for 25 minutes or until cooked. Turn out on to a wire rack to cool. When cold, split carefully into two layers.

Chop most of the cherries and mix well with the sugar and ground almonds. Spread this evenly over one cake layer and replace the other on top.

Spread the icing smoothly over the top layer of the cake. Cut the cake into strips 4cm/1½in wide, then cut diagonally into diamonds 4cm/1½in across. Cut the remaining cherries into quarters. Decorate each cake with a quarter cherry and two small angelica leaves. *About 12 cakes*

Mocha Gâteau (Rich Coffee-flavoured Cake)

	Metric/UK	US
Flour	100g/4oz	1 cup
Castor (superfine) sugar	100g/4oz	½ cup
Eggs	5	5
Butter, melted	2½ Tbsp	2½ Tbsp
Buttercream Icing, flavoured with coffee	225g/8oz	1 cup
Nuts, toasted and chopped	50g/2oz	½ cup

Preheat the oven to moderate (180°C/350°F, Gas Mark 4). Grease and line two × 20cm/8in round sandwich

Madeleines

tins (layer cake pans). Dust lightly with flour.

Make the batter by the whisking method, gently folding in the melted butter until absorbed. Take care not to overmix or the cake will not rise well. Pour into the prepared tins (pans) and bake for 15–20 minutes or until golden brown and springy to the touch. Turn out on to a wire rack to cool.

Sandwich the cakes together with one third of the icing. Use the remainder to cover the top and sides of the cake. Sprinkle toasted chopped nuts over the top and sides of the cake.

Madeleines

These little sponge cakes are baked in a traditional shell-shaped mould.

	Metric/UK	US
Butter, melted	100g/4oz	$\frac{1}{2}$ cup
Flour	100g/4oz	1 cup
Castor (superfine) sugar	100g/4oz	$\frac{1}{2}$ cup
Eggs	4	4
Vanilla essence (extract)	$\frac{1}{2}$ tsp	$\frac{1}{2}$ tsp

Preheat the oven to fairly hot (200°C/400°F, Gas Mark 6). Grease 36 madeleine moulds and dust lightly with flour. Set aside. Make the batter using the whisking method, and lightly fold in the butter.

Fill each mould no more than three-quarters full. Bake for 7–10 minutes or until golden brown and cooked through. Leave to cool for 5 minutes, then turn out of the moulds and cool on a wire rack.
36 cakes

Scones (Biscuits) with Dried Fruit

These traditional British scones (biscuits) are served warm, split and spread with butter.

	Metric/UK	US
Flour	225g/8oz	2 cups
Baking powder	2 tsp	2 tsp
Bicarbonate of soda (baking soda)	1 tsp	1 tsp
Salt	$\frac{1}{4}$ tsp	$\frac{1}{4}$ tsp
Vegetable fat (shortening) or margarine	40g/1$\frac{1}{2}$oz	3 Tbsp
Castor (superfine) sugar	50g/2oz	$\frac{1}{4}$ cup
Raisins	50g/2oz	$\frac{1}{3}$ cup
Currants	2 Tbsp	2 Tbsp
Large egg	1	1
Milk	75ml/3floz	$\frac{1}{3}$ cup

Preheat the oven to very hot (230°C/450°F, Gas Mark 8). Grease a large baking sheet. Sift the dry ingredients into a large bowl. Rub in the fat as in the rubbing-in method. Stir in the sugar and fruit and make a soft dough with the egg and milk. Knead very lightly until just mixed and smooth.

Turn on to a floured board. Flatten out with the hands (a rolling pin knocks out the lightness) to about 1cm/½in thick. Use a 5cm/2in pastry (cookie) cutter to cut the dough into rounds. Re-knead and use up the scraps. Place the rounds on the baking sheet. Bake for 10–12 minutes or until well risen and golden brown. Cool on a rack.

About 12 Scones (biscuits)

Scones (Biscuits) with Sour Cream

	Metric/UK	US
Flour	350g/12oz	3 cups
Bicarbonate of soda (baking soda)	2 tsp	2 tsp
Salt	½ tsp	½ tsp
Vegetable fat (shortening)	50g/2oz	¼ cup
Sour cream	175ml/6floz	¾ cup
TO GLAZE		
Egg yolk	1	1
Milk	2 Tbsp	2 Tbsp

Preheat the oven to very hot (230°C/450°F, Gas Mark 8). Grease two baking sheets and set aside. Make the scones (biscuits) by the basic rubbing-in method, adding the sour cream as the liquid. Divide the dough into 2 rounds, about 20cm/8in in diameter and place on the baking sheets. Cut each dough round with a sharp knife into 8 triangular shapes. Do not separate. Brush with the beaten egg and milk mixture. Bake for 10–15 minutes or until risen and golden brown. Pull apart and cool on a wire rack.

16 scones (biscuits)

Drop Scones (Pancakes)

Use a flat, iron griddle or heavy frying-pan to make these batter scones (biscuits).

	Metric/UK	US
Self-raising (self-rising) flour	225g/8oz	2 cups
Golden (light corn) syrup	2 Tbsp	2 Tbsp
Eggs	2	2
Vegetable oil	2 Tbsp	2 Tbsp
Milk		

Lightly grease the griddle with a little oil. Sift the flour into a bowl. Make a well in the centre and add the syrup, eggs and oil. Beat well together, gradually drawing in the flour. Beat in enough milk to make a batter which is the consistency of thick cream. Drop

Scones (Biscuits) with Dried Fruit.

Nougatines are luscious little sponge cakes.

spoonsful of the batter on to the heated griddle and cook for 3 minutes or until bubbling. Turn over with a spatula and cook the other side until golden. Remove the cooked scones (biscuits) and cover with a clean cloth. Use the remainder of the batter in the same way.
28 scones (pancakes)

Nougatine Cakes

	Metric/UK	US
8 small rectangular cakes, cut from basic Genoese sponge		
Apricot Glaze		
Blanched almonds	8	8

Jamaican Spice Loaf is a sort of gingerbread with treacle or molasses. Serve warm with lots of butter.

PRALINE CREAM FILLING

Castor (superfine) sugar	100g/4oz	½ cup
Almonds	100g/4oz	1 cup
Butter, softened	100g/4oz	½ cup
Icing (confectioner's) sugar	100g/4oz	1 cup
Double (heavy) cream, whipped	50ml/2floz	¼ cup
ICING		
Dark (semi-sweet) chocolate, in small pieces	100g/4oz	4 squares
Fondant Icing	350g/12oz	1½ cups
Sugar syrup (optional)	up to 6 Tbsp	up to 6 Tbsp

To make the filling, in a small saucepan, melt the castor (superfine) sugar over a low heat. When it has melted, increase the heat to high and boil, without stirring, for 1–2 minutes or until a rich golden brown. Add the almonds and stir to coat them evenly. Remove from the heat. Pour on to a cold surface and leave to harden completely. Crush with a rolling pin or put in an electric blender and blend to a fine powder.

Beat the softened butter with the icing (confectioner's) sugar and whipped cream until smooth. Beat in the crushed praline powder and set aside.

To make the icing, melt the chocolate in a heatproof bowl over hot water. Beat in the Fondant Icing, a little at a time until smooth. Dilute with sugar syrup if necessary. Keep hot. With a sharp knife, slice each cake across into three layers. Spread a little Praline Cream over the first two layers and reassemble. Brush the top and sides of each cake with a little Apricot Glaze to stop crumbs from spoiling the icing. Smoothly

coat each layered cake with the hot chocolate Fondant Icing, to cover the top and sides completely. Press a blanched almond on to each cake. Allow to cool completely for 30 minutes before serving.
About 8 cakes

Jamaican Spice Loaf

	Metric/UK	US
Butter	50g/2oz	4 Tbsp
Flour	350g/12oz	3 cups
Bicarbonate of soda (baking soda)	1½ tsp	1½ tsp
Salt	¼ tsp	¼ tsp
Mixed spice (apple pie spice)	½ tsp	½ tsp
Ground cinnamon	½ tsp	½ tsp
Grated nutmeg	½ tsp	½ tsp
Ground ginger	1 tsp	1 tsp
Raisins	75g/3oz	½ cup
Black treacle (molasses)	4 Tbsp	4 Tbsp
Eggs	3	3
Milk	50ml/2floz	¼ cup

Preheat the oven to warm (170°C/325°F, Gas Mark 3). Grease a 1kg/2lb loaf tin (pan) and set aside. Sift the dry ingredients into a large bowl. Add the raisins. Heat the treacle (molasses) and butter and pour into the flour, stirring continuously. Stir in the eggs and milk to make a soft dough. Turn into the tin (pan) and bake in the centre of the oven for about 1½ hours, or until cooked through. Turn out on to a wire rack to cool.

Fruit and Nut Biscuits (Cookies)

	Metric/UK	US
Unsalted butter	175g/6oz	¾ cup
Light brown sugar	50g/2oz	⅓ cup
Castor (superfine) sugar	50g/2oz	¼ cup
Eggs, lightly beaten	2	2
Flour	75g/3oz	¾ cup
Ground almonds	75g/3oz	¾ cup
Hazelnuts, chopped	75g/3oz	¾ cup
Mixed spice (apple pie spice)	½ tsp	½ tsp
Glacé (candied) cherries chopped	2 Tbsp	2 Tbsp
Chopped candied peel	50g/2oz	⅓ cup

Preheat the oven to moderate (180°C/350°F, Gas Mark 4). Lightly grease three baking sheets with a little butter and set aside. Make the dough using the creaming method described earlier in the chapter. Add the nuts, spice and fruit with the flour.

Put teaspoonsful of the mixture on the baking sheets, well spaced to allow the biscuits (cookies) to spread. Bake for 10–15 minutes or until golden brown at the edges. Remove from the oven and transfer to a wire rack and leave to cool.

If you like, these biscuits (cookies) can be sandwiched together in pairs with a little orange and rum-flavoured Buttercream.

About 38 biscuits (cookies)

Chocolate Peppermint Cake

	Metric/UK	US
Self-raising (self-rising) flour	100g/4oz	1 cup
Cocoa powder	50g/2oz	½ cup
Margarine	175g/6oz	¾ cup
Castor (superfine) sugar	175g/6oz	¾ cup
Eggs	3	3
Vanilla essence (extract)	½ tsp	½ tsp
Warm water	1 Tbsp	1 Tbsp

Prepare two 18cm/7in diameter sandwich tins (layer cake pans) by greasing and flouring. Preheat the oven to fairly hot (190°C/375°F, Gas Mark 5). Sift the flour together with the cocoa powder. Prepare the batter using the creaming method. Stir in the water carefully. Divide the batter equally between the two tins (pans) and smooth the tops. Bake for 25 minutes and test to see if they are ready. Turn out and cool. When cold, sandwich the cakes together with a peppermint filling: stir ½ teaspoon of peppermint essence (extract) and a few drops of green food colouring into the basic Buttercream Icing. Dust the top with sifted icing (confectioner's) sugar. Store for up to a few days or serve at once.

Chocolate Peppermint Cake is surprisingly easy to make and has an extra-special minty filling.

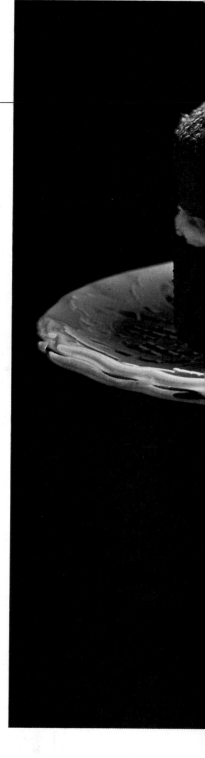

Brandy Snaps

	Metric/UK	US
Butter	75g/3oz	6 Tbsp
Castor (superfine) sugar	50g/2oz	¼ cup
Golden (light corn) syrup	75ml/3floz	6 Tbsp
Flour	50g/2oz	½ cup
Ground ginger	1 tsp	1 tsp

Juice of ½ lemon

Preheat the oven to moderate (180°C/350°F, Gas Mark 4). Grease a large baking sheet and grease the handle of a long wooden spoon with butter to curl the snaps around.

Make the batter by the melting method described earlier in the chapter, beating the liquids carefully into the flour and ginger until smooth. Drop teaspoonsful on to the baking sheet, leaving at least 10cm/4in between each one. Bake for 8–10 minutes or until golden brown.

Turn off the heat and open the oven door. Remove one biscuit (cookie) at a time from the sheet using a palette knife or spatula and curl it around the butter-covered spoon handle. Slide off the handle when set, and on to a wire rack to cool. Repeat with the rest of the batter. If some of the biscuits (cookies) set hard before you are ready to roll them, heat them gently in the oven until pliable again. When all the brandy snaps are cold they can be stored in an airtight container for future use or filled with brandy-flavoured whipped cream to serve.

15–20 biscuits (cookies)

237

Battenburg Cake

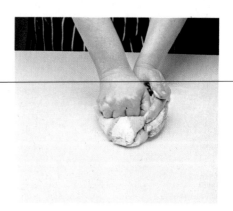

To make *Battenburg Cake,* divide the cake tin in half by pleating a layer of foil carefully down the middle to make a divider.

Now pour white cake batter into one half of the tin and the cocoa-flavoured mixture into the other half. They should not overlap.

Now make the almond paste or knead bought marzipan if preferred, until the mixture is smooth and pliable and ready to roll out.

Cook the cakes and when ready remove from the tin. Carefully cut both cake pieces in half lengthways, as in the picture.

Now join one brown and one white half together using apricot glaze or jam and generously glaze the top of both sides.

Place the other two halves of the cake on top of the first two to make a chequer board pattern. Coat the cake with apricot jam.

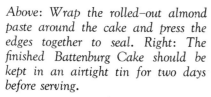

Above: Wrap the rolled-out almond paste around the cake and press the edges together to seal. Right: The finished *Battenburg Cake* should be kept in an airtight tin for two days before serving.

Battenburg Cake

	Metric/UK	US
Butter	225g/8oz	1 cup
Castor (superfine) sugar	225g/8oz	1 cup
Eggs	4	4
Self-raising (self-rising) flour	225g/8oz	2 cups
Vanilla essence (extract)	$\frac{1}{2}$ tsp	$\frac{1}{2}$ tsp
Milk	2–4 Tbsp	2–4 Tbsp
Cocoa powder	2 Tbsp	2 Tbsp
Apricot jam	2 Tbsp	2 Tbsp
Basic quantity of Almond Paste		

Preheat the oven to fairly hot (190°C/375°F, Gas Mark 5). Line a 23×15cm/9×6in rectangular cake tin (pan) with foil, making a deep pleat in the foil down the length of the tin (pan), exactly in the middle. Pull the pleat upright to form a division wall, creating two oblongs of equal size.

Prepare the cake by the creaming method, using the milk to make a soft, dropping consistency. Put one half in half of the tin (pan). Mix the cocoa with the second half and fill the remainder of the tin (pan). Bake for 25 minutes or until cooked. Set aside to cool. Make the Almond Paste as described in the basic recipe earlier in the chapter.

Turn out the cakes and trim the ends. Cut each in half lengthways. Stick a brown length on top of a white length with a little apricot jam. Stick the other two halves together with a little more jam, alternating brown with white. Roll out the almond paste into an oblong big enough to enclose the cake. Coat the cake

This moist delicious Almond Cherry Cake substitutes ground almonds for flour.

with apricot jam and neatly wrap with the almond paste. Place the seam underneath and trim the edges to leave the ends uncovered. Crimp along the borders and score a criss-cross pattern along the top. Keep in an airtight container for about 2 days before serving.

Almond Cherry Cake

Ground almonds are substituted for a proportion of the flour in this recipe, giving a moist, delicious cake which keeps well.

	Metric/UK	US
Butter, softened	100g/4oz	$\frac{1}{2}$ cup
Castor (superfine) sugar	150g/5oz	$\frac{2}{3}$ cup
Large eggs	3	3
Ground almonds	85g/3$\frac{1}{2}$oz	$\frac{3}{4}$ cup
Self-raising (self-rising) flour	40g/1$\frac{1}{2}$oz	$\frac{1}{3}$ cup
Vanilla essence (extract)	1 tsp	1 tsp
Glacé (candied) cherries, cut in half	100g/4oz	$\frac{2}{3}$ cup

Preheat the oven to moderate (180°C/350°F, Gas Mark 4). Grease and flour an 18cm/7in diameter round deep cake tin (pan). Use the creaming method to prepare the batter, adding spoonsful of ground almonds alternately with the eggs. Fold in the flour, vanilla and cherries. Turn into the tin (pan) and bake for 50 minutes or until cooked through. Turn out of the tin (pan) and cool completely before serving.

BAKING WITH YEAST

*Baking bread is an immensely satisfying pastime.
The handling of the yeast, the kneading and punching
of it are almost guaranteed to iron out the traumas of modern
living. And the results from those first warming,
aromatic smells evoking times gone by to the finished
product, duly sliced and dripping with butter and cheese
or jam make the small amount of effort involved
almost incidental. And just compare the home-made
result with the plastic sliced version from your local
supermarket!*

USING YEAST

Using yeast is not difficult providing you remember a few basic facts about it and keep these in mind as you work with it. Above all, remember that yeast is a living organism and needs warmth, food and moisture if it is to work properly. Yeast is the raising agent in dough, and the more efficiently it works, then the better will be the rise.

You can buy fresh yeast in cakes or dried yeast in granules and both are extremely effective. The advantage of dried yeast is that it has good storing properties, while fresh yeast will only last for 4–5 days in the refrigerator. However, it will freeze for a few weeks, which is very convenient. Fresh yeast should smell slightly of mushrooms, be creamy-grey in colour, break cleanly and crumble well. Do not buy fresh yeast that is dark, hard and strong-smelling. Dried yeast looks like small hard granules and is more concentrated than fresh yeast, so use only half the quantity of dried yeast in a recipe giving quantities for fresh yeast.

Yeast is activated by moisture, which is provided by the liquid added; food, which is supplied by added sugar or the sugar in the flour; and by warmth. The yeast is killed off in the process of baking at 43°C/ 110°F, but requires a temperature of between 24°C/ 75°F and 29°C/85°F to produce a good rise. It gives off bubbles of carbon dioxide gas which cause the gluten in the flour to stretch and expand, giving the light open texture which we associate with yeast products.

Note: *All the quantities in this chapter are for fresh yeast, so halve them for dried yeast.*

OTHER INGREDIENTS

Liquid

This can be water or a mixture of milk and water. It is usually heated to lukewarm (about 24°C/75°F to 29°C/85°F) before adding to the flour.

Salt

Always add a little salt to the dough, or the flavour will be rather flat. However, avoid adding too much as this inhibits the action of the yeast.

Flour

Have the flour at room temperature before using it. Almost all flours are soft, household blends which do not produce a well-risen loaf. Aim to buy strong flour, made from hard wheat. This has a high gluten content, which produces a more springy, elastic dough. Choose from white strong flour, wholemeal flour or wholewheat flour. These are available from health-food shops and big supermarkets. You can mix the white and brown flours to produce varying colours and flavours of brown bread.

Eggs, butter or oil can be added to produce a richer mixture. The finished product is yellower in colour, a little lighter in texture and has better keeping qualities.

TECHNIQUES

1. Dissolving the yeast

Crumble fresh yeast into a small bowl, add the sugar (if called for in the recipe) and a small quantity of the warmed milk, or milk and water. Mix to a smooth cream and set aside in a warm place for about 20 minutes until puffed up and frothy.

If you are using dried yeast, dissolve a little sugar in a little warm liquid and sprinkle on the dried yeast. Leave for 10 minutes in a warm place to separate and swell.

The yeast is now active and ready to use.

2. Mixing the dough

Put the dry ingredients (usually flour, salt and sugar) into a large warm mixing bowl. Make a well in the centre and add the liquid ingredients (milk, water, egg, butter, oil, etc.). Use your fingers or a spatula to draw down the flour and mix into the liquids until the flour has all been incorporated. If the dough is too soft and wet, then add a little more flour.

3. Kneading

This can be done successfully in an electric mixer fitted with a dough hook, but hand kneading is a satisfying process. To knead by hand, turn the dough on to a lightly floured board or marble slab. Fold the dough over towards you from the opposite side, then push it away firmly using the heel of your hand. Turn the dough slightly and repeat. Continue doing this for at least 10 minutes until the dough is soft, smooth and elastic. Successful rising depends on this kneading and if you can continue for about 10–15 minutes, so much the better.

4. Rising

Shape the dough into a ball and place in a large bowl. Cover the bowl with a damp cloth or lightly oiled polythene (plastic) sheet to prevent the dough from drying out. The yeast is now evenly dispersed throughout the dough and activated by warmth, liquid and food. Place the bowl in a draught-free place and leave it to rise. If the kitchen is cold, place the bowl over warm

water, but without touching it, to speed up the rise. *Do not* put the dough over heat, in a slow oven or over a pilot-light or hot-plate. This will produce a coarse dough and a grey-looking crumb tasting too strongly of yeast.

The length of time the dough takes almost to double its bulk will vary enormously. But between half an hour and 1½ hours is usually adequate. A high proportion of sugar and fats retards the rising process. Do not let the dough rise too far; it will break the gluten pockets and collapse when cooked.

You can give the dough a 'slow-rise' in the refrigerator overnight, producing a lighter, springier loaf, which keeps well. If you do this, the dough needs longer knocking back and longer proving time.

5. Knocking back

Take the swollen dough and place on a board. Knuckle it down with your fist to expel surplus carbon dioxide and bring the yeast back into contact with its food supply. Knead for 2 minutes.

Use a sharp knife to cut into loaves or rolls and check the size by weighing the pieces. Shape into loaves or rolls, paying attention to the uniformity of the shapes.

6. Proving

This is to ensure that the yeast is still active. Put the dough in the greased tins (pans) and push it out to roughly the shape of the tins (pans), cover with a damp cloth again and place in a warm, slightly moist position for 45–60 minutes. The dough will rise up again and fill the tins (pans).

For a plain finish, dust with a little flour. For a shiny finish brush with a little beaten egg and milk. Cracked wheat can be sprinkled on brown loaves and poppy-seeds on rolls and sweet breads.

7. Baking

Preheat the oven to very hot (240°C/475°F, Gas Mark 9) while the bread is proving. Always place the dough in a very hot oven. Initially, the bread will rise; this is called 'oven spring'. The high temperature kills the action of the yeast and the gluten cells will continue to set while baking. After 15 minutes reduce the oven temperature to the temperature given in the recipe (usually between 190°C/375°F, Gas Mark 5 and 220°C/425°F, Gas Mark 7). Bake for about 25–30 minutes or

until the bread sounds hollow when rapped on the underside with your knuckles. Cool on a wire rack before attempting to cut it. Bread freezes well, so it is well worth making a large batch at one time.

Household White Bread

Bake the bread in a simple loaf tin (pan), braid it or shape it into round loaves.

	Metric/UK	US
Butter	2 tsp	2 tsp
Yeast	25g/1oz	½ cake or 1½ envelopes
Sugar	1 Tbsp plus 1 tsp	1 Tbsp plus 1 tsp
Warm water	900ml/ 1½ pints	3¾ cups
Flour	1.35kg/3lb	12 cups
Salt	1 Tbsp	1 Tbsp

Grease four loaf tins (pans) with the butter. Prepare and cream the yeast with 1 teaspoon of the sugar and 4 teaspoons of the warm water. Proceed following the basic method. Put the 4 loaves to prove. Preheat the oven to very hot (240°C/475°F, Gas Mark 9). When

the loaves have risen up to fill the tins (pans) after about 30–40 minutes, place in the centre of the oven. After 15 minutes, reduce the temperature to hot (220°C/425°F, Gas Mark 7) and put the bread on a lower shelf. Bake for another 25–30 minutes. Tip the loaves out of the tins (pans), test that they are cooked through and put to cool. If not quite ready, return to the oven, upside down, at fairly hot (190°C/375°F, Gas Mark 5) until cooked.

Four 450g/1lb loaves

Wholewheat Bread

	Metric/UK	US
Butter	1½ tsp	1½ tsp
Yeast	25g/1oz	½ cake or 1½ envelopes
Brown sugar	1 tsp	1 tsp
Warm water	900ml/ 1½ pints	3¾ cups
Stone-ground, wholewheat flour	1.35kg/3lb	12 cups
Salt	1 Tbsp	1 Tbsp
Clear honey	2 Tbsp	2 Tbsp
Vegetable oil	1 Tbsp	1 Tbsp

Prepare and cream the yeast with the brown sugar and about 4 teaspoons of the warm water. Proceed as for the basic method, adding the honey and oil with the remaining warm water. Bake in well-greased tins (pans), or flower pots for an attractive, unusual shape. Sprinkle with a little cracked wheat before baking.

Oven temperature and cooking time as for Household White Bread.

Four 450g/1lb loaves

Step-by-Step to Short-Time White Bread

	Metric/UK	US
Fresh yeast	50g/2oz	4 envelopes
Ascorbic Acid tablet	1 × 50mg	1 × 50mg
Strong white flour	1.4kg/3lb	12 cups
Salt	2 Tbsp	2 Tbsp
Castor (superfine) sugar	2 tsp	2tsp
Butter	25g/1oz	2 Tbsp

Warm 900ml/1½ pints (3¾ cups) of water to blood heat. Test temperature by inserting a finger. Crumble the yeast into the liquid.

Crush ascorbic tablet and add to the liquid to dissolve. Mix the flour, salt and sugar together, then cut in fat until in small pieces.

Make a well in the centre and add the yeast liquid. Mix together until the dough binds and leaves the sides of the bowl.

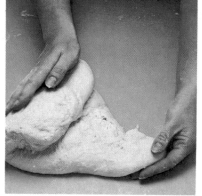

Turn out on to a floured surface and knead and fold it back and forth. Knead for at least 10 minutes, until the dough is shiny and elastic.

Put the dough in a greased polythene (plastic) bag and tie loosely. Put in a warm place and let the dough rise for 5–10 minutes.

Remove the dough from the bag and knock it back. To do this, flatten it by pressing down all over with your knuckles.

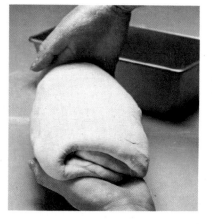

Knead again for 1 minute, then shape it by folding it in three lengthways. Put into a greased loaf pan, seam end underneath.

Put the dough and pan into the bag again and tie loosely. Put in a warm place for 40–45 minutes until doubled. Bake as per the recipe.

Sweet Bread

Sweet Bread can be used in many ways. Make it into buns and rolls or form into a ring and sprinkle with fruit and nuts. If you are making it into a fruit loaf, add about 150g/5oz (1 cup) of mixed candied fruit and peel for each 450g/1lb (4 cups) of flour.

	Metric/UK	US
Butter	100g/4oz plus 1 tsp	½ cup plus 1 tsp
Yeast	14g/½oz	¼ cake or 1 envelope
Sugar	½ tsp	½ tsp
Warm water	3 tsp	3 tsp
Milk	250ml/8floz	1 cup
Flour	700g/1½lb	6 cups
Salt	1 tsp	1 tsp
Eggs, lightly beaten	2	2
GLAZE		
Egg	1	1
Milk	1 Tbsp	1 Tbsp

Grease two tins (pans) with the teaspoon of butter. Prepare and cream the yeast with the sugar and the warm water. Warm the milk to tepid and add the remaining butter. When the butter has melted, set aside to cool before adding to the dry ingredients. Proceed as for the basic method, adding the eggs with the warm liquid ingredients. Add any dried fruit at this time.

Shape the loaves and glaze with the egg beaten in the milk. Bake as before, in an oven preheated to very hot (240°C/475°F, Gas Mark 9) for 10–15 minutes. Reduce to hot (220°C/425°F, Gas Mark 7) for 25–30 minutes until the bread is cooked.

Two 450g/1lb loaves

RECIPES

Brioche

This is a delicious yeast bun which is a little tricky to handle, but absolutely marvellous to eat. It can be made in one large fluted brioche mould or small individual tins (pans).

	Metric/UK	US
Butter	75g/3oz	⅓ cup
Flour	225g/8oz	2 cups
Yeast	14g/½oz	¼ cake or 1 envelope
Salt	1 tsp	1 tsp
Castor (superfine) sugar	2 tsp	2 tsp
Milk	2–3 Tbsp	2–3 Tbsp
GLAZE		
Egg, lightly beaten	1	1

Knead the butter with the heel of your hand or a palette knife or spatula until smooth and soft. Set aside. Flour a board. Draw aside one quarter of the flour and make a well in the centre. Crumble in the yeast and just enough warm water to dissolve it. Mix to a soft dough with your fingers, draw into a ball, cut a cross in the top with a sharp knife and put it into a bowl of warm water to rise. Leave for 8 minutes to double in size, scoop out and put to drain on a cloth.

Use the remaining ingredients to make a dough by the basic method. It will be soft and sticky, but you must beat the dough for 10 minutes by hand—drawing it up and throwing it down until smooth and elastic. Continue beating, but add a little of the butter gradually until it is all worked in, and the dough is of a soft, smooth and barely sticky texture. Mix the yeast ball thoroughly into the dough by hand and put in a bowl to rise in a warm place for about 3 hours, until it has doubled in size. Knock back, cover with foil and refrigerate overnight or for at least 4 hours.

Butter the brioche mould. Turn the dough out on to a board and knead lightly. Cut off one third of the dough and set aside. Roll the remainder into a ball and place in the mould. Make a hole in the centre with three fingers. Roll the remaining dough into a ball and pull out a tapering 'tail' at one end. Fit this into the hole in the large ball. Make a few shallow cuts under the head. Cover and set aside to prove for 15 minutes. Brush with beaten egg. Preheat the oven to

Make brioche into a fabulous dessert by hollowing out centre and inserting whipped cream and strawberries.

very hot (240°C/475°F, Gas Mark 9).

Bake for 20 minutes, then reduce the heat to moderate (180°C/350°F, Gas Mark 4), until golden brown and cooked through when tested with a skewer. Cool for 25 minutes before taking out of the mould.

Large brioches are delicious plain, but they can also be filled with fresh fruit and whipped cream, and brushed all over with glistening caramelized syrup to make an elegant dessert.

To make small brioches, divide the dough into 8 and proceed as for the large brioche using small moulds. The oven temperature should be set slightly lower, at hot (220°C/425°F, Gas Mark 7), but then reduced to the same moderate heat after the first 20 minutes.
1 large or 8 small brioches

Savarin (French Yeast Cake)

A classic French cake soaked in rum or liqueur-flavoured syrup. If possible use a special savarin mould to give the cake its traditional shape.

	Metric/UK	US
Yeast	7g/¼oz	1 Tbsp
Sugar	¼ tsp	¼ tsp
Warm milk	150ml/5floz	⅔ cup
Flour	225g/8oz	2 cups
Salt	½ tsp	½ tsp
Eggs, lightly beaten	4	4
Softened butter	150g/5oz	⅔ cup
SYRUP		
Sugar	175g/6oz	¾ cup
Water	350ml/12floz	1½ cups
Rum	150ml/5floz	⅔ cup
Crème Chantilly and almonds to decorate		

Make a basic dough using all the ingredients except the butter. Beat the mixture for 10 minutes with your hands until smooth and elastic. Cover and leave to rise for 1 hour until doubled in size. Grease a savarin ring mould with 1 tablespoon of butter. Tap the dough until it collapses. Knead in the butter, piece by piece until well blended. Pour into the prepared mould and put to rise in a warm place, covered, for 30 minutes until well risen. Preheat the oven to very hot (230°C/450°F, Gas Mark 8).

Place the mould in the centre of the oven and bake for 20 minutes. Reduce the temperature to fairly hot (190°C/375°F, Gas Mark 5). Bake for a further 15 minutes or until golden brown and cooked through when tested with a skewer. Allow to cool for 5 minutes before turning out on to a rack to cool.

Make the syrup as follows. In a small saucepan dissolve the sugar in the water, stirring continuously. Increase the heat to high and bring to a boil. Simmer for 5 minutes without stirring. Stir in the rum and remove from the heat. Prick the savarin all over with a skewer and pour over the hot syrup. Set aside for 10 minutes. Decorate with Crème Chantilly and almonds.
6–8 servings

Gugelhopf (Austrian yeast cake)

This recipe uses a different method of working with yeast.

	Metric/UK	US
Butter	225g/8oz	1 cup
Fresh yeast	14g/½oz	¼ cake or 1 envelope
Sugar	175g/6oz	¾ cup
Warm milk	250ml/8floz	1 cup
Eggs	4	4
Flour, sifted	450g/1lb	4 cups
Salt	¼ tsp	¼ tsp
Finely grated rind of 1 orange		
Seedless raisins	175g/6oz	1 cup
Chopped walnuts	50g/2oz	⅓ cup
Icing (confectioner's) sugar	2 Tbsp	2 Tbsp

Gugelhopf is a sweet bread popular in Austria and France, containing raisins and walnuts. Serve warm with coffee or tea.

Grease a gugelhopf or large ring mould with butter and set aside. Prepare and cream the yeast with about ½ teaspoon of the sugar and about 4 tablespoons of the warm milk.

In a mixing bowl, cream the butter and sugar until light and fluffy. Beat in the eggs, one at a time, adding 1 tablespoon of the flour with each addition. Stir in the yeast mixture and half of the flour. Add the remaining milk and beat well. Stir in the remaining flour, salt, orange rind, raisins and walnuts.

Turn into the prepared mould. Cover and set aside to rise in a warm place for 2 hours or until doubled in bulk. Preheat the oven to moderate (180°C/350°F, Gas Mark 4).

Place the mould in the centre of the oven and bake for 40 minutes until well risen, golden brown and cooked through when tested with a skewer. Remove from the oven and cool in the mould for 30 minutes before turning out on to a rack. Sprinkle with icing (confectioner's) sugar before serving.
8 servings

*Little Orange Yeast Buns
make marvellous break-
fast breads: they have a
somewhat similar taste to
Danish Pastries.*

Orange Yeast Buns

	Metric/UK	US
Butter	150g/5oz plus 1 tsp	⅔ cup plus 1 tsp
Yeast	14g/½oz	¼ cake or 1 envelope
Sugar	100g/4oz plus ½ tsp	½ cup plus ½ tsp
Warm water	2 Tbsp	2 Tbsp
Milk	125ml/4floz	½ cup
Flour	450g/1lb	4 cups
Salt	1 tsp	1 tsp
Eggs, lightly beaten	2	2
Melted butter	25g/1oz	2 Tbsp
Currants	75g/3oz	½ cup
Grated rind of 2 large oranges		
Chopped mixed (candied) peel	1 Tbsp	1 Tbsp
Ground cinnamon	¼ tsp	¼ tsp
GLAZE		
Icing (confectioner's) sugar sifted	225g/8oz	2 cups
Orange juice	2 Tbsp	2 Tbsp

Proceed as for Sweet Bread, with the basic dough
ingredients. After knocking back and kneading the
second time, roll out the dough into a square. Brush
with the melted butter and sprinkle on the remaining
sugar, currants, orange rind, mixed (candied) peel and
cinnamon. Roll up like a Swiss (jelly) Roll (without the
paper).

Preheat the oven to fairly hot (190°C/375°F, Gas
Mark 5). With a sharp knife, cut up the dough into
4cm/1½in thick slices. Place on a baking sheet, not
quite touching, and leave to prove for 20 minutes, until
the buns have risen up and are touching each other.
Bake for 30–35 minutes until golden brown. Remove
from the oven, cool slightly, then pour over the glaze of
icing (confectioner's) sugar mixed with orange juice.
Leave to cool, then pull apart before serving.
10–15 buns

Danish Pastries

Danish Pastries are made with Croissant dough, rolled like puff pastry. Many mouth-watering flavourings are added as fillings, and they have distinctive shapes.

	Metric/UK	US
Croissant dough	525g/1¼lb	5 cups
GLAZE		
Egg, lightly beaten	1	1
Icing (confectioner's) sugar	4 Tbsp	4 Tbsp
Hot water	2 Tbsp	2 Tbsp

Preheat the oven to hot (220°C/425°F, Gas Mark 7), When the pastries have been shaped, prove and glaze with beaten egg, before putting in the oven for 15 minutes. Mix the sugar and water glaze and paint it on after they are cooked, while still warm.

Suggested fillings

1. APPLE FILLING

Crisp eating apples	2	2
Lemon juice	1 tsp	1 tsp
Apricot jam	4 Tbsp	4 Tbsp

Peel, core and thinly slice the apples. Sprinkle over the lemon juice. Stir in the apricot jam. Use in triangles or combs.

2. ALMOND FILLING

Butter	1 Tbsp	1 Tbsp
Castor (superfine) sugar	75g/3oz	⅓ cup
Ground almonds	75g/3oz	¾ cup
Egg, lightly beaten	½	½
Almond essence (extract)	3 drops	3 drops

Cream the butter with the sugar. Add the other ingredients and stir to make a firm paste. Use in stars.

3. CINNAMON SUGAR FILLING

Butter	50g/2oz	4 Tbsp
Sugar	50g/2oz	¼ cup
Ground cinnamon	2 tsp	2 tsp
Raisins	2 Tbsp	2 Tbsp

Cream the butter with the sugar and stir in the cinnamon and raisins. Use in pinwheels.

4. PINEAPPLE AND BANANA FILLING

Canned, drained pineapple	100g/4oz	4oz
Peeled, chopped bananas	2	2
Lemon juice	1 Tbsp	1 Tbsp

Combine the ingredients. Use in triangles or combs.

Step-by-Step to Danish Pastries

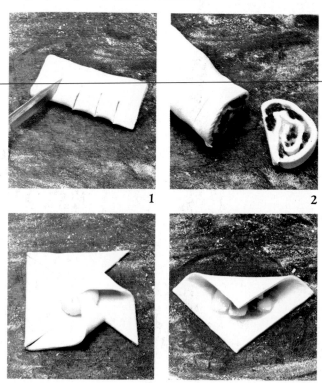

1. *Making slits in combs.*
2. *Roll pinwheels and slice.*
3. *A filled pastry star.*
4. *Pastry filled triangle.*

Traditional shapes

1. COMBS
Cut the dough into squares, place the filling in the centre and fold in half. Make deep cuts along one long edge, cutting through.

2. PINWHEELS
Cut the dough into a large rectangle. Spread with filling and roll up like a Swiss (jelly) Roll. Cut into thin slices.

3. STARS
Cut the dough into squares. Make cuts at each corner and fold every second point to the centre with a spoonful of filling placed in the centre.

4. TRIANGLES
Cut the dough into squares. Place the filling in the centre, fold diagonally and seal with water. Press firmly to seal.

You can fill Danish pastries with almost anything that takes your fancy. The picture on the right gives a selection of different shapes and fillings, from apple to cinnamon, from raisin to almond.

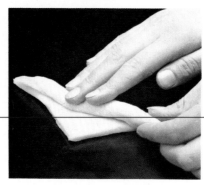

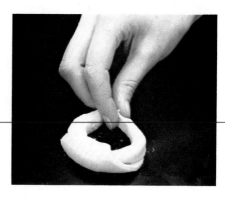

To make croissants, cut out squares about 10cm/4in. Then cut each square into a triangle.

Roll up the triangle, starting at the longest end, tucking the tip over the top.

Bring the two ends round towards each other, to make a crescent shape. Blunt the edges.

Croissants

These are crescent shaped rolls made of a special yeast dough, which is rolled like puff pastry before shaping and baking.

	Metric/UK	US
Yeast	28g/1oz	½ cake or 1½ envelopes
Sugar	1 tsp	1 tsp
Sugar	2 Tbsp	2 Tbsp
Warm milk	250ml/8floz	1 cup
Flour	525g/1¼lb	5 cups
Salt	1 tsp	1 tsp
Chilled butter	275g/10oz	1¼ cups
Eggs, lightly beaten	2	2

Prepare and cream the yeast with the teaspoon of sugar and 2–3 tablespoons of the warm milk.

Sift 450g/1lb (4 cups) of the flour, the remaining 2 tablespoons of sugar and the salt into a mixing bowl. Add 50g/2oz (¼ cup) of butter and cut into small pieces. Rub the butter into the flour until the mixture is like breadcrumbs. Make a well in the centre, add the remaining milk, the yeast mixture and eggs. Draw the flour down until you have a sticky dough. Cover and put to chill in the refrigerator for 1 hour. Shape the remaining butter into an oblong block using a rolling pin. Place in the refrigerator to chill.

Sift the remaining flour on to a clean board. Turn out the dough and knead for 10 minutes until all the flour has been incorporated. Roll out the dough into an oblong 30×20cm/12×8in. Place the chilled butter in the centre. Fold it over to enclose the butter and roll out to a strip about 37cm/15in long. Fold in three and chill for 10 minutes. Roll out and fold three times more, as for Puff Pastry. Chill the dough in the refrigerator for 1 hour.

Preheat the oven to hot (220°C/425°F, Gas Mark 7).

Sprinkle three baking sheets with water. Roll out the dough to a square about 5mm/¼in thick. Cut the dough into 13cm/5in squares, then each square into 2 triangles. Brush the tops with beaten egg to seal the edges. Pull the ends round gently to form a crescent shape, and leave in a warm place for 20–30 minutes until doubled in bulk. Brush the tops with beaten egg and bake for 15 minutes until well risen and golden brown.

About 18 croissants

Croissants are a French specialty now eaten and enjoyed throughout the world. They are made from a pastry of yeast and butter which is similar to puff pastry. They are at their best eaten hot, with butter.

Pizza with Tomatoes, Cheese and Olives

The Italian Pizza is simple to make but has endless variations. It is a large round cake of bread dough spread with a variety of ingredients such as tomatoes, Mozzarella cheese, olives, mushrooms or seafood. It is cooked in a hot oven for 15 minutes until the dough is cooked and the topping melted and hot.

	Metric/UK	US
PIZZA DOUGH		
Yeast	14g/½oz	¼ cake or 1 envelope
Sugar	¼ tsp	¼ tsp
Warm water	125ml/4floz plus 1 Tbsp	½ cup plus 1 Tbsp
Flour	225g/8oz	2 cups
Salt	1 tsp	1 tsp
Olive oil	1 tsp	1 tsp
FILLING		
Oil	1 Tbsp	1 Tbsp
Small onion, finely chopped	1	1
Garlic clove, crushed	1	1
Canned, peeled tomatoes coarsely chopped	400g/14oz	14oz
Dried marjoram	½ tsp	½ tsp
Dried oregano	¼ tsp	¼ tsp
Salt and pepper to taste		
Mozzarella cheese, thinly sliced	175g/6oz	6oz
Capers	2 Tbsp	2 Tbsp
Black olives, halved and stoned (pitted)	20	20

Prepare the dough as for Basic Bread Mixture. Meanwhile, prepare the filling.

In a saucepan, heat the oil over a moderate heat. Add the onion and garlic and fry, stirring occasionally, until soft and translucent. Stir in the tomatoes and can juice, herbs, salt and pepper. Cook for 20–30 minutes, or until the sauce is thick.

Preheat the oven to very hot (230°C/450°F, Gas Mark 8). Grease a large baking sheet with 1 teaspoon of olive oil.

Turn out the risen dough and knead for 3 minutes. Cut the dough in half. Roll out both to a circle about 5mm/¼in thick. Place well apart on the baking sheet. Spoon half the tomato sauce on to each circle. Spread it out. Arrange the Mozzarella slices over the sauce and arrange the capers and olives over them. Moisten by drizzling over each pizza the remaining teaspoon of oil. Bake for 15–20 minutes. Serve hot.

2 servings

APPENDIX

Herbs and Spices

Garnishes

Storage

Wine and Food Chart

SPICES, HERBS AND GARNISHES

SPICES AND HERBS

Quantities

It is important to follow recipes carefully when using herbs and spices, as too much can be overpowering and unpleasant. Start by introducing a very small quantity into a favourite recipe, and you will soon learn how much to add. Freshly ground spices are stronger than old ones, dried herbs than fresh herbs. If a quantity for fresh herbs is given in a recipe, use half the quantity of dried herbs.

Storing

Most spices are hard, and are ground, crushed or grated to powder. They lose their savour gradually after being powdered, so try not to keep them for too long. The same applies to herbs after being dried. Buy both in small amounts and store in airtight jars in a cool, dark place.

Notes on spices

If spices are being used in a savoury dish such as curry, add them to the fat and fry over a low heat for a minute without scorching. This helps develop their aroma.

Spiced foods lose their flavour when frozen for a long time, so use within two or three weeks of freezing.

Chilli powder is a blended powder made of sweet paprika, cayenne pepper, turmeric, cumin, coriander, oregano and cloves. Fresh red or green chillis (chili peppers) should not be substituted.

Pepper is probably the most widely used spice. Peppercorns are available black (sun dried) or white (with outer hulls removed). Black pepper has more flavour, white is hotter. Peppercorns bought whole and ground coarsely in a mill have more flavour than ready-powdered pepper. Use white pepper in white foods where black specks would not look good.

Notes on herbs

Herbs do lose their flavour very quickly if fresh (and picked) and even dried ones become less strong after a few months. Freezing does help to preserve them, however.

Fines herbes are a mixture of freshly chopped herbs, usually parsley, tarragon, chives and chervil. It is traditionally used in omelettes.

Bouquet garni is a mixture of thyme, parsley and bayleaf, and sometimes marjoram, used to flavour stews and stocks. It should be removed before serving if possible.

HERB CHART

BEEF	Garlic	LAMB	Garlic, tarragon
grilled (broiled)		chops	Basil, dill, tarragon
steaks	Tarragon	kebabs	Rosemary
pot roast	Bayleaf, chervil, marjoram, thyme	pot roast	Bayleaf, chervil, marjoram, rosemary, thyme
roast	Basil, marjoram, savory, thyme	roast	Basil, dill, marjoram mint, (as sauce), rosemary, savory, thyme
stew	Basil, bayleaf, chervil, marjoram, parsley, thyme	stew	Basil, bayleaf, chervil, dill, marjoram, mint, parsley, rosemary, thyme
PORK	Marjoram, sage, tarragon	**VEAL**	Sage, tarragon
chops	Chervil, dill, tarragon	pot roast	Bayleaf, chervil, thyme
roast	Dill, savory, thyme	roast	Basil, savory, thyme
sausages	Coriander, sage	stew	Basil, bayleaf, chervil, parsley, thyme
stew	Dill, thyme		
CURRIES	Coriander, dill, garlic	PATE	Bayleaf, garlic
MEATBALLS	Coriander, dill	PIES	Basil, parsley, savory
MINCE (GROUND)		TONGUE	Bayleaf
MEAT	Savory, garlic		
CHICKEN	Rosemary, garlic, savory, tarragon	DUCK	Basil
curry	Coriander, dill	curry	Dill
fried	Basil, marjoram, thyme	roast	Marjoram, thyme
pie	Chervil, parsley, thyme	stew	Sage
stew	Bayleaf, chervil, marjoram, parsley, sage, thyme		
TURKEY	Rosemary, garlic, savory, tarragon	GOOSE	Basil
pie	Parsley, thyme	**STUFFING**	Chervil, coriander, dill, sage, thyme, garlic
roast	Marjoram		
stew	Sage, thyme		

SOUPS		STOCK	
Any soups	Chives (as garnish)	Any stock	Bayleaf, coriander, garlic

Bean	Oregano	Court bouillon	Parsley
Bean, dried	Dill	Poultry and meat	
Borscht	Dill	stocks	Parsley, bouquet garni
Cabbage	Dill		
Celery, cream of	Marjoram		
Chicken	Bayleaf, garlic, rosemary, sage, savory, tarragon, thyme	**EGGS**	
		Any eggs	Tarragon
Chicken, cream of	Marjoram		
Consommé	Bayleaf	Baked	Thyme
Courgette (zucchini)	Dill	Custard	Bayleaf
Cucumber	Dill, mint, savory	Curried	Coriander
Fish	Garlic, rosemary, thyme	Devilled	Basil, dill, oregano, parsley savory, thyme
Lamb broth	Garlic, rosemary		
Minestrone	Basil, oregano	Omelette	Chervil, chives, parsley (together); coriander, marjoram, rosemary, savory
Mushroom	Tarragon		
Onion	Marjoram		
Pea,	Basil, coriander		
cream of	Chervil		
Spinach,	Basil	Scrambled	Chervil, chives, parsley (together); basil, coriander, marjoram, rosemary, savory, thyme
cream of	Chervil		
Split pea	Garlic, savory		
Tomato	Basil, dill, garlic, oregano, rosemary, sage, savory, tarragon, thyme		
		Soufflé	Basil, marjoram, rosemary
Turkey	Garlic, sage		
Vegetable	Basil, garlic, parsley, savory, thyme		

FISH		CHEESE	
Any fish	Basil, bayleaf, chervil, parsley, tarragon, thyme		
Any shellfish	Bayleaf, chervil, parsley		

Casseroles	Rosemary, savory	Canapés	Dill
Crab	Basil, marjoram, thyme	Cheddar (spread)	Sage
Curries	Dill	Cottage cheese	Chervil, dill, parsley, thyme
Grilled (broiled) fish	Marjoram, savory	Cream cheese	Basil, chervil, dill, mint, parsley
Halibut	Dill		
Herring	Dill	Curd cheese	Chervil, parsley
Lobster	Basil, dill, thyme	Fondue	Sage
Prawns (shrimp)	Tarragon, thyme	Omelette	Sage
Salmon	Dill	Soufflé	Parsley
Scallops	Rosemary, thyme	Spreads	Basil, chives, marjoram, thyme
Soused fish	Bayleaf		
Stuffing	Marjoram, parsley, rosemary, savory	Welsh rarebit	Basil
Tuna	Thyme		

VEGETABLES			
Artichoke	Bayleaf, tarragon	Lettuce	Chervil
Asparagus	Basil, marjoram, savory	Lentils	Oregano
Aubergine (eggplant)	Basil, chervil, oregano, parsley, rosemary, sage	Marrow (large zucchini or squash)	Marjoram, sage, savory, tarragon, thyme
Beans, broad (lima)	Basil, chives (as garnish), dill, savory, tarragon, thyme	Mushrooms	Chives (as garnish) oregano, rosemary, tarragon, thyme
Beans, dried	Oregano, tarragon	Onions	Coriander, parsley, sage, tarragon, thyme
Beans, French (green)	Dill, tarragon		
Beetroot (beet)	Dill, sage	Peas	Basil, chervil, chives (as garnish) marjoram, mint, rosemary
Broccoli	Basil, dill, oregano		
Brussels sprouts	Dill, marjoram, sage, savory		
Cabbage	Basil, bayleaf, dill, oregano parsley	Potatoes	Chervil, chives, (as garnish), dill, marjoram, mint, parsley, rosemary, savory, tarragon, thyme
Carrots	Basil, bayleaf, chives (as garnish), mint, rosemary, savory, tarragon, thyme		
Cauliflower	Chives (as garnish), coriander, parsley, rosemary	Spinach	Basil, chervil, coriander, mint, rosemary, thyme
		Tomatoes	Basil, bayleaf, chervil, chives (as garnish), coriander, oregano, parsley, sage, savory
Celery	Basil, chervil, marjoram, parsley, sage		
Courgettes (zucchini)	Basil, marjoram, sage, savory, tarragon, thyme	Turnips	Basil, chives, (as garnish), dill, parsley, rosemary, thyme
Cucumbers	Basil, chervil, dill, savory, mint (in yogurt and cucumber salad)		

SWEET DISHES			
Cooked fruit	Coriander seed	**Herbs are not used in cakes and biscuits (cookies).**	
Fruit salad	Mint		
Melon balls	Mint	See Herb Bread	

Herb and Spinach Flan—an excellent light lunch.

Herb and Spinach Flan

	Metric/UK	US
1 × 23cm/9in flan case (pastry shell), made from Shortcrust Pastry, baked blind and cooled		
FILLING		
Butter	50g/2oz	4 Tbsp
Small onion, thinly sliced into rings	1	1
Lean bacon slices, chopped	3	3
Spinach, washed, trimmed and chopped	½kg/1lb	1lb
Eggs, lightly beaten	2	2
Double (heavy) cream	150ml/5floz	⅔ cup
Salt	½ tsp	½ tsp
Black pepper	¼ tsp	¼ tsp
Dried thyme	1 tsp	1 tsp
Dried basil	½ tsp	½ tsp
Chopped parsley	2 tsp	2 tsp
Cheddar cheese, grated	50g/2oz	½ cup

Preheat the oven to fairly hot (200°C/400°F, Gas Mark 6). In a large frying-pan, melt the butter over a moderate heat. Add the onion and cook, stirring occasionally, until it is soft and translucent. Add the bacon and fry for 5 minutes, stirring occasionally.

Stir in the spinach and cook the mixture, stirring frequently for 3–5 minutes until it is heated through and everything is well blended. Spoon the mixture into the flan case (pastry shell) and set aside.

In a medium-sized mixing bowl, combine the eggs, cream, salt and pepper, thyme, basil and parsley, beating until they are blended. Stir in the cheese and mix well.

Pour the mixture over the spinach and place the flan in the oven. Bake for 30 minutes until the filling has set and the top is brown. Serve hot.
4–6 servings

Herb and Orange Stuffing

This stuffing may be used for duck, lamb or goose, but is particularly good with chicken. The quantities given below will stuff one 2kg/4lb chicken.

	Metric/UK	US
Butter	25g/1oz	2 Tbsp
Large onion, finely chopped	1	1
Lean veal, finely minced	½kg/1lb	1lb
Fresh white breadcrumbs	175g/6oz	3 cups

	Metric/UK	US
Salt	½ tsp	½ tsp
Black pepper	¼ tsp	¼ tsp
Finely grated rind of 1 orange		
Dried marjoram	1 tsp	1 tsp
Dried thyme	½ tsp	½ tsp
Fresh chives, very finely chopped	1 Tbsp	1 Tbsp
Double (heavy) cream	2 Tbsp	2 Tbsp
Fresh orange juice	4 Tbsp	4 Tbsp

In a medium-sized saucepan, melt the butter over a moderate heat. Add the onion and cook, stirring occasionally, until it is soft and translucent. Stir in the veal, breadcrumbs and salt, pepper, orange rind, marjoram, thyme and chives. Cook for 5 minutes, until the veal loses its pinkness. Stir in the cream and orange juice, combine the mixture thoroughly and remove from the heat. The stuffing is now ready.

Herb Bread

Serve hot with salads or fish dishes.

	Metric/UK	US
Large French loaf	1	1
Butter	175g/6oz	¾ cup
Garlic clove, crushed	1	1
Chopped parsley,	1 Tbsp	1 Tbsp
Dried sage	¼ tsp	¼ tsp
Chopped chives	1 Tbsp	1 Tbsp
Black pepper	¼ tsp	¼ tsp

Preheat the oven to fairly hot (190°C/375°F, Gas Mark 5). Using a sharp knife, slice the bread downwards at 2.5cm/1in intervals to within 5mm/¼in of the base, so that each slice is still attached to the bottom of the crust. Set aside.

In a small mixing bowl, cream the butter with a wooden spoon until smooth and creamy. Beat in the garlic, parsley, sage, chives and black pepper, beating until smooth and evenly coloured. With a knife, spread the herb butter on one side of each bread slice, being careful not to detach them. Wrap the loaf in foil and place on a large baking sheet. Put the loaf in the centre of the oven and bake for 15–20 minutes, until the loaf is very hot and the butter has melted into the bread. Remove from the oven and discard the foil. Break the loaf into slices and serve immediately.

20 servings

Herb Bread is easily made from a mixture of butter, garlic, parsley, sage and chives. Serve hot, with spicy savoury dishes.

SPICES CHART

MEAT		
Any meat	Ginger, pepper	

BEEF		LAMB	
pot roast	Allspice, celery seed	pot roast	Allspice, celery seed
roast	Caraway seed	roast	Mustard (made, as coating)
stew	Allspice, anise, caraway seed, celery seed, chilli powder, cinnamon (stick) paprika	stew	Allspice, celery seed

PORK		VEAL	
sausage	Cloves, mustard	chops	Mace
stew	Cayenne pepper Celery seed, paprika	pot roast	Allspice, celery seed,
		stew	Allspice, anise, celery seed, paprika

CURRIES	Cardamom seed, cayenne pepper, cumin seed, turmeric	PIES	Nutmeg
		TONGUE	Cloves

POULTRY		
Any poultry	Chilli powder, pepper	

CHICKEN		DUCK	
braised	Allspice, anise, cloves	pilaffs	Anise, fennel seed
fried	Chilli powder, ginger, sesame seed	roast	Anise, sesame seed
grilled (broiled)	Cayenne pepper, chilli powder, sesame seed	stew	Allspice, ginger
pies	Allspice		
pilaffs	Anise, fennel seed		
roast	Ginger, sesame seed		
stew	Allspice, celery seed, ginger, mace		

GOOSE		TURKEY	
roast	Caraway seed	pies	Allspice
		stews	Allspice

CURRIES	Cardamom seed, cayenne pepper, cumin seed, turmeric	STUFFING	Cumin seed

267

EGGS			
Any eggs	Paprika (as garnish) pepper	All soups	Pepper

Curried	Cumin seed	Borscht	Caraway seed
Custard	Nutmeg	Chicken	Allspice
Devilled	Chilli powder, mustard	Consommé	Allspice
Omelette	Caraway seed, celery seed, chilli powder	Onion	Cloves (ground)
		Pea	Chilli powder, paprika
Scrambled	Celery seed, chilli powder, sesame seed	Potato	Allspice, fennel seed, nutmeg, caraway seed
Soufflé	Celery seed	Tomato	Allspice, chilli powder, nutmeg
		Vegetable	Cayenne pepper

FISH AND SHELLFISH		CHEESE	
Any fish	Chilli powder, pepper, paprika (as garnish)	Any cheese	Mustard, pepper

Baked fish	Fennel seed	Canapés	Cumin seed
Crab	Caraway seed, cayenne pepper, sesame seed	Cottage cheese	Anise, chilli powder
		Fondue	Chilli powder, sesame seed
Curries	Cardamom seed	Marcaroni cheese	Cayenne pepper
Grilled (broiled) fish	Caraway seed, sesame seed	Omelette	Sesame seed
Lobster	Caraway seed, cayenne pepper, cumin seed	Soufflé	Cayenne pepper
Pilaffs	Fennel seed, turmeric	Spreads	Anise, celery seed, chilli powder, cumin seed, sesame seed
Poached fish	Allspice, caraway seed, fennel seed		
		Wafers (crackers) and straws	Cayenne pepper, celery seed
Prawns (shrimp)	Chilli powder, cayenne pepper, cumin seed, sesame seed		
		Welsh rarebit	Cayenne pepper, mace, mustard
Stuffed fish	Caraway seed		

SWEET DISHES		CAKES AND BISCUITS (COOKIES)	
Apple, baked	Anise, cardamom seed, cinnamon, fennel seed, nutmeg	Any cakes and biscuits (cookies)	Anise, caraway seed, cumin seed, sesame seed
		Any biscuits (cookies)	Ginger
pie	Allspice, anise, caraway seed, cinnamon, fennel seed, nutmeg	Danish pastry	Cardamom seed
		Gingerbread	Allspice, cinnamon, cloves, ginger, mustard, pepper
puréed	Cinnamon, cloves, fennel seed, nutmeg	Spice cake	Mustard
Chocolate desserts	Cinnamon, cloves, mace, nutmeg	**BREAD**	
Fruit salad	Allspice, anise		
Lemon, lime and orange desserts	Mace	Banana bread	Nutmeg
Rice pudding	Cinnamon, nutmeg	Sweet breads and rolls	Anise, cardamom seed, cinnamon, cloves, mace, nutmeg, pepper, sesame seed
Steamed puddings	Allspice, cloves, ginger, nutmeg		
Stewed fruits	Anise, cardamom seed, cinnamon, ginger	Rye and pumpernickel	Caraway seed

VEGETABLES

All vegetables	Pepper		
Aubergine (eggplant)	Chilli powder, mace, nutmeg	Lettuce (braised)	Celery seed
Beans, broad (lima)	Chilli powder	Mushrooms	Cloves, nutmeg
Beans, French (green)	Mace, nutmeg	Onions	Caraway seed, chilli powder, cinnamon, cloves, fennel seed, mace, nutmeg
Cabbage	Caraway seed, cayenne pepper, celery seed, fennel seed, nutmeg	Parsnips	Allspice
		Potatoes	Caraway seed, fennel seed
Carrots	Caraway seed, cardamom seed, cinnamon, cloves, ginger	Sauerkraut	Caraway seed
		Spinach	Allspice, nutmeg, paprika
		Spring greens (collards)	Cayenne pepper
Cauliflower	Paprika	Tomatoes	Chilli powder, mace, nutmeg
Celery	Caraway seed		
Corn	Chilli powder, mace, nutmeg, paprika, sesame seed	Turnips	Allspice

*Traditional Gingerbread,
ideal for a picnic. Serve
with butter or cream cheese.*

Gingerbread

	Metric/UK	US
Butter	75g/3oz	$\frac{1}{3}$ cup
Flour	225g/8oz	2 cups
Bicarbonate of soda (baking soda)	$\frac{1}{2}$ tsp	$\frac{1}{2}$ tsp
Ground ginger	$1\frac{1}{2}$ tsp	$1\frac{1}{2}$ tsp
Ground cloves	$\frac{1}{4}$ tsp	$\frac{1}{4}$ tsp
Ground cinnamon	$\frac{1}{2}$ tsp	$\frac{1}{2}$ tsp
Salt	$\frac{1}{4}$ tsp	$\frac{1}{4}$ tsp
Sugar	100g/4oz	$\frac{1}{2}$ cup
Egg	1	1
Treacle (molasses)	175ml/6floz	$\frac{3}{4}$ cup
Sour cream	250ml/8floz	1 cup
Raisins	50g/2oz	$\frac{1}{3}$ cup

Preheat the oven to moderate (180°C/350°F, Gas Mark

4). Lightly grease a loaf tin (pan) with a little softened butter.

Sift the flour, soda, ginger, cloves, cinnamon and salt into a medium-sized mixing bowl. Set aside. Cream the butter and sugar together with a wooden spoon. Add the egg and treacle (molasses) and beat until the mixture is smooth. Stir in the sour cream. Gradually incorporate the flour mixture, beating constantly until the mixture is smooth. Stir in the raisins.

Pour the mixture into the loaf tin (pan) and place in the oven. Bake the gingerbread for $1\frac{1}{4}$ hours, until a skewer inserted into the centre comes out clean.

Garlic Bread

	Metric/UK	US
Butter, softened	225g/8oz	1 cup
Chopped parsley	2 Tbsp	2 Tbsp
Garlic cloves, finely chopped	2	2
French loaves	2	2

Preheat the oven to fairly hot (200°C/400°F, Gas Mark 6). Cream the butter, parsley and garlic together with a wooden spoon. Slice the loaves thickly crosswise to within about 5mm/$\frac{1}{4}$in of the base of the loaves.

Spread the butter mixture generously on one side of each of the slices. Wrap the loaves in foil and place them on a baking sheet in the centre of the oven. Bake for 15–20 minutes until the butter has melted. Serve at once in the foil.

Cinnamon Toast

A delicious change for winter snacks is Cinnamon Toast. Lightly toast slices of white or brown bread on both sides. Spread with butter immediately, then sprinkle a generous pinch of cinnamon over the butter so that the spice melts into the toast with the butter. Serve at once.

Spiced Apple Cake

A moist, spicy cake which can be served plain or iced.

	Metric/UK	US
Flour	225g/8oz plus 1 Tbsp	2 cups plus 1 Tbsp
Salt	$\frac{1}{2}$ tsp	$\frac{1}{2}$ tsp
Baking powder	1 tsp	1 tsp
Ground cinnamon	1 tsp	1 tsp
Ground cloves	$\frac{1}{2}$ tsp	$\frac{1}{2}$ tsp
Butter, softened	100g/4oz	$\frac{1}{2}$ cup
Soft brown sugar	175g/6oz	1 cup
Eggs	3	3
Raisins	100g/4oz	$\frac{2}{3}$ cup
Walnuts, chopped	100g/4oz	1 cup
Apple sauce	225g/8oz	1 cup

Preheat the oven to moderate (180°C/350°F, Gas Mark 4). Grease a 20cm/8in round cake tin (pan) with a little butter and dust lightly with the 1 tablespoon of flour. Sift the remaining flour, salt, baking powder, cinnamon and cloves together. In a separate bowl, beat the butter with a wooden spoon until creamy. Cream in the sugar, then beat in the eggs.

Add the flour mixture a little at a time, stirring until the batter is smooth. Add the raisins, walnuts and apple sauce. Mix well and pour into the cake tin (pan). Bake in the centre of the oven for 80–90 minutes, until a skewer inserted into the centre comes out clean.

Mulled Wine

	Metric/UK	US
Dry red wine	750ml/26 floz (1 bottle)	3$\frac{1}{4}$ cups
Juice and thinly pared rind of 1 lemon		
Grated nutmeg,	$\frac{1}{2}$ tsp	$\frac{1}{2}$ tsp
Cinnamon	5cm/2in	2in
Sugar	3 Tbsp	3 Tbsp
Lemon, thinly sliced	1	1

Pour the wine into a saucepan and add the lemon juice and rind, the spices and sugar. Place over a moderate heat and bring the mixture to a boil, stirring occasionally to dissolve the sugar. Boil the mixture for 2 minutes.

Remove the pan from the heat. Allow the wine to cool slightly, before straining the mixture into a large jug. Garnish with the lemon slices and serve warm.

A traditional, festive bowl of Mulled Wine–easily made from red wine, lemon, spices and sugar.

GARNISHES

The purpose of garnishing food is to make it look pleasing and tempting. A garnish should always be complementary in flavour to the main ingredients of the dish, but may well provide a pleasing contrast in texture and colour. It can be a simple garnish of onion rings, lemon twists, watercress or sliced olives, or it may be a composite garnish of several complementary ingredients, such as glazed baby onions and mushrooms tossed in butter or assorted Julienne strips of vegetables, cooked in butter. The garnish may be hot or cold for a hot dish, but it is always cold for a cold dish. A wide variety of salad vegetables provide colourful garnishes for hot and cold dishes, such as watercress, gherkin (pickle) fans, radish roses and cucumber slices.

Colours

Use bright colours to improve a dull-looking dish: thinly sliced stuffed olives, slices of hard-boiled (hard-cooked) egg, tomato slices, lemon twists and small sprigs of parsley or watercress can transform the appearance of food.

Quantities

The quantity of garnish is dictated by the number of people you are serving. There should always be enough garnish to serve a little with each portion of food. For instance, four servings of fish would be garnished with four lemon twists and perhaps four small sprigs of parsley.

When not to garnish

Some food does not need to be garnished at all. If a dish has many ingredients, some of them brightly coloured, then the food may well look complete in itself. It would simply spoil the dish to add anything to it. Use your discretion with garnishes and keep them immaculate, simple and striking.

Preparation

Prepare the garnishes with care, well in advance, so that it can be put in position quickly when the food is ready to serve.

Olives, black or green, should be stoned (pitted) and cut into thin slices. Hard-boiled (hard-cooked) egg should also be thinly sliced. Use vegetable or aspic cutters, which are available in many small shapes from circles, flowers and petals to squares and half-moons These will enable you to cut any garnish you want from lightly cooked vegetable slices such as carrot or turnip or parsnip and from hard-boiled (hard-cooked) egg whites.

Thin strips of orange or lemon peel can look most colourful, but do be extremely careful to remove all the white pith before shredding it very finely with a sharp knife into uniform lengths.

Button mushrooms should be wiped clean, then cut into thin slices through the cap and stalk, making a mushroom-shaped slice. Either marinate in French Dressing before use, or toss lightly over a low heat in a little melted butter then drain, before arranging in a neat overlapping row.

Various garnishes

Bacon rolls These are easy to make, and delicious with many egg and poultry dishes. Use thinly cut streaky (fatty) bacon slices. Cut off any rind and discard. Smooth and stretch the slice, using the back of a kitchen knife, until thin. Neatly roll up the bacon and cut, forming 2 or 3 rolls from each slice. Thread several uniformly-sized rolls on to a skewer and grill (broil) until crisp. Use hot, allowing one or two rolls per person.

Lemon This is a useful garnish which complements many dishes. It has a bright attractive colour and a sharp but pleasant flavour. Cut into small wedges, removing obvious membranes and pips. Alternatively, cut into wafer-thin slices with a sharp knife, and cut each slice in half. Make twists by cutting through a slice neatly from the centre out to one edge; twist the cut ends in opposite directions and place on the food. Make butterflies by cutting a thin slice neatly in half: cut almost in half again from the outer edge, then twist the narrow 'waist' with a tiny sprig of parsley to form a butterfly or bow.

Salad garnishes

Watercress Wash thoroughly and discard tough stems and ragged leaves. Arrange in small neat sprigs, or perhaps a central bouquet in a ring mould. It looks particularly attractive and gleaming if it is lightly tossed in French Dressing just before using.

Lettuce Wash thoroughly and pat dry. Use small whole leaves as a base for perhaps a stuffed egg hors d'oeuvre, or shred finely and arrange as a neat border on a serving platter.

Cucumber Wipe clean, then slice finely. Alternatively, use a canal knife or the end of a potato peeler to groove the outer skin at intervals all the way down, then thinly slice, to create slices with a patterned outer edge. Arrange cucumber slices in an overlapping, neat row around a platter.

Tomato Slice thinly with a sharp knife to make rings. To 'van-dyke' a whole tomato, start in the fattest 'waist' area of the tomato and, with a very sharp knife, cut a zig-zag pattern deeply all around the waist until it joins. The tomato should pull gently apart to form two small baskets, each with an attractive pointed edge. Fill with hot, cooked, diced mixed vegetables to accompany fish, grilled (broiled) or fried meat. Serve one per person.

Flowers 'Roses' or 'flowers' can be cut from crisp radishes. Wash thoroughly. Cut thin deep cuts almost to the base of the radish, keeping it in one piece. Place in iced water and the 'flower' will gradually open out and curl attractively. Allow plenty of time. This technique of making curls and flowers can be used with crisp celery, leek and almost any firm vegetable.

Gherkins (pickles) Make fans by cutting down from one end to the opposite thinner base many times in parallel cuts, leaving the base intact. The gherkin (pickle) will spread out to make a pretty fan shape.

Some delicious garnishes to serve: Stuffed olives with watercress and anchovies (1) Pineapple cubes wrapped in carrot strips (2) Cheese cubes with cucumber (3) Beetroot (beet) with orange and pickled onion (4) Stuffed olives with shrimp (5) Avocado balls with a grape (6) Stoned (pitted) dates stuffed with cream cheese and topped with a carrot curl (7) A minaret mushroom wrapped in a slice of smoked salmon (8) Cream cheese with celery topped with a black olive (9).

REFRIGERATOR STORAGE CHART

FATS			MILK PRODUCTS		
Butter and margarine Lard and cooking fats	Keep in orginal wrappings or covered containers. Store in special shelf if available in refrigerator.	3–4 weeks	Milk and cream	Keep in bottle or carton.	3–4 days
			Yogurt and sour cream	Keep in original containers.	1 week

EGGS			CHEESE		
Uncooked Cooked (in shells)	Place narrow ends down on rack in refrigerator door.	2 weeks 1 week	Hard: Cheddar, blue etc.	Wrap in foil or cling wrap.	2–3 weeks
			Soft: cream, cottage etc.	Keep in covered containers.	1 week

FISH			FRUIT		
Uncooked	Remove shop wrapping, put on a plate and loosely cover with foil or cling wrap. Store near the coldest part of the refrigerator.	1–2 days	Hard: apples, pears, citrus etc.	Not essential to store in refrigerator. If space is available, wrap in plastic bags or keep in the crisper drawer.	2 weeks
Cooked	Cool and cover with foil.	2–3 days	Soft: raspberries, redcurrants, strawberries etc.	Spread out on shallow trays. Keep in one layer and cover with foil.	1–2 days
Smoked	Wrap in foil.	3–4 days			
Shellfish	Remove shop wrapping and cover with plastic or cling wrap.	1 day			
Frozen	Follow instructions on the packet.				

MEAT			POULTRY		
Large joints Chops, steaks etc. Minced (ground) meat and offal (variety meats)	Remove shop wrapping, place meat on a plate and loosely cover with foil. Store near the coldest part of the refrigerator. If no refrigerator, cover as above then place a mesh meat cover on top.	4–5 days 2–3 days 1–2 days	Uncooked	Remove shop wrapping, place on a plate and loosely cover with foil.	3–4 days
			Cooked	Cool and cover.	3 days
			Frozen	Follow instructions on the packet. Remember to thaw completely before cooking.	
Sausages Bacon and other cured, sliced meats	If pre-packed keep in original wrapping otherwise wrap in foil or cling wrap. This also applies after the packet has been opened.	2–3 days 1 week	**SALAD VEGETABLES**		
Cooked meats	Cool and cover with foil, plastic or cling wrap.	2–3 days		Wash and drain. Store in plastic bags or crisper drawer in the refrigator.	2–3 days

274

FREEZER STORAGE CHART

Food	Preparation	Storage life up to
MEAT Large cuts	Remove bones and excess fat. Pad any projecting bones and seal as snugly as possible in foil or plastic bags. Seal well. Make stock from bones, freeze in ice-cube trays and pack in plastic bags.	9 months beef and lamb; 4 months pork and veal
Small cuts	Remove excess fat, wrap in foil or in plastic bag. Interleave chops, steaks etc with foil or freezer paper, draw out as much air as possible before sealing well in foil or plastic bags.	6 months beef and lamb; 3 months pork and veal
Offal	Prepare and pack as for small cuts. Maintain strict hygiene standards.	2 months
Minced (ground) meat and sausages	Prepare and pack as for small cuts. Freeze only freshly minced (ground) meat and bought sausages. Avoid salt in sausages as this reduces storage life.	1 month
Poultry and game	Remove head, tail and feathers. Clean and truss as for cooking, pad any projecting bones. Do not stuff poultry before freezing. Pack in plastic bags, excluding as much air as possible, and seal well. Make stock from giblets, skim all excess fat after cooling and freeze in tubs or cartons leaving headspace.	Chickens up to 9 months. Ducks, geese, turkeys and game up to 6 months
Poultry joints and quarters	Freeze and wrap individually in plastic bags or foil. Several portions can be frozen in one package providing pieces of poultry are interleaved with foil or plastic sheet.	Chicken up to 9 months. Duck, goose, turkey portions up to 6 months

Food	Preparation	Storage life up to
FISH	Small fish can be frozen whole after preparation. Glaze if preferred and pack in plastic bags or foil. Larger fish should be filleted or cut into steaks. Interleave individual fillets and steaks with aluminium foil, plastic sheet or freezer paper. Pack in flat wax or foil containers. Wrap in plastic or foil.	White fish 6 months; oil 3 months
DAIRY FOODS Eggs	Lightly beat yolks and whites together either with 1 tablespoon sugar or 1 teaspoon salt to every 6 eggs. Pack in waxed carton or tub leaving headspace. Seal well. Alternatively freeze in ice cube tray and store frozen blocks in plastic bag. Seal well. They can also be stored separated.	6 months
Cream	Freeze only double (heavy) cream (not less than 40 per cent butter fat) and whipping cream. Preferably add sugar–one tablespoon to each 600ml (1 pint/$2\frac{1}{2}$ cups) cream. Pack in waxed cartons leaving headspace.	3 months
Ice cream	Store ice cream in original container. Home-made in wax cartons, leaving headspace.	3 months
Butter	Overwrap commercial packaging or tubs with foil. Seal well.	salted up to 3 months: unsalted up to 6 months
Cheese	Hard cheese may become crumbly after freezing. Cream and cottage cheeses mixed with whipped cream make good sandwich fillings. Grated cheese freezes and stores well for use in recipes or for garnishing. Pack in tubs or cartons and grated cheese in plastic bags.	soft cheese up to 3 months; grated hard cheese up to 6 months

VEGETABLES	Preparation	Blanching time in minutes	Storage life up to
Artichokes (globe)	Trim off coarse outer leaves, stalks, tops and stems. Add lemon juice to blanching water.	7	12 months
Asparagus	Wash, scrape stalks, trim to approx equal lengths. Divide up into thick, medium and thin stalks. Pack in rigid containers.	thin–2 thick–4	12 months
Aubergines (eggplants)	Wash well and cut into about 1cm/½in slices with stainless steel knife. Pack in rigid containers.	4	12 months
Beans (broad/lima)	Pick young tender beans. Shell and discard any blemished beans.	3	12 months
Beans (French/green and runner)	Wash and trim ends, leave whole or slice thickly or cut into pieces about 2½cm/1in long.	whole–4 sliced–3	12 months
Beetroot (beet)	Select young and small beets. Cook whole beets until tender, rub off skins and pack in rigid containers. Large beets should be sliced or diced after cooking.	none	6 months
Broccoli	Wash, and trim stalks cutting away any woody stalks. Divide up into thick, medium and thin stems. Pack in rigid containers, sprig to stalk. Separate layers with plastic film or freezer paper.	thick–5 thin–3	12 months
Brussels sprouts	Trim and remove discoloured leaves. Cross-cut the stalks and wash in salted water. Can be frozen individually. Pack in rigid containers or plastic bags.	small–3 large–5	12 months
Cabbage	Trim outer coarse leaves. Wash in salted water. Cut or tear into shreds. Drain well and dry. Pack in rigid containers or plastic bags.	2	6 months
Carrots	Remove tops and tails. Scrape and wash. Leave small new carrots whole, but slice or dice larger carrots. Small whole carrots can be frozen individually.	whole–5 sliced–3	8 months

VEGETABLES	Preparation	Blanching time in minutes	Storage life up to
Cauliflower	Select firm white heads. Remove most of outer coarse leaves. Separate into equal sized sprigs. Wash in salted water, drain and pack in rigid containers. Add lemon juice to blanching water to retain colour.	3	8 months
Celery	Best suited after freezing for use as ingredient in recipes. Remove outer coarse stalks and strings. Cut into 5 to 7½cm/2–3in lengths. Freeze hearts whole. Pack in containers or plastic bags.	hearts–8 stalks–4	12 months
Corn (on the cob)	Remove outer husks, trim ends and wash. Freeze separately and pack in plastic bags.	5 to 8 depending on size	12 months
Corn kernels	Remove outer husks, and scrape kernels off the cob. Wash, drain and pack in rigid containers or plastic bags. Can be added to other vegetables before freezing, eg peas.	5	12 months
Courgettes (zucchini)	Wash and cut into 2½cm/1in slices. Drain and pack into rigid containers interleaving layers with freezer paper or foil.	3	12 months
Leeks	Remove coarse outer leaves and trim root end. Wash well, leave whole or slice and pack into rigid containers or plastic bags. They freeze well in white sauce. Seal well to prevent cross-flavour in storage.	whole–4 sliced–2	6 months

VEGETABLES	Preparation	Blanching time in minutes	Storage life up to
Mushrooms	Wash and peel field mushrooms. Trim stalks. Leave whole or slice. Add lemon juice to blanching water–or sauté in margarine–dry well and pack in rigid containers without blanching. Use only for cooking after freezing.	whole–4 sliced–2	12 months
Onions	Peel, slice into rings. Pack in small rigid containers and seal well to prevent cross-flavour in storage. They freeze well in white sauce.	2	3 months
Parsnips	Choose young and small parsnips, scrape and wash. Cut into quarters or slices. Drain and pack into rigid containers or plastic bags.	3	12 months
Peas	Choose young sweet peas, pod and discard any blemished peas. Blanch in small quantities. Drain well and pack in containers or plastic bags.	1½	12 months
Peppers (red and green)	Wash, halve and remove seeds and stalk. Can then be sliced if preferred. Remove only tops and seeds if later to be stuffed. Freeze individually, whole or sliced. Drain and pack in plastic bags.	2	12 months
Spinach	Choose young tender leaves. Wash well in running water, drain and press out as much water as possible. Pack in rigid containers or plastic bags in portions or family mealtime quantities.	2	12 months
Turnips and swedes (rutabaga)	Remove thick peel and cut into 2½cm/1in cubes. Pack in rigid containers or plastic bags.	3	12 months

FRUIT	Preparation	Storage life up to
Apples	Peel, core and slice. Use ascorbic acid to prevent browning. Blanch (see vegetables) for two or three minutes for dry pack. Alternatively pack in dry sugar or medium sugar syrup with ascorbic acid. Pack in bags or tubs. Leave headspace in syrup pack.	9 months
Apple purée	Peel, core and slice, cook until tender and strain. Add sugar and pack in tubs leaving headspace.	6 months
Apricots	Peel, remove stones (pits) and freeze in halves or slices in medium sugar syrup with ascorbic acid. Pack in tubs leaving headspace.	9 months
Avocados	Peel, remove stone and convert flesh to purée, adding 1 teaspoon of lemon juice to each 600ml (1 pint/2½ cups) of purée. Season with salt and pepper and pack in tubs leaving headspace.	2 months
Bilberries, blueberries and blackberries	Pick firm berries, remove stalks, wash and dry. Freeze as dry pack, individually, or as dry sugar pack or in heavy syrup. Pack in tubs leaving headspace.	9 months
Blackcurrants	Strip firm currants off stem, wash and dry. Freeze as dry pack individually for jam making, or in dry sugar pack or in heavy sugar syrup. Pack in tubs leaving headspace.	9 months
Cherries	Pick fully ripe, firm fruit, wash and dry. Remove stones and freeze as dry pack for jam making or in light sugar syrup. Pack in tubs leaving headspace.	9 months
Citrus fruits: lemons, oranges, grapefruit	Peel and remove pith and pips. Separate into segments and pack in tubs with medium sugar syrup leaving headspace. Alternatively wash, dry and freeze whole, especially Seville oranges for marmalade making.	9 months

FRUIT	Preparation	Storage life up to
Cranberries	Remove stalks, wash and dry. Freeze whole in dry sugar for sauce or strain for purée, then pack in tubs leaving headspace.	6–9 months
Damsons	Wash, halve and remove stones (pits). Pack dry for jam making, in dry sugar pack for cooking and dessert varieties in heavy sugar syrup. Pack in tubs leaving headspace.	9 months
Grapes	Seedless varieties of grapes can be frozen whole; otherwise halve, remove seeds and pack in a light sugar syrup leaving headspace.	9 months
Melon	Peel and halve the fruit to remove the seeds. Cut into slices, cubes or balls and immerse immediately into light sugar syrup. Alternatively sprinkle prepared melon pieces with lemon juice and pack in dry sugar. Leave headspace in cartons or tubs.	9 months
Peaches	Peel, remove stones (pits) and cut into slices. Immediately immerse in medium sugar syrup with ascorbic acid. If dry sugar pack is preferred, dip slices into ascorbic acid solution before sprinkling with sugar.	9 months
Pears	Peel, core and cut into quarters or slices. Immediately sprinkle with lemon juice to avoid discolouration. Then cook for about five minutes in light sugar syrup. Drain the fruit, cool and pack in tubs in medium sugar syrup with ascorbic acid leaving headspace. Freeze and store best as a purée.	6–9 months
Pineapple	Peel and core, then cut into slices, rings or cubes. Pack into light sugar syrup using any juice from the fruit. Leave headspace in tubs and cartons.	3 months
Plums	Wash, halve and remove stones (pits). Pack dry or in dry sugar pack for jam making. For dessert use pack in heavy sugar syrup with ascorbic acid, leaving headspace in tubs.	9 months
Raspberries	Select firm berries and wash only if necessary. Freeze individually or in dry sugar pack.	9 months
Redcurrants	Strip currants off stems, wash and dry. Freeze individually or dry pack for jam making. Alternatively pack in tubs leaving headspace with heavy sugar syrup for desserts.	9 months
Rhubarb	Select only young and tender stalks. Cut into 2½cm/1in pieces and lightly cook. Drain and cool and pack in dry sugar for pie fillings and jam making, or in heavy sugar syrup for dessert use, leaving headspace in tubs.	9 months
Strawberries	Remove hulls and wash only if necessary. Freeze individually or in dry sugar pack.	9 months
Tomatoes	Best frozen as a purée, otherwise wash, dry and freeze individually whole if to be used for cooking.	6–9 months
BREAD AND CAKES	Bake and cool before wrapping in plastic bags, seal and freeze. If sliced, individual bread slices can be toasted without thawing. Freeze breadcrumbs in convenient sized plastic bags.	1 month
Unbaked yeast dough	Yeast does not remain stable very long when frozen. Pack the unrisen dough in greased plastic bags. Leave headspace and seal. Rising time may need to be increased: compensate by adding more yeast in doughs to be frozen.	2 months
Unbaked pastries and pies	Pastry is better frozen unbaked. Prepare in conveniently sized thin slabs. Wrap in foil, roll out after thawing. Pies with a pastry base and/or covering should be prepared as for cooking. Cook and cool savoury fillings before covering with pastry. Fruit does not require cooking. Foil dishes are ideal for packing: over-wrap with foil before freezing.	6 months

WINE AND FOOD CHART

Hors D'Oeuvre	
Pâté, quiche etc.	Fairly strong dry white, such as Traminer, a Rhine wine such as Rudesheimer, rosé such as Rosé d'Anjou or light red, such as Beaujolais
Salad or cold hors d'oeuvre	Dry white, such as Alsatian Sylvaner or Yugoslavian Zilavka or Riesling
Soups	Dry sherry or a light Madeira is served with consommés, otherwise wine is not usually served with soup
White Meat	
Pork	Medium-sweet white, such as Graves or Orvieto or a rosé, such as Côtes de Provence or Mateus
Veal	Strong white, such as Montrachet, Pinot Chardonnay or a light red, such as Valpolicella, Zinfandel or Beaujolais
Ham	Rosé, such as Tavel or Rosé d'Anjou or a light red, such as Macon

Dark Meat	
Beef, roasted or grilled (broiled)	Bordeaux, such as Château Montrose or St. Emilion. (Any good Bordeaux is perfect with a roast.)
Beef casseroles and stews	Sturdy red Burgundy, such as Beaune, a Rhône wine, such as Châteauneuf-du-Pape, a heavier Italian red, such as Barolo or a Hungarian Egri Bikaver or Californian Pinot Noir
Steaks	Bordeaux, such as St. Estephe, a medium red Burgundy, such as Nuits St. Georges, or a Californian Cabernet Sauvignon
Lamb, roasted or grilled (broiled)	Bordeaux, such as a Margaux, a light Burgundy, such as Beaujolais or Macon or a light Italian wine, such as Bardolino
Lamb casseroles, stews and risottos	Bordeaux, such as a Médoc, Cabernet Sauvignon, an Italian wine such as Chianti or Valpolicella
Game (grouse, partridge, pheasant)	Bordeaux, such as St. Emilion or Château Haut-Brion
Hare, venison	Strong red, such as Côtes du Rhône or a heavy Burgundy, such as Chambertin

Fish		**Cheese**	
Grilled (broiled) or lightly poached fish	Light wine, such as Chablis, Pouilly Fuissé or Moselle	Soft (Brie, Camembert etc.)	Medium red Burgundy, such as Beaune or a Bordeaux, such as St. Julien
Fish in rich cream sauce	Heavy white, such as Burgundy (Meursault, Montrachet) or Rhine wine, such as Niersteiner	Medium (Port-Salut, Cheddar etc.)	Light, fruity red, such as Fleurie or Beaujolais, or a spicy white, such as Alsatian Gewurztztraminer or a Tavel
Shellfish	Light white (Chablis is traditional with oysters, for instance), Muscadet, Italian Soave or a slightly flinty Loire, such as Sancerre or Vouvray	Cream or Goat's	Medium white, such as Graves, an Alsatian Traminer or a Rhine wine
Shellfish served as a risotto or with rich sauce	Rosé, such as Tavel, a white Loire wine, such as Pouilly Fumé or a white Burgundy, such as Puligny Montrachet	Blue cheese (Stilton etc.)	Light red such as Bardolino, a medium Burgundy such as Brouilly or a Cabernet Sauvignon
Smoked Fish	Heavy white, such as white Burgundy, Alsatian Traminer or a spicy Rhine spatlese wine		

Poultry		**Desserts**	Sauternes or Barsac are the traditional dessert wines, but any German wine marked spatlese or auslese would also be suitable. For an extra rich dessert, try a Hungarian Tokay
Chicken	Heavier white, such as Hungarian Riesling or a white Burgundy Light red, such as Beaujolais		Generally, wine is not served with desserts containing chocolate
Duck	Heavy white Burgundy, such as Meursault or a rosé, such as Tavel	**After-Dinner**	Port, the heavier Madeiras or, for a change, a mature Hungarian Tokay or the 'queen of Sauternes', Château d'Yquem
Turkey	Heavy white, such as Traminer, a Rhine wine or a rosé, such as Côtes de Provence		

GLOSSARY

BAIN-MARIE (or double boiler)

Vessel containing hot water in which foods can be poached and various dishes and sauces can be kept hot without coming into contact with direct source of heat. The temperature of water in a bain-marie should be kept near boiling point.

BAKE BLIND

To cook dough before it is filled. Flan cases and tartlets are often cooked in this way. Preheat oven to fairly hot. Roll out dough to a circle about 5mm/¼in. thick and fit into flan ring or flan tin. Cover with foil and weigh with dried beans or rice. Bake for 10 minutes. Remove the beans or rice and foil and cook for 5 minutes or until brown.

BARD

To cover the breast of game or poultry for roasting with strips of fat bacon to keep it moist. The bacon can be tied on, or simply laid on. It should be removed 20 minutes before the end of cooking time to brown the meat. Duck and goose do not need barding as they are fatty birds. For other birds, if you have no bacon rub butter generously over the breast before roasting and baste frequently.

BECHAMEL SAUCE

A white sauce which has been enriched by flavouring the milk first with herbs and other seasonings. It is a delicious base for other sauces, such as mushroom, cheese, tomato and shrimp.

BEURRE COMPOSE

Butter transformed by beating various flavourings into it. Beurres composés can be served with grilled (broiled) fish or meat or used to fill hard-boiled (hard-cooked) eggs; they can also be stirred into sauces or soups to give added flavour and sheen.

BEURRE MANIE

Equal amounts of butter and flour creamed or kneaded together for use as a thickener for sauces and stews.

BEURRE NOIR

Butter cooked to a dark nut-brown and sharpened by the addition of reduced vinegar. Used principally for fish, but just as good with eggs, chicken breasts, or calves' brains.

BLANCH

Literally, to whiten, but usually used to mean to boil various ingredients for 1-2 minutes. Some foods previously soaked in cold water are blanched in water gradually brought to the boil, both to cleanse and harden them, and to remove strong taste. Vegetables, fruit and nuts (almonds in particular) are blanched or scaled with boiling water to make them easier to peel.

BOUQUET GARNI

A bunch of herbs containing sprigs of thyme, parsley and bayleaf, and sometimes marjoram, used to flavour stews and stocks.

CALORIE

A unit of heat used in measuring the fuel (energy) value of food, or technically the amount of heat required to raise 1 kilogram of water 1°C. Every adult needs so many calories daily to maintain strength.

CARAMELIZE

To heat sugar slowly, without added liquid, until it melts and takes on a golden brown colour and characteristic flavour.

CARBOHYDRATES

A group of foods essential to a balanced diet, including starches, sugars and cellulose, and containing carbon, hydrogen and oxygen.

CLARIFYING STOCK

A method of removing impurities. Turn the cold stock into a clean enamel

saucepan and warm over low heat. When stock is liquid but still cool, whisk in one large beaten egg white and crushed egg shell, and whisk vigorously. When stock boils, remove from heat and allow it to settle for 10 minutes. The egg white forms a crust and attracts all the cloudy particles, leaving a clear stock. Strain stock through a scalded cloth. Do not squeeze bag or break crust.

COURT BOUILLON
A quickly made vegetable stock, lightly acidulated. It is used for poaching all types of fish, and after the fish is cooked it may be turned into a sauce to accompany, or strained off and kept for future use.

CREME CHANTILLY
A vanilla flavoured, sweetened whipped cream which can be used to decorate cakes or cold desserts.

CREME PATISSIERE
This is also known as pastry custard or confectioner's custard. It has a wide variety of uses from filling choux puffs and éclairs to spreading on cakes and in pastry cases to be topped with fresh fruit. It does not keep for more than a few days in the refrigerator.

CROUTONS
Small cubes of stale white bread, grilled (broiled), dried in the oven or fried to a golden brown. Usually scattered on hot soup as it is served.

DECANT
To pour wine carefully and gently into glass containers known as decanters, in order to leave sediment behind. Spirits are also decanted, but this is chiefly for the pleasant appearance of the coloured liquids in the decorative glass containers.

DEGLAZING SAUCE
A simple brown sauce made with the juices left in the pan after roasting, and brown stock. If you have no stock, you can deglaze with wine, or a mixture of wine and the water in which green vegetables have been cooked

DEGORGE
This process is used to prepare aubergines (eggplants), cucumbers, etc, before they are cooked. Halve, slice or dice the vegetables, sprinkle with salt on the cut surfaces, and leave to drain in a colander for 15-20 minutes. Rinse in cold water, then dry with kitchen paper towels. This operation gives a less bitter taste and makes vegetables firmer in cooking.

DEMI-GLACE SAUCE
Based on a brown sauce, demi-glace sauce is itself often used as a base for other sauces, i.e. sauce bigarade or sauce ivoire. It can also be used by itself as an accompaniment to roasts or steaks. It is a mixture of brown sauce and beef stock reduced and enriched by boiling down to one third of the original quantity.

DEVIL
A very hot, highly spiced sauce served with various foodstuffs. Basic ingredients include Worcester or other piquant sauces, garlic, mustard, vinegar, cayenne, paprika, chilli, etc.

DRY PACK
A term used in freezing to describe a method of freezing fruit. Fruit with relatively tough skins, gooseberries and currants, for instance, are usually dry packed—that is washed, dried and packed in closed polythene (plastic) bags. Dry sugar pack is also suitable for most fruits—just sprinkle the fruit to be frozen with sugar (about 125g/4oz/$\frac{1}{2}$ cup to each 450g/1lb of fruit), and stir in gently before closing the bag.

FINES HERBES
A mixture of freshly chopped herbs, usually parsley, tarragon, chives and chervil. Used classically in omelettes, or as a flavouring for rich stews.

GAME

Refers to wild animals and birds which are hunted for sport and then eaten; it includes wild goose, duck and turkey, grouse, partridge, pheasant, wild pigeon, quail, woodcock, and other small birds, known as 'feathered' game; and also hare, rabbit, venison (deer) and boar known as 'ground' game or 'furred' game.

GLAZE

Brushed on dough before baking to give it a good finish. Beaten egg yolk, lightly beaten egg white, egg white and sugar, whole beaten egg, milk, milk and sugar, or cream can be used. Egg yolk gives the shiniest glaze. Sweet pastry can be brushed with water and then sprinkled with sugar for a pretty sparkling finish.

JULIENNE

A term used to indicate the size and shape to which vegetables or other garnishes should be cut for certain dishes. A julienne strip is the length of a matchstick, about 4cm/1½ inches long and about 2mm/⅛ inch wide.

KNEADING

A stage in bread-making after mixing the dough. To knead by hand, turn the dough on to a lightly floured board or marble slab. Fold the dough over towards you from the opposite side, then push it away firmly using the heel of your hand. Turn the dough slightly and repeat. Continue doing this for at least 10 minutes until dough is soft, smooth and elastic. Kneading can also be done in an electric mixer fitted with a dough hook.

KNOCKING BACK

A stage in bread-making after the dough has risen. Take the swollen dough and place on a board. Knuckle it down with your fist to expel surplus carbon dioxide and bring the yeast back into contact with its food supply. Knead for two minutes.

KNOCKING UP (Fluting)

This prevents the edges of double crust pies from coming apart during cooking. Make a series of shallow parallel cuts, at right angles to the edge, with the back of a knife in the dough edges, press with the prongs of a fork, or crimp the pastry with the thumb and forefinger.

MACERATE

To soak. A term generally applied only to fruit soaked in liqueur or syrup.

MARBLING

An effective but simple decoration for cakes covered with white glacé icing. Add a few drops of food colouring to 1 tbsp. of prepared glacé icing. Using a small forcing (pastry) bag, draw parallel lines over the surface of the cake with the coloured icing. Use a skewer to draw aside the icing in lines at right angles to the coloured lines.

MARINATE

To souse or soak. Applied to meat or game soaked in wine and oil with herbs and vegetables to flavour before cooking. The object is to make the meat more tender, moist, and well-flavoured.

MINERALS

There are about 10 mineral elements to be derived from daily food. The chief ones are Calcium (found in cheese, herrings, watercress and other vegetables, and eggs, etc.), Phosphorus (found in sweetbreads, cheese, fish, meat, eggs, bread, milk), and Iron (found in kidney, liver, beef, herrings, watercress, spinach, celery, cabbage, raisins).

PASTA

Pasta is made from durum wheat flour and water. Eggs are added, and sometimes spinach to give green noodles. Pasta is usually dried before being sold. It comes in hundreds of shapes and sizes, from thin ribbon noodles, to wide sheets of lasagne and the well-known macaroni, spaghetti and vermicelli shapes. There are

also novelty pasta shapes, twisted spirals, shells, bows and letters of the alphabet. These smaller varieties are ideal for adding to soups, casseroles and salads. Fresh pasta (available from Italian delicatessens) should be cooked on the same day it is bought.

PARBOIL
To boil until partly cooked.

PAUNCHING
To remove stomach and intestines of rabbit and hare.

POT ROASTING
A slow method of cooking, usually with liquid which is good for less tender and small cuts of meat. The meat is usually left whole, first browned in fat over high heat then finished, covered, over a low heat.

PROTEINS
Any of a class of nitrogenous substances consisting of a complex union of amino acids. Proteins occur in all animal and vegetable matter and are essential to the diet of animals. They are body-builders and energy producers.

ROUX
A preparation of equal amounts of fat and flour, used for thickening sauces and soups. In a white sauce the roux is cooked for only a minute or two before adding the liquid: it is known as a *roux blond*. If the fat and flour are allowed to colour to a rich brown before liquid is added, the roux is a *roux brun*, the basis of many brown sauces.

ROES
The eggs of fish; can be either hard or soft. The hard roe is that of the female and the soft of the male.

REDUCE
Method of thickening sauces, by decreasing the quantity of liquid by evaporation during long, slow cooking. Reducing also enriches flavour.

SMOKING FISH
There are two methods of smoking fish: hot smoking and cold smoking. Hot-smoked fish is already cooked and does not need further cooking. Smoked cod roe, buckling, mackerel, salmon and trout are all hot-smoked. Cold-smoking flavours but does not cook the fish, so it needs cooking. This group includes smoked cod, haddock, kippers and sprats.

SUGAR SYRUP
Another method used to freeze fruit. Sugar is added to boiling water and simmered just long enough for the sugar to be dissolved. Cool before adding to fruit. Syrups usually come in one of three strengths: light (about 225g/8oz/1 cup sugar to 600ml/1 pint/2½ cups water); medium (about 350g/12oz/1½ cups sugar to 550ml/17floz/2 cups water); and heavy (450g/1lb/2 cups sugar to 500ml/17floz/2 cups water).

VITAMINS
Organic substances found variously in most foods and essential, in small amounts, for the normal functioning of the body. The principal known vitamins include:
Vitamin A: found in fish-liver oil, egg yolk, butter, etc., and in carrots and other vegetables.
Vitamin B: found in yeast, wholemeal (wholewheat) flour and bread, pork bacon, offal (variety meat), cabbage, lettuce, potatoes, leeks, milk, black treacle (molasses), meat extracts.
Vitamin C: found in citrus fruits, tomatoes and various vegetables.
Vitamin D: found in fish-liver oils, milk, egg yolks, cheese, etc.
Vitamin E: found in whole wheat, lettuce, black treacle (molasses), etc.
Vitamin K: found in green vegetables, fish meal, hempseed, etc.

RECIPE INDEX

Aioli, 43
Almond(s):
  cake, 227
  cherry cake, 239
  filling for Danish
  pastries, 252
  with fish balls, 80
American apple pie, 210
Anchovy sauce, 36
Apfelstrudel, 201, 212
Apple:
  cake, spiced, 271
  coriander fruit
  crumble, 178
  filling for Danish
  pastries, 252
  fritters, 177
  pie, American, 210
  and quince turnovers,
  212
  sauce, 45
  strudel, 201, 212
Apricot:
  condé, 132
  glaze, 224
  salad, 167
Asparagus quiche, 207
Aubergine (egg plant),
  in Moussaka, 107
Austrian yeast cake see
  Gugelhopf

Bacon:
  rolls, as garnish, 273
  with scrambled eggs,
  57-8
Banana:
  flambé, 168
  fritters, 178
  and pineapple filling,
  252
Battenburg cake, 238-9
Beans, red kidney, in
  chili con carne, 106-7
Béarnaise sauce, 40-1
Béchamel sauce, 35-6
Beef:
  chili con carne, 106-7
  goulasch, 105
  grilled (broiled)
  porterhouse steak, 102
  with olives, 106
  pot roast with brandy,
  101
  steak and kidney

pudding, 205
Stroganoff, 100-1
Beurres composés see
  Butters, flavoured
Biscuits (cookies):
  brandy snaps, 236-7
  chocolate refrigerator,
  229-30
  fruit and nut, 236
  ginger and cream,
  wafers, 230
  shortbread, 230
  Viennese fingers, 229
  see also Cakes
Blue cheese sauce, 43
Boeuf Stroganoff, 100-1
Bombe Coppelia, 185
Borscht, 24
Brains
  in butter, 99-100
  in egg and breadcrumbs,
  94
Brandy:
  with mixed vegetables,
  151
  with pot roast, 101
  sauce, with lobster,
  81
  snaps, 236-7
Brawn, 94
Bread:
  brioche, 249
  cinnamon toast, 271
  croissants, 255
  garlic, 270-1
  household white, 244-5
  orange yeast buns, 251
  pizza, 255
  sweet, 247
  wholewheat
  (wholemeal), 245
  see also Cakes
Bread sauce, 44
Brioche, 249
Brown stock, 15
Butter(s), flavoured, 41
  watercress, 102
Butter cream cake
  filling, 220

Cabbage see Coleslaw
Cakes:
  almond, 227
  almond cherry, 239
  Battenburg, 238-9

cherry-filled, 230-1
chocolate peppermint,
  236
chocolate roulade, 228
Danish pastries, 252
Dundee, 227
gingerbread, 270
gugelhopf, 250
Jamaican spice loaf,
  235
Madeira, 228-9
madeleines, 232
mocha gâteau, 231-2
nougatines, 234-5
orange fingers, 227
savarin, 249
see also Bread;
  Biscuits (cookies)
Caper sauce, 36
Carrot soup, cream, 25
Chamonix, 186-7
Charlotte Russe, 185
Cheese:
  with grilled (broiled)
  fish, 77
  sauce, 36
  soufflé, 55-6
  straws, 205-6
Cheesecake, 208-9
Cherry:
  almond cherry cake,
  239
  -filled cakes, 230-1
  stuffing, 121
Chestnut purée, 186-7
Chicken:
  diced, in Nun's salad,
  158
  Florentine, 123-4
  with prawns (shrimp)
  122
  sautéed, in Madeira-
  flavoured cream sauce,
  123
  soup, cream of, 27-8
Chicory (endive),
  braides, 150
Chili con carne, 106-7
Chocolate:
  Bavarois, 188-9
  ice-cream, 182
  peppermint cake, 236
  refrigerator biscuits
  (cookies), 229-30
  roulade, 228

Choux puffs, 212-13
Cinnamon:
  sugar filling, 252
  toast, 271
Clam chowder, New
  England, 27
Cock-a-Leekie, 28-9
Coffee:
  ice-cream, 182, 184
  soufflé, 177
Coleslaw, with caraway,
  158-9
Consommé Madrilène,
  25-6
Cookies see biscuits
Coquilles Saint-Jacques
  à l'Ail, 76-7
Coriander fruit crumble,
  178
Country pâté, 105
Courgettes (Zucchini),
  stuffed, 150-1
Court bouillon, 66
Crab meat flan, 78-9
Crème au beurre, 220
  meringe, 220
  mousseline, 220
Crème caramel, 173
Crème chantilly, 221
Crème pâtissière, 220-1
Crepes:
  batter, 174
  Suzette, 179
Croissants, 255
Crumble(s), 172
  coriander fruit, 178
Cucumber:
  garnish, 273
  with lamb chops, 98
Custard:
  baked, 173
  sauce, 173

Danish pastries, 252
Deglazing sauce, 38-9
Dijon kidneys, 95
Dried fruit compote, 168
Drop scones see Scones
Dumplings see Gnocchi
Dundee cake, 227

Egg(s):
  Benedict, 56
  and bacon scramble,
  57-8

INDEX

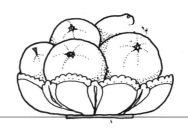

Picture Credits

Rex Bamber: 32/3, 36/7
Theo Bergstrom: 125
Delu/PAF International: 81, 106, 133, 151, 195, 248
Alan Duns: 16, 18, 39, 48/9, 56, 69, 78, 99, 108/9, 115, 123, 126/7, 135, 148/9, 152/3, 160/1, 162/3, 170/1, 180/1, 182, 183, 184, 187, 197, 198, 203, 206, 209, 212/3, 216/7, 226, 229, 232, 234, 235, 236/7, 251
John Elliot: 140/1
Geoffrey Frosh: 154/5
Melvin Grey: 14/5, 26, 112, 128/9, 214/5, 244/5, 253, 272/3, 276/7
Jerry Harpur: 100
Gina Harris: 254
Anthony Kay: 12/3, 118/9
Paul Kemp: 50/1, 52, 54, 84/5, 86, 93(b), 104, 124, 130, 136, 164, 172/3, 242, 243, 247
David Levin: 21, 34, 38, 53, 68, 90, 92, 114, 117, 194, 196, 216, 218, 219, 221, 223, 224, 225, 246
David Melbrum: 40, 145, 174, 175, 188, 201, 210/1, 238, 239
Key Nilsson: 156
Roger Phillips: 10/1, 19, 22, 25, 28, 29, 30/1, 42/3, 45, 46/7, 57, 58, 59, 62/3, 70, 71, 72, 74/5, 76, 77, 82/3, 91, 98, 101, 103, 110/1, 120, 131, 132, 138, 142/3, 150, 158, 159, 169, 178, 179, 186, 190/1, 192/3, 200, 204, 228, 230/1, 233, 240/1, 250, 252, 258/9, 263, 264, 269, 270, 275, 282/3
Iain Reid: 79, 80, 95, 107, 165, 166, 176
Kim Sayer: 155
David Smith: 122
Tessa Traeger: 60/1
Paul Williams: 20, 222
George Wright: 35, 271